THE CARDINAL VIRTUES: AQUINAS, ALBERT, AND PHILIP THE CHANCELLOR

Translated by
R.E. Houser

These translations from the Latin works of Thomas Aquinas, Albert the Great, and Philip the Chancellor concentrate on the four cardinal virtues —prudence, justice, courage, and temperance—first identified by Plato as essential requirements for living a happy and morally good life.

An historical introduction traces the development of the doctrine of four cardinal virtues from Greek philosophy through the thirteenth century. The treatment isolates three stages in this development: (1) Greek and Roman *Philosophi*: Socrates, Plato, Aristotle, early Stoics, Cicero, and Seneca; (2) early Christian *Sancti*: Ambrose, Jerome, Augustine, and Gregory; and (3) medieval schoolmen (*Magistri*): Master Peter Lombard, Philip the Chancellor, Albert, and Aquinas.

The bulk of the book is devoted to translations of texts on the topic of the cardinal virtues: Philip the Chancellor, "On the Four Cardinal Virtues" and "On Virtue in General: Continuation" (from the *Summa on the Good*); Albert the Great, "On the Division and Sufficiency of the Virtues" (from the *Parisian Summa*), and *Commentary on the Sentences*, Book 3, Distinctions 33 and 36; and Thomas Aquinas, *Disputed Question on the Cardinal Virtues*. Two appendices contain translations of shorter supplementary texts on the cardinal virtues by Ambrose, Augustine, Jerome, Gregory, Bernard of Clairvaux, Peter Lombard, and as well as from Thomas Aquinas' *Commentary on the Nichomachean Ethics*. Also included are three charts showing the development of the doctrine of the "parts" of courage, temperance, and justice; a glossary of Latin terms; a bibliography; and an index.

MEDIAEVAL SOURCES IN TRANSLATION 39

STUDIES IN MEDIEVAL MORAL TEACHING 4

The Cardinal Virtues: Aquinas, Albert, and Philip the Chancellor

translated by

R.E. Houser

Pontifical Institute of Mediaeval Studies

Publication of this volume
was made possible by the support of
The Medieval Moral Teaching Fund
Pontifical Institute of Mediaeval Studies

NATIONAL LIBRARY OF CANADA CATALOGUING IN PUBLICATION

Thomas, Aquinas, Saint, 1225?-1274.
The cardinal virtues : Aquinas, Albert and Philip the Chancellor / translated by R. E. Houser.

(Mediaeval sources in translation, ISSN 0316-0874 ; 39)
(Studies in medieval moral teaching ; 4)
Translated from the Latin.
Includes bibliographical references and index.
ISBN 0-88844-289-0

1. Cardinal virtues — Early works to 1800. I. Albertus, Magnus, Saint, 1193?-1280. II. Philip, the Chancellor, d. 1236. III. Houser, Rollen Edward, 1946- . IV. Title. V. Series VI. Series: Studies in medieval moral teaching ; 4.

BV4645.A78 2004 179′.9 C2003-906932-X

Pontifical Institute of Mediaeval Studies
59 Queen's Park Crescent East
Toronto, Ontario, Canada M5S 2C4

www.pims.ca

Printed in Canada

For

A.A. Maurer CSB

Joseph Owens CSSR

E.A. Synan †

J.A. Weisheipl OP †

quattuor magistri principaliores

Contents

Introduction

AUTHORS, TEXTS, EDITIONS

The present volume was originally conceived as simply a translation of Aquinas's *Quaestio disputata de virtutibus cardinalibus*. Br. Thomas presented his doctrine of the cardinal virtues in three different works: his *Scriptum* on the *Sententiae* of Master Peter Lombard, Bk. 3, d. 33 (written 1252-1256); the *Summa theologiae*, 1-2, q. 61 (1268-1271); and the *Quaestio disputata de virtutibus cardinalibus*, which was disputed at the time he was composing *Summa theologiae* 2-2 (1271-2).[1] In addition, he made some important remarks about the cardinal virtues in the course of treating the general nature of virtue in *Quaestiones disputatae de virtutibus in communi* (1271-2). For understanding his views about the cardinal virtues, the *Quaestio disputata de virtutibus cardinalibus* seems to be the most appropriate of these four texts to translate.

The main reason for choosing this work is that it was probably written last, thereby containing Br. Thomas's final word on the subject. When writing his youthful *Scriptum*, Aquinas was more under the sway of his master Albert than he would be later. The treatment of the cardinal virtues in *Summa* 1-2, written earlier in his second teaching period at Paris, contains his mature doctrine, but the presentation for "beginners" in theology is so condensed and simplified that it cries out for the kind of elaboration found only in a disputed question, when Aquinas had the opportunity to set out his own views at generous length and with all the sophistication at his disposal.

To take but one example, Aquinas has three different arguments for the cardinal virtues. Viewing them conjointly is important for understanding the true nature of the cardinal virtues, as what he calls both "special" and

[1] Dates taken from G. Emery, "Brief Catalogue of the Works of St. Thomas Aquinas," in J.-P. Torrell, *St. Thomas Aquinas, Vol. 1: The Person and his Work*, tr. Robert Royal (Washington: Catholic University Press, 1996).

"general" virtues. But at *Summa* 1-2, q. 61, Aquinas had separated arguments for "general" cardinal virtues (in Art. 2) from that for "special" cardinal virtues (Art. 3). Even so perceptive an interpreter of Aquinas as Anton Pegis dropped Art. 3 from his abridgement, *Introduction to St. Thomas Aquinas*, thereby offering the reader a partial and distorted view of Aquinas's doctrine. The other work on virtue that Aquinas composed during 1271-2, the *Quaestiones disputatae de virtutibus in communi*, has the disadvantage of focusing on the general nature of virtue as such, rather than specifically on the *cardinal* virtues. The causal approach to virtue Aquinas took there led him to focus on the "powers" of the soul, but it also led him to ignore the two other arguments crucial for understanding his doctrine of the cardinal virtues. Aquinas himself seems to have recognized this problem and so for the first and only time he brought together as a 'package' all three arguments elucidating the nature of the cardinal virtues in Art. 1 of the disputed question translated here.

Choosing to translate this little work immediately presented a textual problem. The Marietti text, while readily available, looked suspicious at several key points, especially in Art. 1.[2] These suspicions were confirmed by looking at five manuscripts kindly supplied to me by Fr. Emile Deronne op, the editor of the as yet unpublished Leonine text. Consequently, as a Latin text I have used the Marietti edition, as corrected by these five manuscripts, which I have read in light of the editorial principles guiding recent Leonine work on the disputed questions.[3] Fr. Deronne is of course not responsible for any erroneous readings of the Latin texts.

In the course of translating Aquinas, a second and more substantial issue arose. The more closely I looked, especially at the level of detail contained in the numerous objections and replies found in a disputed question, the more clearly a point of capital importance came into view. In approaching the cardinal virtues Aquinas took his inspiration, not so much from Aristotle, who had dismissed the Platonic theory of four virtues, as from his teacher Albert. The more I read Albert, the clearer became the inadequacies

[2] In his translation of both *De virtutibus in communi* and *De virtutibus cardinalibus* entitled *Disputed Questions on Virtue* (South Bend, IN: St. Augustine's Press, 1999) Ralph McInerny seems to use the Marietti edition.

[3] See *De malo*, ed. Leonina, 23: 21*-72*. The sigla I have used in the textual notes follow the forthcoming Leonine edition, vol. 24.2: P^7 = Paris, Nat. lat. 15811 (Shooner 2415); Am^2 = Amiens 244 (Shooner 33); As = Assisi 112 (Shooner 62); O^2 = Oxford, Balliol 49 (Shooner 2082); Ve^2 = Venezia, Lat. III, 85 (Shooner 3601); M = Marietti.

of the centuries old tradition, exemplified by Cajetan, of reading the *Summa* alone (or in conjunction with Aristotle), and the even older tradition, exemplified by Capreolus, of reading his *Scriptum* on Lombard. Both these traditions tend to separate his thought from the historical context in which it actually developed.[4] It thus became clear that the most accurate way to present Aquinas's thought would be also to translate Albert, his immediate source.

The texts of Albert led me in turn to Philip the Chancellor. Significant recent work has been done on thirteenth century Dominican "moral manuals."[5] As Dominicans, Thomas and Albert were aware of such works: Raymond of Peñafort, *Summa de casibus* (1224; 1234-5), Hugh of St.-Cher, *Speculum ecclesiae* (1240), William Peraldus, *Summa vitiorum* (1236) and *Summa virtutum* (1249-50), and Vincent of Beauvais, *Speculum maius* (1244, 1259). It has been claimed "that Aquinas modeled the second part of the *Summa* on William Peraldus's *Summa of Virtue* and *Summa of Vice*," on the grounds that Peraldus began with a treatment of virtue in general, followed by consideration of the three theological and four cardinal virtues, and finally treatment of a host of other virtues fitting "under" these seven.[6]

But this is to go too far. Such confessor's manuals were only marginally influential on the virtue theory of Albert and Aquinas, and Aquinas in

[4] For one recent example limiting the study of Aquinas's virtue theory to the *Summa*, see Jean Porter, *Moral Action and Christian Ethics* (Cambridge: CUP, 1995) which never mentions the *Quaestiones disputatae de virtutibus*. Porter claims that for Aquinas "the cardinal virtues, considered as specific and discrete virtues, are *all* necessarily present in the character of the truly virtuous person." Aquinas is then "forced by the logic" of this claim to say that "the virtues possessed and exhibited by our imperfect selves are *not true virtues*," with the result that "Aquinas *himself* recognizes that the person of perfected acquired virtue represents an *ideal*, rather than an attainable possibility" (160, 161, 163; my emphasis). This interpretation stems immediately from not properly distinguishing the general from specific cardinal virtues and comes ultimately from trying to read the *Summa* in isolation from the disputed questions.

[5] See Leonard Boyle, *The Setting of the Summa theologiae of Saint Thomas* (Toronto: PIMS, 1982); M. Michele Mulcahey, *"First the Bow is bent in Study...." Dominican Education before 1350* (Toronto: PIMS, 1998), 527-552; Torrell, *St. Thomas Aquinas* 119; also the ongoing study of the cardinal virtues headed by I. Bejczy: www.let.kun.nl/~I.Bejczy/Genealogy.html.

[6] So John Inglis, *On Aquinas* (Belmont, CA: Wadsworth/Thomson, 2002), 25-6, 80.

particular treated such second level works gingerly. Philip the Chancellor's *Summa de bono* was far more important for Albert's own *De bono*, as comparison of the texts translated below shows. Moreover, while earlier Franciscan and Dominican authors quoted Philip without attribution, Albert recognized his debt to the Chancellor and so was the first both to quote and name him. Far from thinking of themselves as originators in theology, both Vincent of Beauvais and William Peraldus were also happy to acknowledge their use of Philip.[7] More specifically, the structure of treating the virtues in general, then the three theological virtues and the four cardinal virtues, was not originated by William Peraldus; it goes back to Philip.[8] Albert's texts, then, establish a direct historical line running from Aquinas through Albert to Philip. In addition to knowing certain doctrines of the Chancellor through Albert, Aquinas also seems to have read Philip's work himself. It was Philip's *Summa de bono*, then, written 1225-8, well before all the works of the manualists (save the first edition of Raymond), that was the fundamental source for the development of Dominican moral thought in the thirteenth century. To be sure, that thought included confessor's manuals, but the more profound treatises of moral theology written by Philip and Thomas are its beginning and ending points. To show this, it became necessary to translate Philip as well as Albert.

Fortunately, several of their texts have been well edited. For Philip the Chancellor's *Summa de bono* I had the signal advantage of using N. Wicki's superb edition, Bern: Editiones Francke, 1985, one that may form the basis for renewed interest in this underestimated figure. Philip took up the topic of the cardinal virtues in two different sections of his work. The first, entitled "On the Four Cardinal Virtues" (pp. 84-98 below), was concerned with the nature of the cardinal virtues and it corresponds roughly to Peter Lombard, *Sent.*, 3, d. 33; the other, entitled "On Virtue in General. Continuation"(pp. 99-115 below) deals with the connections among the virtues, the issue raised by the Master at *Sent.*, 3, d. 36.

Albert the Great came to Paris in 1243 and left for Cologne, along with Br. Thomas, in 1248. The City of Light was for him an intellectual illu-

[7] N. Wicki, introduction to Philip, *Summa de bono* (Bern: Editiones Francke, 1985), 41*: "Des solutions de la Somme (of Philip) sont alléguées *et attribuées* au Chancelier par Vincent de Beauvais dans sa *Speculum Maius* et par Guillaume Peyrant dans sa *Summa de virtutibus*" (my emphasis).

[8] In Wicki's edition: *De virtutibus in communi*, 525-561; *De virtutibus theologicis*, 561-744; *De quatuor cardinalibus virtutibus*, 744-1069.

mination and Albert embraced the Aristotelian learning he found there. He wrote two kinds of works then *au courant* at Paris: a commentary on Lombard, even though he was well past the normal age for doing so, and a *Summa* of theological knowledge which took more than its title from the *Summa de bono* of Philip the Chancellor. The sections of these two works devoted to the cardinal virtues are translated here. His treatment of the cardinal virtues in the *Summa parisiensis*, Part Six, entitled *De bono* (pp. 118-124 below) focuses on their nature, covering roughly the same material as his commentary on the *Sent.*, 3, d. 33 (pp. 126-139 below); but these treatments are different enough to warrant translating both here. Albert's commentary on *Sent.*, 3, d. 36 (pp. 140-153 below) treats the connections among the virtues, the same material found in the text of Lombard he was commenting upon and in Philip's "continuation." For Albert's *De bono* (written 1246-9), I have used the fine edition of H. Kühle, *et al.*, vol. 28 of the Cologne edition. For his commentary on the *Sent.,* 3 (written 1246-8), I have used the Borgnet edition, vol. 28.

Aquinas was enough of a traditionalist to maintain the distinction between the nature of the cardinal virtues and their connections that he found set out in Peter Lombard, Philip, and Albert; but he could not help but put his own distinctive stamp on these two topics. In *Summa theologiae* 1-2, after treating the essence of virtue (q. 55) and its "subject," the powers of the soul where the virtues actually exist (q. 56), his treatment of the acquired virtues began with the intellectual virtues (q. 57), turned to the moral virtues (qq. 58-60), and culminated in the four cardinal virtues (q. 61). He then took up the three theological virtues (q. 62) before clarifying the difference between humanly acquired and divinely inspired virtues (q. 63). After presenting the nature of the cardinal and other virtues in this way, Aquinas rounded out his treatment of virtue with four questions devoted to "certain properties" of the virtues, where property has the Aristotelian meaning of an attribute deemed to flow as an effect from the nature of something. He situated the traditional topic of the connections among the virtues as one of four such "properties": the Aristotelian "mean" found in every virtue (q. 64), their connections (q. 65), their "equality" (q. 66) and their "duration after this life" (q. 67).

This arrangement of the properties of the virtues, while clever enough, has one disadvantage: it turns the "mean" into an effect rather than a cause–the formal cause–of virtue. Aquinas realized this problem and attempted to overcome it when using the four "properties" of virtue in the *Summa* as the model for *On the Cardinal Virtues*. Art. 1 of this disputed question contains his account of the causes–the material and formal causes –of the cardinal virtues. Arts. 2-4 then follow with the final three "properties" from the *Summa*: their connection, equality, and duration after the present life. In this way, the four articles of *On the Cardinal Virtues* recast qq. 64-67 of *Summa* 1-2, though in the disputed question the virtues covered are limited to the four cardinal virtues.

In the historical introduction that follows I have attempted to set the story of scholastic philosophizing about the cardinal virtues against a background of classical and patristic thought. The historical narrative begins with Socrates and ends with Aquinas. While just a sketch, it may go some way toward showing that Philip, Albert, and Aquinas were not just the heirs but fully the equals of Plato, Aristotle, and the Stoics in the development of the doctrine of the four cardinal virtues.

History of the Doctrine of the Cardinal Virtues

The theory of four cardinal virtues was a medieval Christian doctrine. Its origins go back to Socrates, to be sure, and Plato was the first thinker to set out an explicit theory about the four virtues of prudence, courage, temperance, and justice. But the phrase "cardinal virtues" seems to have been invented by Ambrose, Christian Bishop of Milan. Born of anguish and hope, it was first pronounced in the funeral oration he delivered over the body of his brother Satyrus. The Fathers of the Christian Church were able to baptize the Platonic virtues, but a rigorous and thorough doctrine of the cardinal virtues had to wait almost a millennium, for the founding of universities and the teaching of their Masters. The present translation is designed to exhibit the contribution of three thirteenth century theologians: Philip the Chancellor, Albert the Great, and Thomas Aquinas. All three placed the cardinal virtues within a larger scheme of seven fundamental virtues–four cardinal and three theological–that guide the Christian life. This scheme will be familiar to those acquainted with Aquinas's *Summa of Theology 2-2*, but it was not peculiar to Thomas. Medieval artisans, for example, illustrated these seven virtues in their manuscripts, set them into their stained glass, and carved them into their cathedrals.[9] Philip, Albert,

[9] Adolf Katzenellenbogen, *Allegories of the Virtues and Vices in Medieval Art*, tr. A. Crick (New York: Norton, 1964). Fig. 8b shows the four cardinal and three theological virtues as knights led by humility, in Herrad of Landsberg, *Hortus delici-*

and Thomas consciously built on the work of three groups of thinkers: pagan philosophers (*philosophi*), Christian Fathers (*sancti*), and other schoolmasters (*magistri*).

1. *Philosophi*

It is arguable that the Western tradition of virtue theory began with the sophists, the new teachers who emerged with Greek democracy in the fifth century B.C. They developed techniques of rhetorical analysis for citizen-orators speaking in the popular assemblies and law courts; and they also used their techniques to criticize the traditional Greek morality of earlier sages (*sophoi*). The Persian War brought recognition of cultural differences and led the sophists to make morality a matter of individually or culturally relative custom (*nomos*) rather than of unvarying human nature (*physis*). Such is the meaning of the revolutionary principle that began Protagoras's *On Truth*: "Of all things the measure is man." Sophists adjusted their claims to knowledge accordingly. Correct action is to be guided by right opinion rather than certain wisdom, and they coined the name "sophist (*sophistes*)" as a sign of their epistemological downsizing. The position of the sophists can be summarized thus: If your opinion is right by the standards of yourself or your family or your tribe or city, then your action will be good (RO $\supset$ GA).[10]

---

arum, fol. 200r, late 12th C. Fig. 67 shows a "tree of virtues" with the same seven virtues as branches rooted in humility, from *De fructibus carnis et spiritus*, Salzburg, Studienbibliotek, MS. Sign.V.1.H.162, fol. 75v, 12th C. Emile Mâle, *The Gothic Image*, tr. D. Nussey (New York: Harper and Row, 1958) 104, points to the same eight virtues at Chartres.

[10] Paul Woodruff, "Rhetoric and Relativism: Protagoras and Gorgias," *The Cambridge Companion to Early Greek Philosophy* (Cambridge: CUP, 1999) 309, concludes: "For the arena of human action and decision, where knowledge *cannot* obtain a grip, teaching good judgment and the art of words takes the highest practical value. This is the main teaching of the sophists. Its unexpected legacy has been the enduring challenge it has provided to philosophers." On the sophists: G.B. Kerferd, *The Sophistic Movement* (Cambridge: CUP, 1981). J. De Romilly, *The Great Sophists in Periclean Athens* (Oxford: Clarendon, 1992) 211, points to the way Isocrates sums up the sophistic view. He "believes that it is human *opinions* that provide the authority in matters of morality." Cf. Isocrates, *Antidosis*, sec. 271; R.E. Houser, "*Chronos* and *Logos*: Rhetoric and the Rise of Philosophy," *ACPQ* 68 (1994) 247-258. For a less subjectivist interpretation of Protagoras, see Edward Sciappa, *Protagoras and Logos* (Columbia, SC: USC Press, 1991) 117-130. For bibliography:

a. Socrates

Socrates[11] turned sophistic techniques against their creators. He thought that moral goodness is based on nature, not on custom, that good action comes from virtue understood on the model of a craft like carpentry or a skill like horsemanship, and that virtue must find its necessary and sufficient conditions, not in opinion but in certain knowledge. To generate knowledge, Socrates developed sophistic analysis into a technique of cross-examination (*elenchos*) designed to answer the question "what is it?" by uncovering the true and abiding natures of the virtues. As Xenophon presents him, Socrates found in such knowledge the necessary and sufficient condition for real virtue:

> For just actions, and all things done virtuously, are fine and good. Whoever knows these will never choose anything else ($W \supset V$), and whoever does not know them cannot do them and, even if he tries, will fail ($\sim W \supset \sim V$). Thus, the wise do what is fine and good; the unwise cannot, and even if they try, they fail ($W \equiv V$).[12]

Cambridge Companion 391-394.

[11] Socrates here is the real, historical figure. Knowledge of him comes from Plato's dialogues, Aristotle, the Athenian general Xenophon, and Aristophanes. Leo Strauss advocated for Xenophon as witness in *Xenophon's Socrates* (Ithaca: Cornell, 1972). Gregory Vlastos, *Socrates: Ironist and Moral Philosopher* (Cambridge: CUP, 1991) found the Socrates of Plato's early dialogues to be quite different from the Socrates of the middle dialogues and to be the primary source for knowing the historical Socrates, followed by Aristotle, then Xenophon. Terence Irwin, *Platonic Ethics* (Oxford: OUP, 1995) 15, followed Vlastos: "Plato's early dialogues present the views of the historical Socrates." Julia Annas, *Platonic Ethics, Old and New* (Ithaca: Cornell, 1999) 1-7, has recently tried to move away from this "developmental" view of Plato in favor of the "unitarian" approach found in "the ancients," especially the Middle Platonists. They found a consistent Platonic teaching throughout the dialogues, one unified under the "one final end" of "becoming like God"; but she admits that their quest for such unity of doctrine was "too optimistic." For understanding the historical Socrates, as distinct from Plato, my own view is that Xenophon and Aristotle are the primary witnesses, the strongest evidence coming when they are corroborated by Plato's early dialogues. On the historical Socrates, see Paul VanderWaerdt, ed., *The Socratic Movement* (Ithaca: Cornell, 1994); H. H. Benson, ed., *Essays on the Philosophy of Socrates* (Oxford: OUP, 1992). For bibliography, see Richard Kraut, ed., *The Cambridge Companion to Plato* (Cambridge: CUP, 1992) 502-505.

[12] Xenophon, *Memorabilia* 3.9.5. This Socratic claim reducing virtue to wisdom is corroborated by the reduction of courage to wisdom in Plato's *Laches* and the

The *logical* identity of wisdom and virtue–their mutual entailment–seems to have led Socrates to an even stronger claim, their *ontological* identity; and so he reduced virtue to wisdom: "Therefore, since just actions and all other types of fine and good activity are done virtuously, it is clear that justice and every other type of virtue *is* wisdom."[13] Here virtue is reduced to wisdom in the negative sense of eliminating moral virtue as something distinct from knowledge. What is called virtue is simply knowledge under a different name; knowing the good is doing it; and so-called *akratic* behavior, that is, knowing what is right but doing what is wrong, is impossible:

> When asked further whether he thought that those who know what they ought to do but do the opposite are wise and strong (*egkrateis*), he said: No, rather, they are unwise and weak (*akrateis*).[14]

Socrates, then, answered the sophists and defended objective moral norms by resorting to an unrelenting intellectualism. Whether he thought it possible actually to obtain the wisdom that constitutes virtue was a question about which even his followers did not agree. Plato's early dialogues end in *aporia* and his Socrates claims no wisdom for himself; while Xenophon's Socrates does have the wisdom that is virtue. Socrates's reductionism condemned the sophists to vice because of ignorance; but it runs counter to normal experience and implicitly condemned the average Athenian citizen, as well. This perhaps explains why traditionalists could combine forces with the avant-garde in condemning him to death. As a theorist, Socrates reduced the broad moral spectrum to two extremes, to sages and sinners, and in doing so he found no room for the morally mediocre middle.

b. Plato

In several early dialogues, Plato presented the Socratic hypothesis that reduced virtue to wisdom, but by the time he wrote the *Republic* he opted for a more complicated reductionism, one that reduced all other virtues to

---

reduction of temperance to wisdom in Plato's *Charmides*. Cf. Terence Irwin, *Platonic Ethics* 38-44.

[13] Xenophon, *Memorabilia* 3.9.5.

[14] Xenophon, *Memorabilia* 3.9.4. Vlastos 100-101 holds that *akratês* at 4.5.6 should be translated "intemperate" rather than "weak-willed" or "incontinent," a stronger rendering which can work here as well.

the four that would eventually be called cardinal virtues: wisdom, courage, temperance, and justice.[15] His argument for them is ontological, based on the geography of a soul that cannot be seen directly but can be approached indirectly, through the social structure observable in the city. The *Republic* follows the up and down story of the origin, development, and demise of the four virtues, in both city and individual soul.

Every city must have three classes, because there are three functions that must be performed in community life. The first and most obvious is producing goods and providing services, the function of the "craftsmen." When they learn how to subordinate their desire for wealth to the end of producing goods useful to the *polis*, the craftsmen develop the virtue of temperance. This first step up makes the city just to a limited degree. The business class, however, is notoriously unwise and timid, so its temperance arises primarily from external pressure rather than internal motivation, pressure that comes from competition within the class of craftsmen and from compulsion administered by the next class, the warriors. Theirs is the police and military function, and they become virtuous when they learn that courage is even more important than victory. The warriors do not lack temperance, but it is not their predominant virtue; and when they add courage to the temperance of the craftsmen, justice in the city grows. Generals, however, are ill-equipped to set goals in war or peace, which is why Plato calls this class "auxiliaries." They are the instruments of the highest and ruling class, who become true "guardians" when they learn to eschew power in favor of wisdom. When this virtue becomes their predominant trait, the city becomes fully just, because each class has attained its appropriate virtue: temperance for the craftsmen, courage for the auxiliaries, wisdom for the guardians.[16]

The three classes found in a city lead to understanding the three corresponding parts of the soul: reason (*logistikon*), emotion (*thumos*), and desire (*epithumia*), whose virtues are respectively wisdom, courage, and temperance. Wisdom is found wherever reason knows and chooses the good; courage is found wherever the emotions overcome obstacles to the good; and temperance is found wherever desire for pleasure is so con-

[15] The reduction of virtue to wisdom is most prominent in *Laches*, *Charmides*, *Euthyphro*, *Euthydemus*, *Protagoras*. The four virtues are treated in *Republic* 4 (427d-445e); see Irwin, *Platonic Ethics* 203-261. Bibliography: Irwin 393-405; R. Kraut, *Cambridge Companion to Plato* (Cambridge: CUP, 1992) 507-509.

[16] *Republic* 4 (369a-434d).

trolled as to lead to the good rather than away from it. Each of these virtues is broadly conceived, since it functions in each and every good act of that part of the soul. Justice, however, is in a way ontologically homeless, for it is a harmony produced when each of the three parts functions well. To explain the relation of justice to the other virtues, Plato emended Socrates' thesis that wisdom is a necessary and sufficient condition for virtue, by substituting the combination of wisdom, courage, and temperance for Socrates' single virtue of wisdom. Taken together, these three virtues are the necessary and sufficient condition for justice: "That which preserves and fosters this inner harmony is called a just and fine action" ($(W \cdot C \cdot T) \supset J$); and "an action which destroys this harmony is unjust" ($\sim (W \cdot C \cdot T) \supset \sim J$). Plato thereby reduced justice to the other three virtues, but he did not do so through a negative reduction that eliminates one virtue in favor of another, but through a positive reduction that shows the connection of one virtue with another. He thereby achieved a kind of unity of function without making the virtues identical in nature with each other, in the way Socrates had done. There is no true courage without temperance, no full justice without wisdom, for they are four distinct virtues which are unified functionally with each other.[17]

The trip down to vice is the reverse of the trip up to virtue. The harmony of virtue is eaten away step by step, so that although "there is but one form of virtue," the four virtues of the philosopher king or the aristocrat, "there are unlimited forms of vice, four of which are worthy of examination."[18] The first step down from the full justice of the aristocrat occurs when wisdom gives way to opinion in the timocrat, who loves the honor that accompanies good action more than the goodness that such action produces. Courage predominates in the timocrat, while temperance

[17] Plato, *Republic* 4 (443e5-444a1). Terence Irwin, *Platonic Ethics* 237-239, is sure the Socratic position that there is but one virtue–wisdom–is different from the Platonic position in the *Republic*; but he is not sure whether Plato held that there are four virtues ontologically different but operationally unified, or only one virtue–justice. He concludes: "It must remain uncertain, then, whether Plato takes the accounts of the virtues to show that they are distinct, although inseparable, or that they are really one and the same virtue. But even if he maintains the Unity Thesis, he disagrees sharply with Socrates' reasons for maintaining it. Since Socrates believes that there is nothing to virtue besides the right sort of knowledge, he lacks the basis for distinctions among the virtues that rests on the tripartition of the soul."

[18] *Republic* 4 (445c).

and justice also remain in his soul. Truly courageous, temperate, and just acts are still performed, but they have lost their inner life because they are no longer energized by true wisdom. Consequently, all three are so reduced in stature that Plato's global moral evaluation is that such a *polis* or such an individual is vicious, not virtuous. Next goes courage, loss of which produces the rich oligarch. His outstanding virtue is temperance, which enables him still to produce quality goods, amass the wealth that comes from them, and maintain some real, though diminished level of justice, both in his soul and in the community he runs. When temperance is eclipsed by exaggerated love of freedom and equality, the oligarch becomes a democrat, who loves justice dearly but thinks it can be maintained without wisdom, without courage, without temperance. Such justice is but a pale imitation of true justice, for its claim to the name of virtue is that some genuine goods, notably equality and freedom, are still prized, though they are attained in more and more unjust ways. Finally comes the last step downward, from democrat to tyrant, where mind is so enslaved by the basest desires that the vestiges of all the virtues are lost in the tyrant's soul and in his regime, for he reduces the good for all to the good for him. And so is completed the circle from vice to the highest virtue and back again to utter vice.[19]

Vices, then, are distorted images of the virtues. While there is no true wisdom or justice in vicious souls, their opposites–the vices of imprudence or injustice–still reflect these virtues. On the way up to true virtue, humans can attain temperance of a sort before becoming courageous or wise, a kind of temperance that is still properly speaking a vice because not engendered by wisdom and courage, but one that allows the craftsman to control his desire for wealth, produce goods, and contribute somewhat to the good of his whole soul and the whole *polis*, even if for reasons he does not understand or for the wrong reasons. On the way down, we come to understand that such a craftsman has an oligarchic soul, one in danger of becoming democratic through losing what it still has of temperance, just as it has already lost wisdom and courage. The demise of the soul is the story of how the virtue of each part of the soul becomes more and more distorted in itself and less and less able to cooperate with the others. Total chaos in the soul, however, would make it impossible for us to do anything. Consequently, just as all four virtues operate together in the aristocrat, so in the souls of vicious men the four distorted images of the virtues–what used to

[19] *Republic* 8-9 (543a-592b).

be virtues but are in the process of turning into vices–still work together, though less and less efficiently as one descends the ladder of virtue and vice. If they did not, the vicious would accomplish nothing, not even vice.

Plato's theory of four virtues, then, is an account of how to achieve inner harmony and perfection, one that shows justice is intrinsically good for us and also is good in its consequences. This harmony is produced through functional unity, not, as Socrates thought, through ontological unity. Plato's doctrine can be summed up as follows: following Socrates, Plato held that whoever truly has one virtue has all the virtues, and whoever lacks one virtue lacks all true virtue. But he departed from his teacher in recognizing four virtues, not just one. Because these virtues exist on their own, they can be gained and lost one by one. Until all four are present together in the soul of the truly just person, however, they are only images of true virtues and therefore really are vices.

c. Aristotle

If Plato introduced a doctrine of four virtues his most illustrious pupil turned his back on them. To Aristotle's mind, Plato made practice depend too much on theory, so that his conclusions about the virtues were only as sure as his dubious account of the soul. To minimize the dependence of ethics on the vagaries of theoretical psychology, Aristotle abandoned arguments based on the soul's powers.[20] Instead he turned to Plato's account of justice, which took its bearings from the end of justice, not some power of the soul. Here was a model for philosophical ethics, Aristotle thought; and using it he found that the fundamental fact of ethics is the goal-oriented character of human actions. Moral virtues are means to the single ultimate end which dominates every human life: the drive for "happiness."[21] Socra-

[20] Aristotle limits psychology to one chapter of the *Nic. Eth.* 1.13. Aristotle goes out of his way to reject Plato's mode of argument based on the difference between the "rational" and "irrational" parts of the soul: "Whether these are separated as the parts of the body or of anything divisible are, or are distinct by definition but by nature inseparable, like convex and concave in the circumference of a circle, *does not affect the present question*." (1102a29-33) tr. Ross.

[21] *Eudaimonia*, also translated as "success" (Hutchinson) or "flourishing." For a general view of Aristotle's ethics, see: Sarah Broadie, *Ethics with Aristotle* (Oxford: OUP, 1991); Richard Kraut, *Aristotle on the Human Good* (Princeton: Princeton University Press, 1986); Nancy Sherman, ed., *Aristotle's Ethics: Critical Essays* (New York: Rowan and Littlefield, 1999). For more focus on the virtues, see D.S. Hutchinson, "Ethics," in *The Cambridge Companion to Aristotle* (Cambridge: CUP, 1995)

tes was right to understand virtue as a kind of craft for living well, but Aristotle thought he had over-intellectualized it. Virtues are *moral* habits–that is, character traits acquired through repeated actions–not some kind of intellectual knowledge. And while Plato was right in saying that understanding such interior habits needs to be founded on some objective reality outside the soul, that reality is not Plato's city. Virtue should be understood as Aristotle understood sensation, where each sense power is best described through its object, as sight is directed to color and hearing to sound.[22] For Aristotle, then, knowing a virtue depended on two things: (1) knowing its *formal* character, that is, attaining a middle point between the extremes of excess and defect, which are the two vices opposed to it,[23] and (2) knowing this "mean" concretely, not abstractly, by limiting each virtue to a precise area of moral life. What resulted was a host of *specific* virtues. Aristotle gave no indication of having obtained an exhaustive list of virtues, but the ones he did consider fit into his polemic against Plato.

Aristotle multiplied Platonic wisdom into five different virtues: the theoretical virtues of wisdom (*sophia*), understanding (*nous*), and knowledge (*episteme*), productive craftsmanship (*techne*), and finally prudence (*phronesis*), which is different from the others because it guides practical life. He then adopted Plato's three moral virtues–courage, temperance, and justice–but he transformed them into *specific* virtues by limiting the scope of each. Finally, he added nine other specific virtues, in areas where Plato had seen only vice. The alternative to the timocrat's vicious love of honor are the virtues of proper ambition (when the honors are small) and magnanimity (for great honors). While Plato thought love of money always a vice, Aristotle said money could be used virtuously, in magnificence (by the wealthy) and liberality (for small sums). Even the democratic soul Plato seemed especially to despise can develop virtues, such as shame (in the realm of desires), good temper (which controls emotions), and truthfulness, friendliness, and wittiness (three rational virtues). Aristotle's list of moral virtues seems designed to counter Plato's dismissal of timocrats,

195-232, with an excellent bibliography, 357-372; D.S. Hutchinson, *The Virtues of Aristotle* (London: OUP, 1986); Nancy Sherman, *The Fabric of Character: Aristotle's Theory of Virtue* (New York: OUP, 1989). The best detailed treatment of each of the virtues is still Thomas Aquinas, *Sententia libri ethicorum* (Rome: Santa Sabina, 1969) ed. Leonina, 47, tr. C.I. Litzinger, rpr. (Notre Dame, IN: Dumb Ox Press, 1993).

[22] Aristotle, *On the Soul* 2.6-11.

[23] Aristotle, *NE* 2.6 (1106a14-25). Cf. Hutchinson, *Cambridge Companion* 217-219.

oligarchs, and democrats as necessarily vicious men.[24]

Most importantly for the development of the doctrine of the cardinal virtues, Aristotle's theory of specific virtues led him to reject the Socratic unity of the virtues and also Plato's doctrine that true virtue is limited to the person who has all four cardinal virtues. In their place he substituted a doctrine of the *connection* between each *specific* moral virtue and the practical intellectual virtue of prudence. While Socrates and Plato had said full-blown wisdom is the necessary and sufficient condition for moral virtue, Aristotle thought they had misidentified the intellectual virtue required. That virtue is not wisdom, but prudence, construed narrowly as good practical decision-making: "It is clear, then, from what has been said, it is not possible to be good in the principal way without prudence ($\sim P \supset \sim V$); nor prudent without ethical virtue ($\sim V \supset \sim P$)."[25] Aristotle recognized the consequent logical identity between prudence and each moral virtue ($P \equiv V$), but he thought it did *not* entail a Socratic ontological identity between them, nor does it require the virtuous person to be virtuous in every area, as Plato maintained. Imprudence ($\sim P$) is a kind of blindness which prevents the exercise of a moral virtue because one cannot see how to apply it in a specific area of morality; while lack of a virtue ($\sim V$) prevents one from putting prudence into practice in a limited moral realm, owing to not wanting to do the good even when one knows how. Prudence and virtue, then, must work together. But they are by no means the same thing, and being virtuous in one area of life is no guarantee of virtue in another.

Aristotle lowered the intellectual requirements for virtue by separating the prudent person from the sage. Moral virtue requires only prudence, not wisdom; and he thought the psychological habits of prudence and virtue are gradually built up from repeated acts. On the other hand, while moral virtue does not demand the wisdom of the sages, it does require more than the mere opinions advocated by the sophists. This is the limited extent to which Aristotle followed the intellectual elitism of Socrates and Plato ($\sim P \supset \sim V$), but without either succumbing to Socratic over-intellectualism or to the way Plato confused the virtuous with the "blessed (*makarios*)." Many people may make a prudent choice now and then, but these correct choices do not come *from* the habit of prudence. Aristotle was similarly elitist about

[24] Listed at *Nic. Eth.* 2.7, treated in detail 3.6-5.11. Cf. Hutchinson, *Cambridge Companion* 219-228.

[25] *Nic. Eth.* 6.13 (1144b30-32).

the moral virtues on which prudence depends ($\sim V \supset \sim P$). While one can recognize something like courage, for example, anywhere humans face obstacles, Aristotle limited the *virtue* of courage, properly speaking, to those who face death and do so on the battlefield, fighting freely for their own country. Making the moral virtues into *specific* virtues has the effect of limiting the virtuous to a small moral elite. In short, Aristotle showed how it is possible to be courageous, for example, without being temperate, and he also recognized a mediocre moral middle made up of those who perform virtuous actions but not out of virtue. But since he regarded the occupants of this middle ground as not truly virtuous, he did not see any reason to base philosophical ethics on their behavior.

The way Aristotle treated the moral vision of Socrates had a cost: he sacrificed Plato's central insight that there are four virtues linked closely to human nature. It seems never to have occurred to him that in doing so he fell victim in the area of moral virtue to the same error he had attributed to Socrates and Plato in the area of intellectual virtue, namely, setting the standards for virtue too high. While he recognized moral acts and habits at work in everyday life, he reserved the term "virtue" for the outstanding excellence of the few. It is one thing to say that the private courage of a wife or merchant is a lesser form of courage than the public, martial courage of an Achilles; it is quite another to say their courage is not really courage at all. And such a residue of Platonism seems to have stuck to Aristotle's theory of virtue, for this is precisely what he said.[26]

d. The Stoics

The schools of philosophy which dominated late antiquity–Skepticism, Epicureanism, and Stoicism–were all inspired more by Socrates than Plato or Aristotle.[27] The Skeptics took their inspiration from the "human" wisdom

[26] John Casey, *Pagan Virtue* (Oxford: Clarendon, 1990) defends the tradition which "runs from Homer to ... the theorists of Republican virtues of the Renaissance," who thought of courage (and the other virtues) "as being preeminently a public virtue" in contrast with the more private conception of courage found in "liberal individualism" which comes "from both Christianity and Kant" (51-2). While Aristotle's conception of courage was public and Kant's private, Aquinas self-consciously strove to cover both sides of this distinction by developing multiple, analogous senses of each cardinal virtue.

[27] A.A. Long, "The Socratic legacy," *The Cambridge History of Hellenistic Philosophy* (Cambridge: CUP, 1999) 617-641, esp. "The Socratic presence in Greek ethics" 618-623.

Socrates admitted he had in the *Apology*, a wisdom that ironically consists in recognizing what one does *not* know. Rather than thinking such a confession of ignorance the starting point from which philosophy builds, the skeptics took it as the end for which philosophy strives. The Epicureans found in Socrates' preference for the views of "the few" inspiration for preferring the cultured pleasure brought by wisdom over the baser pleasures of "the many."[28] But when early Christians encountered these philosophies they judged both to be at odds with revelation. However skeptical his bent, a Christian cannot be a Skeptic because Christian dogma demands belief; and pleasure simply is not God, even if seeing God face to face brings pleasure that surpasses all understanding.

In Stoicism, by contrast, early Christians found much that was attractive.[29] The school took its name from the "painted porch (*stoa poikile*)" alongside the Athenian market-place, where Socrates had conversed but Plato and Aristotle had abandoned when founding their own schools. By returning the life of philosophizing there, Zeno of Citium (ca. 334-262 B.C.), its founder, served notice that the philosophical doctrines of Stoicism would return to the radical and critical spirit of Socrates; and he did so by writing a new *Republic* that corrected Plato's, a critique further developed in *On the Republic* by his disciple Chrysippus (ca. 280-206 B.C.).[30]

Immediately attractive to Christians was a new philosophical principle the Stoics professed. Zeno and Chrysippus construed Socrates's personal divinity–his daimon–as a cosmic force of universal reason (*logos*), one identified by Cleanthes († 232 B.C.) as Zeus, the author of nature. This cause was similar enough in name and function to the *logos* in the Gospel

[28] On Epicurus († 271/270 B.C.) and Epicureans: M. Erler and M. Schofield, "Epicurean ethics," *The Cambridge History of Hellenistic Philosophy* 642-675; Phillip Mitsis, *Epicurus' Ethical Theory* (Ithaca: Cornell, 1988) esp. 70-79; J.M. Rist, *Epicurus: an Introduction* (Cambridge: CUP, 1972) 100-163. On Skeptics (Pyrrho † 275 B.C.; Sextus Empiricus, † ca. 200 A.D.): R.J. Hankinson, *The Skeptics* (London: Routledge, 1995) 262-272.

[29] B. Inwood and P. Donini, "Stoic Ethics," *The Cambridge History of Hellenistic Philosophy* 675-738; J.M. Rist, *Stoic Philosophy* (Cambridge: CUP, 1969) 1-111; Marcia Colish, *The Stoic Tradition from Antiquity to the Early Middle Ages* (Leiden: Brill, 1985).

[30] Diogenes Laertius, *Vitae* 7.121, 131; tr. Inwood and Gerson 143, 145. M. Schofield, *The Stoic Idea of the City* (Cambridge: CUP, 1991); "Social and Political Thought: vi Zeno's *Republic*," *The Cambridge History of Hellenistic Philosophy* 756-760.

of John[31] for early Christians to take notice. The first rule of Stoic ethics was to submit one's mind to it. The Stoics then absorbed the fundamental doctrines of Platonic-Aristotelian teleology–that the good is an end (*telos*), the ultimate end of human life is happiness, happiness is achieved through virtue–by attaching them to this new principle.

> Zeno first, in his book *On the Nature of Man*, said that the end was to live in agreement with nature, which is to live according to virtue. For nature leads to virtue.... To live according to virtue is equivalent to living according to the experience of events which occur by nature, as Chrysippus says in book one of his *On Ends*. For our natures are parts of the nature of the universe. Therefore, the end becomes to live consistently with nature, that is, according to one's own nature *and* that of the universe, doing nothing which is forbidden by the common law, which is right reason penetrating all things, being the same as Zeus who is the leader of the administration of things. And this itself is the virtue of the happy man and a smooth flow of life, whenever all things are done according to the harmony of the divinity in each of us with the will of the administrator of the universe.[32]

The Stoic *logos* proved more intelligible, more personal, and more amenable to religious devotion than Plato's "good" or Aristotle's "happiness." It was variously known as reason or nature or Zeus, and Zeno's punning definition of virtue is based upon it: to be virtuous is "to live in agreement (*homo-logoumenos zên*)," in agreement with reason and in agreement with nature, which, since they encompass the divine in us, is to live in agreement with God.

When Zeno and Chrysippus turned to the virtues that "living in agreement" involved, they followed Plato's four principal virtues and also his claim that they mutually entail each other. But they thought Plato underestimated the logical consequences of his own position. If the four virtues entail each other, they should be "equal" to each other; and their opposing vices should be "equal" too, even if Plato tried to moderate his position by saying there are four unequal levels of vice, not just one level.[33] They also

[31] Goulven Madec, "Verus philosophus est amator Dei: S. Ambroise, S. Augustin, et la philosophie," *Revue des Sciences Philosophiques et Théologiques*, 61 (1977) 549-566.

[32] Diogenes Laertius, *Vitae* 7.87-8, tr. Inwood and Gerson 136.

[33] Diogenes Laertius, *Vitae* 7.127, tr. Inwood and Gerson 144; Stobaeus, 2.66-7, tr. Long and Sedley 1: 379-80.

spurned Aristotle's attempts to moderate virtue theory. Diogenes Laertius († ca. 250 A.D.) reported that "while the Peripatetics say that *progress* lies between virtue and vice," the Stoics "believed there is nothing between virtue and vice,"[34] a moral rigorism encapsulated in a striking image:

> For just as those who are submerged in the ocean cannot breathe, whether they are so close to the surface that they are just about to emerge or they are down deep ... so too whoever is making a little progress toward the habit of virtue is no less in misery than one who has progressed not at all.[35]

These innovations produced a new exemplar of virtue: not a well-rounded ideal like Plato's "philosopher-king" or even Aristotle's "great-souled" man, who has the practical and political attainments of the philosopher-king minus the burden of too much theory; they found their ideal in a lopsided "sage" like Socrates himself, obsessed with understanding the intentions behind our actions. By putting a cosmic and cosmopolitan twist on Socrates' search for universal definitions, the Stoics thought his single-minded devotion to the *logos* allowed him to submit with equanimity to death, seemingly the worst of evils, a philosophical ideal clearly attractive to early Christians, whose first moral exemplar was the martyr who could withstand death out of single-minded devotion to Christ.

The Stoic sage was conceived as a paragon of moral virtue. Zeno's account of virtue took off from the *Republic*, where Plato had argued that virtue is good for humans and vice bad, not just extrinsically through their consequences, but intrinsically. There Plato noted that what is good intrinsically but not in its results, such as fleeting feelings of joy or pleasure, is quite the opposite of something not good intrinsically but only in what results from it, such as physical training, medical drugs, the skill of the physician, and money. In turn, both of these senses of goodness are different from things good both intrinsically and in their consequences, good things such as sight and health.[36] Plato thought virtue good in both ways

[34] Diogenes Laertius, *Vitae* 7.127, tr. Inwood and Gerson 144.

[35] Cicero, *De finibus* 3.14.48. Cf. Augustine, *Letter 167 to Jerome*, 12-13, below pp. 209-12; Plutarch, *Com. not.* 1063ab, tr. Long and Sedley 1: 382.

[36] Plato, *Republic* 2 (357b): "Tell me, do you think there is a kind of good (*agathon*) which we welcome not because we desire its consequences (*ton apobainonton*) but for its own sake (*auto hautou heneka*): for example, joy (*charein*) and all the harmless pleasures (*hêdonai*) which have no further consequences beyond the joy which one finds in them?" tr. Grube.

and vice good in neither, because only on this account could virtue affect all three factors involved in every moral action–the inner states and intentions that cause actions, real actions themselves, and consequences that result from actions. Of these three, Plato thought the most important one, virtue's 'payoff,' as it were, is found in the actions performed, and Aristotle agreed, defining happiness as "*activity* of soul in accord with virtue." From Plato's own examples, however, Zeno drew a different and more radical conclusion. It struck him that Plato was wrong to say that health and wealth are good in different ways, for both are good only in their consequences. The evidence for this evaluation is that both can be badly used, as when a thief uses his good health to outrun the authorities. Zeno therefore concluded that virtues are not one among many things that are intrinsically good, they are the *only* things that are good intrinsically (*agathon, kalon*; *honestum*); and likewise the only thing intrinsically bad is vice (*kakia*; *vitium*). Everything else is morally neutral, for which he coined the term "indifferent (*adiaphoros*; *indifferens*)":

> The virtues–prudence, justice, courage, temperance and the others–are good (*agatha*); and their opposites–imprudence, injustice, and the others–are bad (*kaka*); neither good nor bad are those things which neither benefit nor harm, such as life, *health*, pleasure, beauty, strength, *wealth*, good reputation, noble birth, and their opposites death, *disease*, pain, ugliness, weakness, *poverty*, bad reputation, low birth, and such things.... For these things are not good, but things *indifferent* (*adiaphora*) in the category of *preferred* things (*proêgmena*). For just as heating, not cooling, is a property of the hot, so benefitting, not harming, is a property of the good; but *wealth and health* do not benefit any more than they harm; therefore, neither wealth nor health is good.[37]

Humans obviously choose things that are intrinsically "indifferent" on the Stoic scheme. To explain how this is possible, *without introducing any intrinsic goodness into them*, the Stoics developed a completely new moral vocabulary, replete with neologisms designed to avoid the Platonic-Aristotelian error of positing intrinsic goodness in things that are intrinsically indifferent. Animals and humans do have "impulses (*hormê*; *appetitio animi*)" for and against things intrinsically indifferent. When humans deem

[37] Diogenes Laertius, *Vitae* 7.102-3, tr. Inwood and Gerson. Cf. Long and Sedley, *The Hellenistic Philosophers* 1: 354-359. Latin terms come from Cicero, *De finibus*.

such things of "value" or "worth (*axion*; *aestimabile*)" they are "preferred (*proêgmenon*; *praepositum, selectum*)" out of their intrinsic indifference; while things rejected are deemed to have "dis-value (*apaxion*)" and are "dis-preferred (*apoproêgmenon*; *reiectum*)" by us. Such language can look like a retreat to sophistic subjectivism, so the Stoics turned to "nature" as a criterion of choice. An action that is "in accord with (*kata*)" my nature is one that should be done; one that is not in accord with my nature should not be done. My nature is in turn guided by the cosmic nature that resides in the cosmic *logos* and is manifested through the "common" natural law. Those actions in accord with our nature are "proper (*oikeion*)," while those not in accord are "alien (*allotrion*)." "Proper" actions are also called "dutiful" or "appropriate (*kathêkon*)," a term "first used by Zeno, and derived from the phrase 'applying to certain people (*kata tinos hêkein*)', for it is an action (*energêma*) that is proper (*oikeion*) to arrangements that are according to nature." When Cicero translated *kathêkon* as *officium* he understood this term to mean 'duty based on one's nature,'[38] a notion that had a profound effect on subsequent moral philosophizing.

Duty alone, however, does not ensure virtue. In his *De finibus* (44 B.C.), Cicero set out five steps of moral development, steps distinguishing how one follows what is "dutiful (*kathêkon*; *officium*)." Virtue is attained only at the last step. He began with the innate inclination all animals, including humans, have toward self-preservation: "(1) the first [step] is to preserve oneself in the condition of one's nature." After securing life, however, one must go on to live it. Steps (2) through (4) focus on learning how to live by acting through "preference" for "duty": "(2) then one holds onto what is according to nature and rejects what is contrary, and once one masters 'preference' and 'dis-preference,' (3) then follows 'dutiful preference,' and (4) then comes 'permanent dutiful preference'." These three intermediate steps focus on bringing our actions and their consequences in line with the natural law. Though such improvements make one morally better, they do not produce virtue: "and then (5) at the end preference becomes unwavering and in harmony with nature, and here *for the first time* what can truly be called good [that is, virtuous] begins to be present in us and to be understood."[39]

To take the final step to virtue requires a fundamental and counter-intuitive reorientation: away from actions and their external consequences,

[38] Diogenes Laertius, *Vitae* 7.107; Cicero, *De finibus,* 3.20.

[39] Cicero, *De finibus*, 3.20.

inward toward mental states. At first we concentrate on "things *done* in accord with nature," but virtue refocuses on "seeing the *order* of things that should be done," order that is not an individual action but the plan that organizes individual actions. Virtue leads us to perform actions with consequences that are "finely done (*honeste facta*)," to be sure, but virtue consists essentially in "the fine itself (*ipsumque honestum*)," that is, in the inner character and habit of virtue. The sage focuses on inner intention and character (*diathesis*), because these are what constitute virtue, properly speaking. The Stoic conception of virtue, then, manifests "the exaltation of moral intention."[40] To bring the point home Cicero ends with a Stoic twist on a favorite Peripatetic example. The "ultimate end" of the archer is not to succeed in hitting the target, as Aristotle had incorrectly thought. Because external factors like the wind play a role there, his ultimate end is merely "to do all he can do to aim straight," something interior to him and well within his control.[41] The strength of will required to concentrate on inner attitudes and character, rather than external actions and consequences, set the grand theme for the later Stoics–Seneca, Epictetus, and Marcus Aurelius.

The Stoics set out the content of virtue in two ways: they focused negatively on eclipsing the passions and positively on developing the four cardinal virtues. Their attitude toward the passions of the soul was founded on rejecting both the Platonic teaching that the soul has three parts, that they correspond to the class structure of the *polis*, and that virtue and vice are a function of the relations among these parts, as Aristotle had done, and also in going beyond Aristotle to reject the very notion of the soul having parts:

> All [the Stoics] commonly hold that virtue is a certain character (*diathesin*) and power of command in the soul, generated by reason, or

[40] P. Donini, "Stoic Ethics," *The Cambridge History of Hellenistic Philosophy* 717. Cf. I. Kant, *Grounding of the Metaphysics of Morals*, who, after beginning with the Stoic division of the sciences, famously says: "Nothing in the world–indeed nothing even beyond the world–can possibly be conceived which could be called *good without qualification* except a good will."

[41] Cicero, *De finibus*, 3.22. Cf. 3.24: "We think that wisdom is *not* like the arts of the helmsman or the physician [as Plato and Aristotle held], but more like those of the actor, as I just said, or the dancer, since its end (*extremum*), that is, the effect of the art, is found within it, it is not sought outside," as the movement of the ship or the healing of the patient are effects existing "outside" their arts.

> rather, virtue is reason, consistent and firm and unchangeable. And they think that the passionate and irrational part is not distinguished by some distinction in nature from the rational part of the soul, but the same part of the soul, which they call the reasoning and commanding part, when as a whole it turns or changes during passions or changes in character or habit it becomes vice or virtue. It has nothing irrational in itself, but is called irrational when a strong and dominant excessive impulse has carried it off toward something wrong and contrary to reason.[42]

If moral goodness comes from having the whole, unitary soul act rationally in accord with a common, divine reason, moral evil comes from it being under the sway of private passion. The Stoic rejection of the Aristotelian-Platonic doctrine of different psychic powers affected both their definitions of the passions and their account of how to remove oneself from their control. "According to Zeno, passion is an irrational and un-natural movement in the soul, or an excessive impulse," a definition Chrysippus clarified by adding that the doctrine of the unitary soul implies that "passions are intellectual judgments (*kriseis*)."[43] As a sign of how important passion was for Stoic ethics, the list provided by Diogenes Laertius runs to twenty-six species of passions, though there are but four main types: (1) Before we attain what we want, we are subject to desire (*epithumia*), defined as "irrational appetite" for what appears good, and (2) fear (*phobos*), which is "expectation of bad." Obtaining an object we want can result in (3) pleasure (*hêdonê*), which is "irrational elation at obtaining what seems worthy of choice," while (4) pain (*lupê*) is the "irrational contraction" brought on when we fail to get what seems good.[44]

One rectifies these passions, not by channeling them to work under the guidance of reason, as Plato and Aristotle held, but by achieving "passionlessness (*apatheia*)," a kind of freedom from the influence of the passions achieved by stamping them out altogether. This state replaces passions with their opposites, called "good-passions (*eupatheia*)." Opposed to desire is (1) "willing (*boulêsis*)," defined as "rational appetite"; while the opposite of fear is (2) "caution (*eulabeia*)," that is, "rational avoidance"; and the oppo-

[42] Plutarch, *De virtute morali*, 441cd; cf. Long and Sedley 61B, 1: 378. See B. Inwood, *Ethics and Human Action in Early Stoicism* (Oxford: OUP, 1985).

[43] Diogenes Laertius, *Vitae* 7.110.

[44] Diogenes Laertius, *Vitae* 7.111-114; Stobaeus, 2.88.8-90.6; cf. Long and Sedley 1: 410-411.

site of pleasure is (3) "joy (*charan*)" or "rational elation."[45] Since both are states of a soul whose thoughts and emotions go together, the passions are irrational, the "good-passions" rational. Nothing opposed to pain is listed, but following the logic of the descriptions of pleasure and pain it would have to be a sort of 'rational expansion' of the mind, rejoicing in avoiding the seeming good and acquiring the truly good. Such an expansion seems but another word for virtue. The pathology of the four passions, then, uncovers the primary function of virtue: when virtue dethrones pain, it also brings the soul good will, caution, and joy.

The positive Stoic account of the life of virtue focused on the four Platonic virtues. They accepted the Socratic thesis that wisdom is the necessary and sufficient condition of moral virtue and they were aware that there was more than one ontology of the virtues compatible with this logical relation. An orthodox Platonist and no friend of the Stoics, Plutarch, first century (A.D.) author of the *Parallel Lives*, explained the views of Zeno and Chrysippus by conceiving their positions as extremes falling away form the Platonic doctrine he embraced that there are four and only four virtues, ontologically different but operationally connected.

"Zeno admits many different virtues, like Plato, that is, prudence, courage, temperance, and justice, as being not separate yet other and different from each other." The way he defined the cardinal virtues, however, "carried" Zeno logically to the Socratic position that "virtue is one, though it seems to differ in its actions in relation to its dispositions relative to things." For Zeno "defined prudence in distributions as justice, prudence in choices as temperance, and prudence in endurance as courage," definitions that effectively reduce all the virtues to a single virtue–prudence or knowledge–just as Socrates had done.

Chrysippus then marched off in the opposite direction. He recognized that the four principal virtues must be operationally unified, but in addition he thought that each virtue has its own "peculiar quality" which distinguished it from all other virtues. Consequently, "Chrysippus ... unwittingly stirred up, in Plato's words [*Meno* 72a], a 'swarm of virtues' both unusual and unknown," many more than four. As a Platonist, Plutarch berated him for "filling philosophy with many absurd names that it does not need"; but in truth Chrysippus made a great contribution to virtue theory, by showing how to make room for more than Plato's four virtues while keeping those four. He did so by inventing the distinction between four "primary" virtues

[45] Diogenes Laertius, *Vitae* 7.117, tr. Inwood and Gerson 142.

and the other virtues "subordinate to them."[46] Chrysippus thereby avoided two extremes: too much reductionism, as found in Socrates, Plato, and Zeno; and too little, as in Aristotle's hodge-podge of virtues related only by prudence. This 'moderate' position would come to dominate Stoicism and prove attractive to virtue theorists from Cicero to Aquinas.

e. Cicero

The works in which Chrysippus set out the doctrine of subordinate virtues have been lost, though scattered references in Greek listing primary and subordinate virtues as they had become canonical are found in Plutarch; in Diogenes Laertius (ca. 200-250 A.D.), author of the uneven but invaluable *Lives and Opinions of Eminent Philosophers*[47]; and in the late compiler Stobaeus (ca. 400 A.D.).[48] The earliest and best source for them, however, is Cicero's *De inventione*, written in Latin about 87 B.C. Throughout his writings, Cicero (106-43 B.C.) returned repeatedly to the Stoic doctrine of the four virtues, because they constitute the "duty (*kathêkon*; *officium*)"

[46] Plutarch, *De virtute morali* 440e-441d, who says Chrysippus reasoned thus: "For just as in the courageous man there is courage and in the mild man mildness and justice in the just man, so also in the graceful man there is gracefulness and in the noble man nobility and in the great man greatness and in the fine man fineness, and other such clever, easily conceived virtues were posited." Cf. *De Stoicorum repugnantiis* 1034c-e. Long and Sedley 1: 377-8; 2: 373-6.

[47] Diogenes Laertius, without naming a particular author says: "Of virtues, some are primary and some are subordinate to these. The primary virtues are these: prudence, courage, justice, and temperance. Species of these are magnanimity (*megalopsychian*), continence (*egkrateian*), patience (*karterian*), quick-wit (*agchinoian*), and good counsel (*euboulian*)." 7.92. "Good counsel (*euboulia*) and understanding (*sunesis*) follow on prudence, orderliness (*eutaxia*) and seemliness (*kosmiotês*) on temperance, equity (*isotês*) and considerateness (*eugnômosunê*) on justice, and on courage firmness (*aparallaxia*)and good tone (*eutonia*)." 7.126.

[48] Stobaeus, 60.9-24, without naming a particular author, says the Stoics held: "The primary virtues are four: prudence, temperance, courage, justice . . . To prudence are subordinated good counsel (*euboulian*), good reasoning (*eulogistian*), quick-wit (*agchinoian*), understanding (*nounecheian*), and resourcefulness (*eumêchanian*); to temperance are subordinate orderliness (*eutaxian*), seemliness (*kosmiotêta*), modesty (*aidêmosunên*), and continence (*egkrateian*); to courage are subordinated patience (*karterian*), confidence (*tharraleotêta*), magnanimity (*megalopsychian*), cheerfulnes (*eupsychian*), hard work (*philoponian*); and to justice are subordinated piety (*eusebeian*), honesty (*chrêstotêta*), good fellowship (*eukoinônêsian*), and fairness (*eusunallaxian*)." Cf. Long and Sedley 1: 380; 2: 376.

that motivates the virtuous person, especially in his mature and masterful *De officiis* (44 B.C.), which took its very title from this Stoic concept. But *De inventione* is more important for the history of the doctrine of the cardinal virtues, for two reasons. First, in this juvenile work Cicero followed a lost Greek original, which helps in reconstructing the "subordinate" virtues as earlier Stoics understood them. Second, and looking forward, it would so happen that *De inventione* survived and became known to the scholastics of the thirteenth century.[49] So it was from Cicero that Philip, Albert, and Thomas learned about the subordinate virtues.

Cicero's treatment of virtue in *De inventione* was Stoic and over-simplified, as might be expected of a student effort. The "invention" in Cicero's title is skill at finding arguments, one of five skills covered in ancient rhetorical manuals.[50] In treating the three kinds of speeches–legal, political, and display oratory–Cicero organized his treatment of political speeches in a Stoic manner.

He began with a Stoic rendering of the distinction between things good intrinsically and extrinsically. The intrinsic good he calls the "honorable good (*bonum honestum*)" and following the Stoics he reduces all such goods to virtue: "all things of this type are included under one meaning and one term, namely, virtue." Things extrinsically good and intrinsically neutral are exemplified by money and called "useful goods (*bona utilia*)."[51]

Virtue is then given a Stoic definition: "Virtue is a habit of the mind in agreement with the way of nature and reason."[52] Cicero's definition con-

[49] Also known were the lists of virtues drawn up in the Greek Aristotelian *De passionibus*, attributed to Andronicus of Rhodes (1st C. B.C.), and in the Latin work on the *Somnium Scipionis* of Cicero by Macrobius (ca. 400 A.D.).

[50] The others are arrangement, style, memory, and delivery. See G. Kennedy, *The Art of Persuasion in Greece* (Princeton: Princeton University Press, 1963); E.P.J. Corbett, *Classical Rhetoric* (Oxford: OUP, 1990).

[51] Cicero, *De inventione* 2.157-159. Cicero's latent Platonism leads him incoherently to add a third type: "something that joins together both of these, which by its own power and dignity leads us to it and beyond its own nature produces some utility we seek, such as friendship or good reputation." On Cicero, see: M. Colish, *The Stoic Tradition*, 1: 61-158; Maximilian Forschner, "Theoria und stoische Tugend: Zenons Erbe in Cicero, Tusculanae disputationes V," *Zeitschrift für philosophische Forschung* 53 (1999) 163-187; and still helpful for Thomists is E.K. Rand, *Cicero in the Courtroom of St. Thomas Aquinas* (Milwaukee: Marquette, 1946).

[52] 2.159: Nam virtus est animi habitus naturae modo atque rationi consentaneus.

tains Stoic themes: virtue is an inner "habit" because the life of virtue focuses on inner states rather than external actions or their consequences; it is a habit of "mind," not soul, reflecting the Stoic elimination of ontological parts within the mind and identity of virtue with intelligence; Cicero's "agreement (*consentaneus*)" is clearly an echo of Zeno's "to live in agreement (*homologoumenos zên*)"; and what the individual mind should agree with is cosmic "reason (*ratio*; *logos*)," the principle that includes "nature" and the "law of nature." Cicero then turns to the four primary Stoic virtues, defining each and identifying their subordinate "parts." Both his definitions and the parts he identifies will be developed by Philip, Albert, and Aquinas.

Prudence is defined using the three Stoic categories: the morally good, bad, and indifferent. "Prudence is knowledge of things that are good or bad or neither. Its parts are memory, understanding, and foresight."[53] Of these three parts, only understanding seems to have Stoic overtones; but the parts of the other three virtues are clearly connected with Stoic subordinate virtues.

Cicero next turned to justice, defined as "the habit of mind that preserves the common utility while also giving to each what is his due."[54] As with his general definition of virtue, Cicero gives this definition a Stoic shape by beginning with "habit of mind." This focus manages to turn inward what would otherwise be the most outer-directed of the virtues. By calling the common good the "common utility" Cicero indicates that the external results of justice are happy consequences of the virtue, but not its essence. In this way, the traditional Platonic and Aristotelian matter of Cicero's definition–concern for the common good and the private good of others–is given a Stoic form. Cicero then divides justice using the Stoic notion of law to distinguish the "law of nature (*ius naturae*)," which provides justice its beginnings, from the "law of custom (*consuetudine ius*)," which provides for its development. Under the law of nature Cicero locates six parts of justice: religion, piety, consideration, retribution, honor, and truth. After allowances are made for differences in language, authors' interests, and time, Cicero's list overlaps those of Diogenes Laertius and Stobaeus remarkably; and all six species will be adopted by Aquinas. Under

[53] 2.160: Prudentia est rerum bonarum et malarum neutrarumque scientia. Partes eius: memoria, intelligentia, providentia.

[54] 2.160: Iustitia est habitus animi communi utilitate conservata suam cuique tribuens dignitatem.

the "law of custom" Cicero located "agreements, equity, and written judgments." Equity clearly came from the Stoics and will be adopted by Aquinas, while the other two are peculiar to Cicero's legal interests.[55]

Cicero then turned to courage, which he defined as "considered undertaking of dangers and endurance of hardships." Gone is Aristotle's insistence of mortal danger as the object of courage. "Consideration" at the beginning of the definition sets the Stoic motif of rationality, one enhanced by the fact that Cicero manages to define courage without reference to passion or fear, which have been expunged from the mind on the Stoic conception of courage. The most Stoic feature of his treatment, however, are the parts of courage: "magnificence, confidence, patience, and perseverance."[56] Cicero's definition of magnificence shows he actually had magnanimity in mind, and with this emendation the list of virtues subordinate to courage is thoroughly Stoic, and all four will be adopted by Philip, Albert, and Aquinas.[57]

Cicero ended with temperance, defined as "domination of reason over

[55] 2.161: Naturae ius est quod non opinio genuit, sed quaedam in natura vis insevit, ut religionem, pietatem, gratiam, vindicationem, observantiam, veritatem. 162: The parts of consuetudine ius are pactum, par, iudicatum. Note especially the following correlations among Greek and Latin terms for the subordinates of justice: 1) piety: eusebeia; religio, pietas; 2) equity: isotês, par; 3) consideration of others: eukoinônêsia, eugnômosunê; gratia, observantia; 4) fairness: eusunallaxia; vindicatio; 5) honesty: chrêstotês,veritas. Cf. nn. 47, 48.

[56] 2.163: Fortitudo est considerata periculorum susceptio et laborum perpessio. Eius partes magnificentia, fidentia, patientia, perseverantia. The Greek and Latin subordinates of courage are related thus: 1a) magnanimity: megalopsychia; magnanimitas, 1b) magnificence: megaloprepeia; magnificentia; 2) confidence: aparallaxia, tharraleotes; fidentia; 3) patience: karteria; patientia; 4) perseverance: philoponia; perseverantia, constantia.

[57] 2.163: Magnificence is planning and carrying out things that are great and lofty, out of a full and clear consideration by the mind: Magnificentia est rerum magnarum et excelsarum cum animi ampla quadam et splendida propositione cogitatio atque administratio. This definition does not mention outlay of money, as did Aristotle's, but serves well as a definition of magnanimity. Diogenes and Stobaeus exclusively use megalopsychia not megaloprepeia for the Stoic virtue subordinate to courage. Thus, although Cicero used magnificentia and magnanimitas rather interchangeably, his Stoic sources probably read megalopsychia consistently. Cf. *De off.* 1.21.72, 1.23.79, where Cicero uses magnificentia for magnanimitas; 1.19.63, 1.43.152, where he uses magnanimitas. The confusion created for Latin readers was finally resolved by Aquinas.

desire and over other incorrect inclinations of the mind, domination that is firm and attains the mean."[58] As before, this definition is thoroughly Stoic. Most prominent is the fact that guidance over human life is provided by reason (*ratio*), the Stoic *logos*. The guidance it provides is not just advice, as would be appropriate for a Platonically conceived 'political' rule of reason over desire, it is domination, the kind of rule a master (*dominus*) has over a slave. Once again, the soul is called "mind," implying psychic unity of a Stoic sort. And the dominance is not limited to the realms of nutrition and sex, as it had been for Aristotle, but in addition to governing such desires (*libido*), Cicero uses a Stoic technical term to widen the domain of temperance: it governs any improper inclination (*impetus*; *hormê*). Only at the end of his definition does Cicero tack on the Peripatetic notion of following the mean.

There are three virtues subordinated to temperance: continence, clemency, and modesty. Clemency, defined as sympathy of the higher ranks for the lower, seems a peculiarly Roman virtue and original with Cicero. The other two virtues were Stoic in origin. In Plutarch, temperance referred to the broad area of human choices (*en haireteois*), and continence (*egkrateia*) in Diogenes and Stobaeus seems to refer broadly to the 'strength of will' that allows one to make choices for the good, in any area of moral life. Cicero translated *egkrateia* as *continentia* and defined it thus: "Continence is that by which cupidity is ruled by the governance of good counsel."[59] If "cupidity" means broadly 'any desire,' then Cicero seems accurately to have reflected the Stoic understanding; but "cupidity" might be limited to nutritional and sexual desires, and was so understood later. The term "continence" is ambiguous, and the scholastics would spend some efforts trying to determine its true nature. The other subordinate Stoic virtue–modesty–involved no such ambiguity and was readily adopted by the schoolmen.

For later virtue theorists, the important role Cicero played was to present the results of the Stoic attempt to integrate the four primary virtues–stemming ultimately from Plato–with the many specific virtues–stemming ultimately from Aristotle. Since they did not have access to Greek Stoic texts, later thinkers sometimes were unaware of the specifically Stoic features of the doctrine of the cardinal virtues in Cicero's presentation, and

[58] 2.164: Temperantia est rationis in libidinem atque in alios non rectos impetus animi firma et moderata dominatio. Eius partes continentia, clementia, modestia.

[59] 2.164: Continentia est per quam cupiditas consili gubernatione regitur.

Cicero himself tended toward syncretism. The main challenge for the scholastic masters was to try to bring to life a millenium-old Stoic skeleton present in lists of virtues they found in old books like Cicero's. It is to their philosophical credit that they did so well, as we shall see.

f. Seneca

The final pagan Roman in the story of the cardinal virtues was Seneca (4BC-65AD). His thought was deeply influential on early medieval thinkers, in part because he was deemed not a pagan at all, but a Christian who corresponded with St. Paul.[60] The reality was considerably less elevated. Ambitious son of an ambitious father, Seneca followed his father's footsteps from Cordoba to Rome and used his considerable gifts in rhetoric and philosophy to rise to heights of power and wealth. Almost sentenced to death by Caligula (r. 37-41), he attained a position at court under Claudius but was soon banished to Corsica in 41 on the probably accurate charge of a liaison with Julia, niece of the Emperor and daughter of the much mourned Germanicus. Recalled to court in 49 to tutor Nero, he retired in 62 and facing the charge of complicity in conspiracy he committed suicide in 65.

Though a clever man and fine stylist, Seneca was not an original thinker in philosophy, nor even so interested in how the Greek Stoics had developed their conclusions as Cicero. But he was keenly concerned with the reality of living out Stoicism and he initiated a new phase in Stoic writing. Followed by Epictetus (†140) and the Emperor Marcus Aurelius (†180), Seneca concentrated on real-life attempts to attain *apatheia* and virtue, in the words of Epictetus "to endure and abstain." Seneca accepted the scheme of the cardinal virtues as part of the Stoic patrimony, something to be used in writing short humane works of advice and consolation. Most influential were 124 moral epistles to his friend Lucilius. Seneca also knew the doctrine of virtues subordinate to the four major virtues and he composed treatises on some of them, *De constantia* and *De clementia*. His influence was paramount in the early middle ages and the most notable doctrine about the cardinal virtues that this favorite of emperors handed onto the medievals was the way he gave it a secular and political interpretation. For Seneca, the four virtues were virtues for a political elite, virtues of para-

[60] On Seneca as correspondent of Paul, see Paul Berry, *The Correspondence between Paul and Seneca, A.D. 61-65* (Lewiston, NY: Mellen, 1999). On Seneca, the definitive work is still Miriam T. Griffin, *Seneca: A Philosopher in Politics* (Oxford: Clarendon, 1976).

mount importance for emperors and rulers, because they produce "tranquillity of mind" when in power, "consolation" when not, and resolution when faced with "the shortness of life" and the prospect of death, all titles of Senecan tracts. From Seneca, then, readers learned that the four Stoic virtues were the best guides to practical life, that they come together as a 'package' of four virtues necessarily united together, that they involve other virtues connected with them, and above all that they are most fitting for emperors and princes.

Though the Latin Fathers initiated a wholly new approach to the cardinal virtues, as we shall see, the influence of Seneca especially, as representative of a Stoic and political understanding of the four virtues, lasted well into the twelfth century.[61] As an example, the sixth century is especially interesting. While Pope Gregory I (†604) followed the new understanding of the cardinal virtues initiated by Ambrose, two of his contemporaries followed the older, Stoic conception of them. Both were churchmen living in Seneca's home province now called Spain. Martin of Braga purported to be the author of a short and much copied treatise on the cardinal virtues entitled *Formula vitae honestae*. This little work does not mention God and its four virtues are the virtues of a prince, to whom it is dedicated. It was composed (or copied) by Bishop Martin in the spirit (and perhaps the letter) of Seneca, and may well be a lost work of Seneca's, to whom it was later attributed. The other author was Isidore of Seville.[62] For both authors the cardinal virtues are such as could have come from the pen of Seneca himself.

Though Christians and Latin writers, Martin and Isidore can serve as an appropriate stopping point for consideration of the initial phase of the development of the doctrine of the four cardinal virtues. This phase saw the origin and perfection of a doctrine of four virtues, a doctrine that derived from prolonged meditation on Socrates and whose primary exponents were Plato, Aristotle, and the Stoics. But as much as these three great ethical schools had done, they had not made the cardinal virtues 'cardinal.' This innovation required the wholesale revolution in thought known as Christian wisdom.

[61] See, for example, G. Verbeke, *The Presence of Stoicism in Medieval Thought* (Washington: Catholic University of America, 1983) 8-11.

[62] On this period see: R. Newhauser, *The Treatise on Vices and Virtues in Latin and the Vernacular* (Turnhout: 1993); Colish, *The Stoic Tradition*, 1: 16.

2. *Sancti*

It has recently been argued that Augustine inaugurated a new period in the history of philosophy, a period called "the Latin Age" that extended from the Bishop of Hippo through the late scholastic writers of the seventeenth century.[63] The history of the development of the doctrine of the cardinal virtues fits this theory well, for Christian writers of the fourth century certainly inaugurated a new way of considering the cardinal virtues. They thought of them as Christian virtues and invented the phrase "cardinal virtue" as a sign of their new conception. This new age in thought about the four virtues, however, was not begun by Augustine but by his teacher Ambrose, Bishop of Milan.

a. Ambrose

Ambrose seems to have invented the term "cardinal virtues" because he was an inveterately allegorical thinker.[64] In *On Paradise* (ca. 377) he set out an allegorical explanation of *Genesis*: the fertile land of paradise is like a fertile soul; Adam is like its intellect and Eve like its senses. The four rivers in Eden are in reality the four great rivers of the earth. These rivers in turn are analogous to the four Platonic virtues within the soul, because each is "principal" within its own realm.[65] Platonic analogy turned into Christian allegory when Ambrose connected the two sides of the compari-

[63] J. Deely, *Four Ages of Understanding: The First Postmodern Survey of Philosophy from Ancient Times to the Turn of the Twenty-first Century* (Toronto: University of Toronto Press, 2001) 161-484.

[64] See (I. Brady) ed., *Magistri Petri Lombardi Sententiae in IV Libris Distinctae* (Rome: Grottaferata, 1981) 2: 188 n. 3: "primus autem qui eas cardinales vocat est Ambrosius." On virtue theory and the Christian fathers see: Colish, *The Stoic Tradition*, vol. 2; R.E. Houser, "The Cardinal Virtues: Aquinas and the Fathers," in B. C. Bazan *et al*, ed., *Les philosophies morales et politiques au Moyen Âge* (Ottawa: LEGAS, 1995) 2: 699-708. On Ambrose and philosophy, see: Andrew Lenox-Conyngham, "Ambrose and philosophy," *Christian faith and Greek philosophy in late antiquity* (Leiden: Brill, 1993) 112-128; G. Madec, *S. Ambroise et la philosophie* (Paris: Études Augustiniennes, 1974); B. Ramsey and C. Harrison, ed., *Ambrose* (New York: Routledge, 1997); H. Savon, *Ambroise de Milan* (Paris: Desclée de Brouwer, 1997).

[65] Ambrose, *De par.* 3.18, CSEL 32.1: 277. For ms. illuminations of the picture Ambrose paints, see Katzenellenbogen 49 n. 1, fig. 68-69. Cf. J. Moorhead, *Ambrose: Church and Society in the Late Roman World* (London: Longman, 1999) 177-180.

son–the four rivers with the four virtues–through a common point of reference, namely, through God, who is at once the cosmic artisan who created the rivers of paradise and, in the person of Jesus Christ, the wisdom producing virtue in individual men. Allegorical exegesis, then, gave the Platonic virtues a cosmic import they would not otherwise have.

In the funeral oration for Satyrus (ca. 378), Ambrose read the life of his brother allegorically, as he read Scripture. Though he was a quiet man whose external deeds did not live up to antique ideals of civic excellence, his brother did indeed exhibit the four Platonic virtues, and he did so in a way that broke through the limits which had been imposed on these virtues by the *philosophi*. Ambrose christened them "cardinal virtues," a phrase he seems to have coined for the occasion. After beginning with a series of intensely emotional personal remembrances showing how his brother was his "other self," Ambrose devoted the second half of his oration to showing how his brother exhibited all four cardinal virtues. After covering his prudence, courage, and temperance, Ambrose said:

> What remains, in order to complete the cardinal virtues, is that we also show the parts of justice in him (Satyrus). For even though the virtues are born together and perfected together, nevertheless one desires to know the form and outline of each one of them, and especially of justice.[66]

To signify the new life now present in the old virtues, Ambrose chose the adjective "cardinal (*cardinalis*)," which is derived from the noun *cardo*, an unusual term with a number of seemingly unrelated meanings. For the mason, *cardo* meant the hinge on which a door turns, or the tenon and mortise which dovetail together in the door's frame. For the Roman surveyor, it meant the baseline for his measurement of a field, and more broadly the term was used to refer to a geographical district, region, or

[66] *De excessu fratris Satyri* 1.57, CSEL 73: 239: Superest, ut ad conclusionem *cardinalium virtutum* etiam *partes* in eo debeamus advertere. Nam etsi cognatur sint inter se concretaeque virtutes, tamen singularum quaedam forma et expressio desideratur maximeque iustitiae. P. Courcelle, "Aspects variés du platonisme ambrosien," in *Recherches sur les Confessions de S. Augustin* (Paris: Boccard, 1968) 323, found Ambrose here depended on Apuleius, *De Platone et eius dogmate* 2.7.229, ed. Beaujeau (Paris: Les Belles Lettres, 1973) 84: Per has tres animae *partes quartam virtutem, iustitiam*. Ambrose coined "cardinal" in place of Apuleius's "fourth." Cf. M. McGuire, tr., *Funeral Orations by Gregory Nazianzen and St. Ambrose* (New York: Fathers of the Church, 1953) 22. J. Moorhead, *Ambrose* 36-39.

boundary. More commonly, and the only way Ambrose himself used the word, *cardo* is a cosmological term, and as such it was applied to the earth's poles, points on the ecliptic, the days when the seasons change, and the four winds.[67] This cosmic import is apparent in Apuleius, whose textbook Ambrose read during his cram course in Platonism after becoming bishop.[68] These meanings, however, are not haphazard but are united by the notion of something which is extraordinarily important, in no small part because it is a point of transition. A *cardo* allows for movement from one room to another, from one field to the next, from one district, or region, or season to another. Indeed, its poles (*cardines*) are what allow the spheres in the Ptolemaic universe to spin around the earth in the first place. When applied to the lives of men, *cardines* are those critical points which seem to sum up the meaning of a human life and often bring with them fundamental transformations. Of these, what more ultimate point of transition is there than death? Earlier Roman writers had recognized this fact and had used the term *cardo* to refer to the end of life and even to death itself.[69] But none of them had called the virtues which help humans face death "cardinal."

Ambrose did so, first of all, because the four virtues gave Satyrus the ability to face death, though on this point Ambrose was no different from his illustrious Roman forebears. But he went beyond them to the other side of death, when all men face the author of the cosmos. The virtues which prepared him to face that 'cardinal' moment invested his brother's life with cosmic significance and so deserve to be called "cardinal" themselves. That preparation was not achieved by fixating on death and attempting to en-

[67] P.G.W. Clare, *Oxford Latin Dictionary* (Oxford: OUP, 1982) 276. Lewis and Short, *A Latin Dictionary* (Oxford: OUP, 1879) 291. *Cardo* was used for the poles by Varro, Pliny, Cicero, Ovid, Statius, and Seneca; for days when the seasons change by Pliny; for points on the ecliptic by Quintilian. Servius, a contemporary of Ambrose, used *cardinalis* of the four winds, in commenting on Virgil. Ambrose uses *cardo* three times: on Good Friday "the *foundations* of the earth shook," *De fide 5 ad Gratianum Augustum* 1.17.114, PL 16: 577; "a wind did not come from the four *directions* of the earth," *De spiritu sancto* 3.19.150, PL 16: 846; and on the first day God created heaven and earth, "for these two things are like unto *foundations* for things" created later, *Exemeron* 1.7.25, CSEL 32.1: 23.

[68] P. Courcelle, "Aspects variés," 336. In *De mundo* 1.289-290, 122, Apuleius says he uses *cardo* to translate *kentron* in holding the earth is the center of the universe. For Ambrose, of course, the center of the cosmos is God, not *terra firma*.

[69] Seneca, *De beneficiis* 4.22.1; *Troades* 52; Lucan, *Bellum civile* 7.381; Silius Italicus, *Punica*, 9.140.

gender a Stoic equanimity in the face of it. Ambrose turned to Plato to explain his brother's life, not his death, because Plato's four virtues are designed for living, for living the whole of life with an eye to the good. Ambrose simply replaced the abstract Platonic good with the God of Abraham, Isaac, and Jacob, and in so doing he gave Plato's four virtues a more concrete end than the philosophers ever had. This teleological orientation toward God would always be maintained by Ambrose's patristic and medieval descendants. In Ambrose's conception, then, three features make the four virtues "cardinal": they involve death, judgment, and orientation toward God. Thus did he transform the four Platonic virtues linguistically and doctrinally into *Christian* virtues, the "principal" virtues of the Christian life.[70]

Re-conceiving the four virtues as Ambrose did quite naturally raises the question of their connection with the beatitudes, conceived as rules for the Christian life; and he asserted such a connection between the four cardinal virtues and the four beatitudes listed in Luke's Gospel. "Blessed are the poor" enjoins Christians to temperance, whereby they trample out the seduction of the present life. "Blessed are they who hunger and thirst" enjoins them to justice, which derives from compassion and largesse to neighbor. "Blessed are you who weep" enjoins a kind of Christian prudence that weeps for what is worldly and seeks what is eternal. "Blessed are you when men hate you" enjoins courage, which "suffers persecution because of faith" and reminded Ambrose that the martyr's "crown of suffering" is "the consummation of courage" for a Christian.[71] Apart from this last, profound connection, the other three correlations, though clever, are strained and had little influence on subsequent thinkers. But this attempt uncovered a more profound problem, one whose solution did have a deep impact on the development of the doctrine of the cardinal virtues.

Ambrose was too honest a thinker not to face the obvious problem of two accounts of the beatitudes. While he could set out an easy correlation between the cardinal virtues and Luke's four beatitudes, how would the four virtues square with Matthew's eight beatitudes. Even more, how could

[70] *De sac.* 3.2.9, CSEL 73: 42. Et omnes quidem virtutes ad spiritum pertinent, sed istae quasi cardinales sunt, quasi principales. *De off. min.* 1.29.142, PL 16: 70: Fundamentum ergo est iustitiae *fides*. Colish, *The Stoic Tradition* 2: 55-70, focused her treatment of Ambrose's doctrine of virtue on *De Ioseph* and *De officiis ministrorum*. "Ambrose seeks to bring the Stoic sage into the fullness of being through Christian redemption."

[71] *Exp. ev. sec. Lucam* 5.64-67, CCSL 14: 157.

the two Gospel accounts be consistent with each other at all? Ambrose was sure that all the beatitudes are present in both Gospel accounts and that the different numbers have some allegorical significance: "the four are in the eight and the eight in the four."[72]

There are two ways to make the accounts consistent: either each one of Matthew's eight beatitudes is correlated with some one or another of Luke's four, and consequently with one of the four cardinal virtues; or each beatitude actually contains *all* the others, all of Luke's four and all of Matthew's eight, with the consequence that each cardinal virtue also must entail *all* the other cardinal virtues. One might expect Ambrose to have taken the first option, but he chose the second, for it recognizes the fact that each beatitude leads beyond itself. "Whoever is poor in spirit is not greedy, whoever mourns is not proud, whoever is meek is also peaceful." While he did not work out all the logical implications of this view, Ambrose clearly saw that each beatitude logically entails *all* the others. If so, given the correlation between beatitudes and cardinal virtues, each cardinal virtue should also entail the other cardinal virtues. In the funeral oration for Satyrus, Ambrose followed the Platonic view that the four virtues, though ontologically distinct, are unified operationally,[73] while in the commentary *On Luke* he took an even stronger stance: "Therefore, the virtues are so connected and chained together, that whoever has *one* seems to have them all; and there accrues to the saints [though not to the pagans, he implies] *one* virtue."[74] Here Ambrose crossed the line separating Platonic virtues which are essentially multiple while operationally united, to a more Socratic view where Christian virtue is essentially one while operationally many. His method of reconciling the Gospels ensured that the philosophers' doctrine of the unity of the cardinal virtues influenced both the "saints" and the medieval "masters."

[72] *Exp. ev. sec. Lucam* 5.49, CCSL 14: 152.

[73] *De excessu* 1.57, CSEL 73: 239.

[74] *Exp. ev. sec. Lucam* 5.62-3, CCSL 14: 156-7. Colish, *The Stoic Tradition* 2: 69: "Ambrose restores an authentically Stoic emphasis to the idea that all the virtues imply each other, even though he rejects the correlative principle that all sins are equal. However, the unity which he sees underlying the virtues is a corollary not only of the functional interrelationships but also of their common foundation in faith and charity."

b. Jerome, Augustine, Gregory

Ambrose's "cardinal virtues" were immediately adopted by other Church Fathers. In a letter about Paulina (397), Jerome endorsed the unity of the cardinal virtues: "The Stoics [here quoted with approval] say the four virtues are so closely connected to each other and mutually conjoined that whoever does not have one, lacks all." The unity of virtue provided Jerome–not a man sympathetic to half measures–with a rigorist interpretation of *James* 2:10: "Whoever shall keep the whole law, and yet offend in one point, is guilty of all." To Jerome, St. James meant that "whoever lacks one virtue lacks them all."[75]

It fell to Augustine, however, to draw the full logical and rhetorical consequences of the Ambrosian doctrine. He accepted the most rigorous, Socratic interpretation of them in his early work, *On the Practices of the Catholic Church* (388). Augustine explained Catholic "practices (*mores*)" through the two love commandments and defined virtue in terms of love: "But if virtue leads us to the happy life, I would say that virtue altogether is nothing other than the highest love of God. For what is called fourfold virtue is named, so far as I can tell, from certain varied affections of love itself." Defining all four virtues through love allowed Augustine to *reduce* all four cardinal virtues to love, much as Socrates had reduced all virtue to knowledge. He then concluded there are no longer four virtues which must be unified but *one* "fourfold virtue," four manifestations of one love which is "not of things in general but of God."[76] Because there is but one God, there is but one virtue and that virtue is charity.

Two centuries later, in his *Moralia on Job*, Pope Gregory the Great followed Ambrose and Augustine in using the beatitudes to argue for the same conclusion about the cardinal virtues. There may seem to be people who are chaste but not humble, humble but not merciful, or merciful but not just. In truth, however, each beatitude entails the other beatitudes, as Ambrose had said. By analogy with the beatitudes:

[75] Jerome, *Ep. 66 ad Pammachium* 3, CSEL 54: 649. Colish, *The Stoic Tradition* 2: 88. On Jerome, see J.N.D. Kelly, *Jerome, his Life, Writings, and Controversies* (London: Duckworth, 1975).

[76] Augustine, *De moribus ecclesiae* 15.25; PL 32, 1322. On Augustine, see Colish, *The Stoic Tradition* 2: 217-220; J.M. Rist, *Augustine: ancient thought baptized* (Cambridge: CUP, 1994) 168-173; James Wenzel, *Augustine and the Limits of Virtue* (Cambridge: CUP, 1992); N.J. Torchia, "Stoics, Stoicism: Ethics," in A.D. Fitzgerald, ed., *Augustine through the Ages: An encyclopedia* (Grand Rapids, MI: Eerdmans, 1999) 818-819.

> perfected *virtues* can in no way be disjoined, because there is not true prudence which is not just, temperate, and brave; nor perfected temperance which is not brave, just, and prudent; nor integral fortitude which is not prudent, temperate, and just; nor true justice which is not prudent, brave, and temperate.[77]

The Fathers were nothing if not moral rigorists, as the "philosophers" before them had been. Their account of the cardinal virtues might seem to describe true Christians as completely virtuous and pagans as vicious, being at once too easy on the former and too hard on the latter, and leaving no middle ground for truly virtuous pagans and vicious Christians. This gap is but a Christian rendering of the distance between Stoic sage and the rest of mankind, a fissure begun by that old stone-mason, Socrates himself. Writing to Jerome in 415, Augustine tried mightily to avoid the logical consequences of the position they had taken, by uncovering some middle ground which would at least find room for sinful Christians to improve. He argued from reason and Scripture, countering the Stoic image of suddenly breaking into full wisdom and virtue, like a drowning swimmer finally breaking the surface, with a Platonic image of moral and intellectual improvement which is like a gradual move from darkness to light.[78] But counter-arguments and alternative images are no substitute for an adequate theory; and no such theory was developed in the patristic period.

c. The Early Medieval Period

The long period from Gregory the Great (†604) to Peter Lombard (†1160) saw some Christian authors make use of the Christian conception of the cardinal virtues initiated by the Fathers, a conception that formed a second stream that paralleled the Stoic stream found, for example, in Martin of Braga and Isidore of Seville. The Stoic conception was so powerful, however, that its cross-currents drew in Christian writers. During the Carolingian period, Alcuin (†804), advisor on religion and education to

[77] Gregory, *Moralia in Job* 22.1.2, PL 76: 212CD. See Colish, *The Stoic Tradition* 2: 264-266.

[78] Augustine, *Ep. 167* to Jerome, see pp. 209-12 below. Ralph Hennings, "The correspondence between Augustine and Jerome," *Studia patristica* 27 (1993) 303-310. T.H. Irwin, "Splendid Vices? Augustine For and Against Pagan Virtues," *Mediaeval Philosophy and Theology* 8 (1999) 105-127, marshals Augustinian texts for and against "pagan virtues," but makes them consistent only by reducing Augustine's view to that of Aquinas.

Charlemagne, founder of royal and monastic libraries, and Abbot of Tour, wrote on the cardinal virtues and took an explicitly Augustinian line in approaching them. And so did his student Rabanus Maurus (†864), abbot and archbishop. Both authors, however, couched their treatment of the cardinal virtues in works of advice to their royal patrons, clear evidence of the Senecan, political conception of the cardinal virtues.

Arguably the finest representative of the early medieval conception of the cardinal virtues, however, was Bernard (†1153), Abbot of Clairvaux. He too wrote a treatise that dealt with the cardinal virtues. Its title and addressee, however, show that even the finest abbot in Christendom was under the influence of the Senecan political conception of the cardinal virtues. For this work was not one of the numerous "conferences" Bernard addressed to the monks under his care, even though it was addressed to a monk, one of his own, or rather, to a former monk who had risen to the most powerful position in the Latin world, Pope Eugenius III. Bernard's conception of the cardinal virtues was not so very different from the conception of Alcuin and Rabanus Maurus after all, for he still thought of them as virtues needed by the ruler, in this case, an ecclesiastical ruler. And the title Bernard gave his work, "On Consideration (*De consideratione*)," underscored the Stoic influence on his thought, for of the many terms for rational thought available to him, "consideration" was loaded with Stoic connotations, as we have seen, the meaning of which he learned from Cicero and Seneca.[79] In its content, too, the Stoicism present in the section of Bernard's work devoted to the cardinal virtues is palpable, for the main themes running through it are how unified the virtues are, how important it is for the head of Christendom to rule using them, and how necessary it is for him to cultivate the leisure necessary to allow these ruling virtues to blossom, Senecan themes all, even if addressed to a Christian prince for Christian purposes.[80] Transforming the cardinal virtues to qualities essential to the moral life of every Christian, not just the Christian prince, was a task not taken up before the scholastic masters developed the principles set out by Ambrose and Augustine, a task begun by Master Peter Lombard.

[79] Cicero's definition of courage includes the term considerata, n. 56 above.

[80] See the translation of Bernard, below pp. 216-9.

3. *Magistri*

a. Peter Lombard: Magister sententiarum

Between 1224 and 1229, Alexander of Hales initiated the custom of commenting on the *Sententiae,* a florilegium of theological texts plucked from the writings of the Fathers by Peter Lombard, Master of Theology and Bishop of Paris (†1160) and arranged in four books: God, creation, Christ the "Incarnate Word," and the sacraments. Commenting on the *Sententiae* soon became a requirement for Masters of Theology. After a discussion of the ontology of Christ, Bk. 3 describes the benefits God showers on us: the theological virtues (d. 23-32), gifts of the Holy Spirit (d. 34-5), and the Ten Commandments (d. 37-40). Nestled within what is essentially a treatise on grace is one short distinction on the cardinal virtues (d. 33) and another on the connections among the virtues (d. 36). Thirteenth-century theologians developed a detailed doctrine of cardinal virtues by amplifying Lombard's few remarks.[81]

The Master centered his consideration of the theological virtues on their existence in Christ and began by asking "whether he had faith and hope, along with charity, since Christ is filled with grace."[82] Drawing on definitions taken from Augustine, Lombard concluded that Christ did not possess faith and hope; he had only charity, whose pre-eminence the Master explained through two powerful, patristic metaphors. Ambrose had called charity the "*mother* of the virtues," and Augustine argued that if "the root of all evil is cupidity" (*1 Tim.* 6:10), then charity must be the "*root* of all good."[83]

The Master found the four cardinal virtues in Scripture (*Wis.* 8:7), though only when suitably construed by tradition. And he recited some rather too narrow definitions from Augustine: "Justice consists in helping the miserable, prudence in taking precautions to avoid traps, courage in enduring difficulties, and temperance in restraining depraved pleasures."[84] Another Father helped with the unusual term "cardinal": "These virtues are called cardinal, as Jerome says, 'by which in this mortality one lives well' and afterwards arrives at eternal life." Lombard, not dawdling over definitions, moved quickly to what interested him: whether Christ has these

[81]On Peter Lombard: Marcia Colish, *Peter Lombard* (Leiden: Brill, 1994).

[82] Peter Lombard, *Sent.* 3. d. 23, 2: 141.

[83] Peter Lombard, *Sent.* 3. d. 27, 2: 162; d. 23, 2: 142; d. 31, 2: 183.

[84] Lombard, *Sent.* d. 33. 1.2, 2: 188. Cf. Augustine, *De trin.* 9.12, CCSL 50A: 439.

four virtues. He used *John* 1:16 to argue that Christ fully possesses all four cardinal virtues, because it is "Christ 'from whose fullness we have received' them."[85] But they do not function in Christ in exactly the same way as in humans. For Christ they have the same "use" in heaven and on earth, but for humans they have different "uses." For Lombard, then, the cardinal virtues are clearly Christian virtues: they are caused by God, and they lead us to "eternal life." Not distinguishing sufficiently between final and efficient causality, Lombard seems to have thought that, simply because they lead to the Christian end, the cardinal virtues must be "infused," that is, caused efficiently by divine grace rather than by human effort.[86]

In d. 36 Lombard rounded out his consideration of virtue by turning to the connection and equality of the virtues. The thesis of a strong unity among the virtues, both theological and cardinal, he found "probable": "Since charity is the *mother* of all the virtues, wherever the mother, that is, charity, is found, there her children, that is, the virtues, are rightly believed to be." About their equality, that is, whether all one's virtues are present to the same degree, his authorities seemed in conflict: biblical heroes seem eminent for different virtues–Job for patience, David for humility; but Augustine clearly said the virtues were all equal. To reconcile his authorities, Lombard distinguished two ways one can possess the virtues "all at once and equally": either "with regard to the mental habit and essence of each" virtue, or "in act." This distinction led him to say about continence, the virtue governing sexual relations: "A just man, making use of his spouse (*utens coniugio*) does not have continence in act, though he does have it in habit." This conclusion is bizarre, to be sure, for one would think the just husband's *action* would also be virtuous. But far more important than Lombard's logic is the moral realism he shows. Here, quite clearly if incoherently, the moral rigorism of Lombard's tradition has been diluted by the common sense of a practically minded school-master and bishop–by no means brilliant, but a sage confessor.

For the development of the doctrine of the cardinal virtues, Lombard

[85] *Sent.* 3. d. 33, 2: 188. Cf. *John* 1:16: "from his fullness we have all received, grace upon grace."

[86] On the "identification of virtue and grace," see J. Müller, *Natürliche Moral und philosophische Ethik bei Albertus Magnus* (Münster: Aschendorff, 2001) 136, who quotes Lottin, *Psychologie* et morale 3: 101: "il n'y a pas de difference entre la vertu et la grâce." Cf. Lombard, *Sent.* 2. d.27.1, 1:480: Virtus est, ut Augustinus ait, bona qualitas menis, qua recte vivitur et qua nullus male utitur, quam Deus solus in homine operatur.

initiated a new age. In his *Sentences*, thirteenth-century Masters, whose greater knowledge of Aristotelian principles allowed them to move far beyond the Master's rudimentary ideas, saw several things of importance: seven virtues–three theological and four cardinal; seven Christian virtues, designed for the sake of returning us to our "heavenly homeland (*patria*)"; and cardinal virtues that are infused by God and as connected and equal to each other as are the theological virtues. And in Lombard they met vestiges of antique and Patristic moral rigorism; but only vestiges, for he approached morality with a new spirit. This was perhaps his most important bequest to the century to follow. His thought may not have been sophisticated but his moral canvas was wide; at least it was wide enough to incorporate ordinary folk along with saints and sinners. In this respect, he can be said to have begun the scholastic drive for an all-encompassing moral vision, one which radically revised the doctrine of the cardinal virtues inherited from the Fathers.

b. Philip the Chancellor

The first considerable step was taken by Philip, Chancellor of the University of Paris and patron of the Dominicans.[87] He helped the friars obtain their two chairs in the Theology faculty, during the great strike by masters and scholars (1229-1231),[88] an intervention resented by the secular Masters and revived in their bitter opposition to Aquinas and Bonaventure in 1255-6. The gratitude of the Dominicans manifested itself in the profound

[87] Philip the Chancellor is perhaps the least studied major figure in 13th-c. thought. For a sketch, see Houser, "Philip the Chancellor," *Blackwell Companion to Medieval Philosophy*, 534-5. See O. Lottin, "L'influence littéraire du chancelier Philippe," *Psychologie et morale aux xiie et xiiie siècles* (Paris: Gembloux, 1960) 6: 149-169, for his general influence on 13th-c. thought; W. Principe, *Philip the Chancellor's theology of the hypostatic union* (Toronto: PIMS, 1975), includes a general study of his thought; T. Potts, *Conscience in Medieval Philosophy* (Cambridge: CUP, 1980) and "Conscience," N. Kretzman, ed., *The Cambridge History of Later Medieval Philosophy* 690-5, for his doctrine on conscience and the precepts of the natural law, which greatly influenced Albert and Aquinas; Jan Aertsen, *Medieval philosophy and the transcendentals: the case of Thomas Aquinas* (Leiden: Brill, 1996), for his important influence on the doctrine of the transcendentals; Johannes Baptist Schneyer, *Die Sittenkritik in den Predigten Phillip des Kanzlers*, in *BGPhMA* 39/4 (Münster: Ashendorff, 1963), on his ethics.

[88] Philip the Chancellor, *Summa de bono*, ed. N. Wicki (Bern: Editiones Francke, 1985) 1: 26*-27*.

impact Philip's *Summa on the Good* (1225-8) had on Dominican theologians, especially Albert and Thomas. They were enamored of his *Summa*, which moved far in the direction of realizing Lombard's promise of a full treatment of the vast range of moral excellence and depravity, and all the stages between them. To do so, Philip had to move well beyond Lombard's brief remarks about the cardinal virtues.

Philip's first step concerned organizing his treatise. The philosophers, especially Avicenna, had taught that goodness, along with being and truth, are transcendentals, that is, analogical features of reality (along with our ideas of them) which transcend Aristotle's ten categories. So, taking a cue from *Genesis*, where from the third day on God "saw" that what he had done was "good," even "very good," the Chancellor began his *Summa* with a short treatise on the transcendentals, followed by two sets of questions on two different senses of goodness. The concept of the "good of nature" helped him rework Book 2 of the *Sentences* into a treatise on the *exitus* of creatures from God: angels, corporeal creatures, and humans. Then came questions on the "good of grace," a masterful transformation of part of Book 3 of the *Sentences* into a full-blown treatise on how the seven principal virtues–three theological and four cardinal–aid humans in their *reditus* to God. In addition to a title, then, Aquinas found in Philip's *Summa* two structuring principles he could follow: Philip's work was organized overall on the *exitus* and *reditus* of creatures, and his treatise on moral theology, the first one in the thirteenth century,[89] was based on the seven principal virtues.

The Chancellor introduced the cardinal virtues with three questions about their nature which arose straightforwardly from reading Lombard, Bk. 3, d. 33: the "division and number" of the four cardinal virtues, their order of priority, and "why they are called 'cardinal' virtues." Philip then added something Lombard had not even thought to attempt: a detailed treatment of all four virtues, running to over 300 pages in the modern critical edition.[90] In a third and final section, he somewhat awkwardly re-

[89] S. Pinckaers, *The Sources of Christian Morality* 218.

[90] Philip's influence on Albert's approach to the virtues can be documented in Albert, *De bono*, ed. Cologne 28; see ix-xv for Albert's sources and doctrine, 320 for references to Philip. Albert's pupil Ulrich of Strasbourg in turn followed the same plan in his own *Summa de bono*, whose Bk. 6 was devoted to the virtues. For the plan of Ulrich's work see J. Daguillon, *La Summa de bono, lib. 1* (Paris: Vrin, 1930) 12*-29*; also F.J. Lescoe, *God as First Principle in Ulrich of Strasbourg* (New York: Alba, 1979) 15-36. Cf. Ulrich, *De summo bono*, ed. K. Flasch and L. Sturlese (Corpus

turned to the two general topics Lombard had treated in d. 36: the twin issues of the connection and equality of the virtues.

If Peter Lombard had the mind of an encyclopedist, content merely to repeat traditional doctrines such as the four cardinal virtues, Philip the Chancellor had a naturally philosophical mind, one that wanted to understand what he inherited from tradition. To do so, he made efficient use of what little of Aristotle was available to him. Of the Philosopher's moral works, only the *Ethica vetus* (*Nicomachean Ethics* 2-3) had been translated into Latin; but careful reading taught him principles which could illuminate the cardinal virtues.

First, the Chancellor knew Aristotle's four causes and recognized that Aristotle had used them as principles to develop a philosophical explanation of moral virtue. For example the Philosopher had said that repetition of good actions produces virtue, making man the *agent* cause of virtue (2.1), and that finding the mean between excess and defect is the *form* moral virtue takes (2.2). Philip's account would likewise be a causal account.

Second, from Aristotle's moral psychology he took the view that each human has a soul with distinct powers which are the proximate sources of its actions and passions. He also appropriated the method Aristotle had devised for the difficult task of peering inside the soul. The soul and its powers are understood through their acts, while those acts in turn are understood through their objects: "Powers differ based on acts, and acts based on their *objects* or causes of motion."[91] *Object* in Philip's usage meant that feature of a real thing or set of real things which serves as the term of a cognitive relation between things and their knowers. The *object*, then, provides an external and real basis for understanding the inner workings of the soul, a perceptible basis for knowing what is not directly perceptible and especially for distinguishing powers, acts, and passions from each other. Philip knew that Aristotle had used their *objects* to distinguish the five senses from each other and that this account of sensation had provided the model for his account of virtue: "act, properly speaking, has a definite *matter*, such as seeing has color, hearing has sound."[92]

Philosophorum Teutonicorum Medii Aevi) 1 (1989), 2.1-4 (1987), 4.1-2 (1987).

[91] *Summa de bono*, 1: 227. Cf. L. Dewan, "*Obiectum*: Notes on the Invention of a Word," *Archives d'histoire doctrinale et littéraire du moyen age* 48 (1981) 37-96, esp. 42, 50-52.

[92] 2: 959.19-20.

Third, Philip recognized that the causal and psychological principles he took from Aristotle had to be related to each other. Here the material cause turned out to be especially important, because it has two distinct senses: Since the *object* in its technical sense gives content to our understanding of a power, Philip thought of that object as a kind of *matter*.[93] On the other hand, since a virtue perfects some power of the soul, he also thought of such powers as matter. As Philip used the term, then, *matter* can refer either to the power of the soul which is delimited by the object of its activity (this is the *subjective* sense of matter) or to that object which so delimits a power or act (its *objective* sense).

Equipped with these Aristotelian principles, the Chancellor proposed to do fully and completely for the cardinal virtues what Aristotle had done only sketchily for moral virtue in general. He would use their final, efficient, formal, and material causes to explain the cardinal virtues, concentrating especially on the two senses–objective and subjective–of their matter. To justify the tradition of the four cardinal virtues, then, became an ambitious project falling into two parts: consideration of the nature of the cardinal virtues, followed by treatment of the wide range of human virtues which are best understood as "parts" subordinate to the cardinal virtues.[94]

c. Philip: The Nature of the Cardinal Virtues

In Q. 1, Philip was initially inclined to look inside the soul, at its powers, the subjective matter of the cardinal virtues. The Platonic tendencies of his mind led him to hope for a one-to-one correlation between the psychic powers and the four cardinal virtues, since such a neat correlation would support the cardinal virtues in the strongest possible way, by identifying one virtue for each power of the soul. Obj. 1 bears witness to his frustration over the impossibility of such a tidy solution, since the Augustinian tradition in which Philip had been raised recognized only three powers in the soul: reason, emotion, and desire.[95] But if matter alone could not do

[93] Cf. 2: 206.2-207.6: "Therefore, diversity of rational powers is based on diversity of acts; but diversity of acts is based on specific diversity of their *matter*."

[94] His account of the cardinal virtues is in fact only half of the story. Philip follows the same two-step procedure for the three theological virtues, *Summa*, 2: 489-743.

[95] Isaac of Stella, *Epistola de anima*, PL 194: 1878D; also in the influential pseudo-Augustinian *De spiritu et anima* 4, PL 40: 782. Philip adopted Isaac's description of the three powers of the soul: rationabilitas, irascibilitas, and concupiscibilitas.

the job, perhaps form, its correlative principle, would do. The Chancellor knew that Aristotle had explained matter as power and form as act. If a power of the soul is the matter of a virtue, should not its form consist in some sort of act? If so, then "the number of the virtues is not taken from the number of *powers* but from their principal *acts*."[96]

The first thing the Chancellor noted about such acts was what any Platonist would notice: their relation to reason. The good we desire and the evil we hate engender in us the four Stoic passions: joy and hope, sorrow and fear. "Now these sorts of affections, that is, those belonging to desire or emotion, should be ruled by reason; and then they are worthy of praise." For "temperance is taken based on an act of desire as it is subject to the order of reason, that is, to restrain our cupidities. Courage is taken based on an act of emotion which has been ordered, that is, to confront what produces fear." Courage and temperance, then, share only partially in the rule of reason. Prudence, however, is fully rational because, seated in the power of reason itself, it is "taken from the act of distinguishing good from bad." Though he never read the *Republic*, Philip half considered justice as "an act in relation to *all* these powers, not just one,"[97] but in the end he concluded that "both justice and prudence are based on acts of *reason*," since justice "orders us in relation to neighbor."[98] The initial benefit of turning from matter to "act," then, was that it led Philip to a Platonic conclusion, one of the first importance for Albert and Aquinas, and medieval ethics generally: the virtuous life is a rational life, one lived within faith, to be sure, but dominated by the rule of reason.

In Q. 3, where the Chancellor asked "why they are called cardinal," he again looked at the cardinal virtues as "acts of the powers" of the soul. The first of three "reasons" offered defending the traditional four "cardinal" virtues resulted from one of those extraordinary co-incidences which are sometimes found in the history of thought. For the Chancellor seems to have gathered together every bit of information available to him about the cardinal virtues, and on his desk lay open the *De consideratione* of Bernard of Clairvaux, along with an important but particularly difficult passage in Aristotle.[99]

[96] P. 86.

[97] P. 86. Our "proximate end" is the end of the cardinal virtues, which lead *ad deum*, as distinct from our ultimate end, the end of the theological virtues, which lead *in deum*. Cf. p. 97.

[98] P. 86.

[99] P. 95.

The Philosopher's long dialectical argument for the general definition of moral virtue[100] made considerable use of the Socratic analogy between technical crafts (*artes*) and moral virtues; but there is also an important disanalogy between them. The goodness of an art is found only in its products, but the goodness of a virtue does not reside solely in its products, that is, in moral actions. Rather, moral actions "brought about by virtue, even if they have the right quality, are not done justly or temperately, unless the agent acts while having a certain quality: first, if knowing, second, if willing for the sake of these, third, if holding himself resolutely and unchangeably, he acts."[101] In order to distinguish the small class of truly virtuous actions from actions which are morally good but not truly virtuous, Aristotle here set out four conditions for virtue: in addition to exhibiting the "right quality," a morally virtuous action must also come from the knowledge, will, and habit of the agent. While what these conditions mean in detail is far from clear, Aristotle's overall intent seems to have been that truly virtuous actions must come from a good *habit* in the agent, while other morally good actions do not have to derive from habits.

When the Chancellor read this passage, however, he passed over habit and understood the text to mean there are four "universal conditions" for the very "existence (*esse*) of virtue," conditions he construed as "acts" rather than habits. Of the four conditions in Aristotle's text, only the second–knowledge–seems fairly clear. While a good deed may come from opinion or even ignorance, Aristotle's elitist conception of virtue required that a virtuous action come from true knowledge (*sciens*). Philip simply supplied Aristotle's own term for such practical knowledge: prudence. But what the Philosopher meant by the other three conditions was not readily apparent. To understand them, he took inspiration from what St. Bernard had said about the cardinal virtues.

Aristotle's examples of "right quality"–performing a just or temperate action–meant simply that the action itself must be morally good. The Chancellor asked what in general makes such actions morally good and found the answer in the way Bernard had described the cardinal virtue of

[100] *Nic. Eth.* 2.1-7.

[101] *Nic. Eth.* 2.4 (1105a29-b1). Translated from the *Ethica vetus* Philip used. Ed. R.A. Gauthier, *Aristoteles Latinus* 10.18-22: "Ea autem que secundum virtutes fiunt, non si illa qualiter habent, iuste et caste operantur, set si qui operatur qualiter habens operatur; prius quidem si sciens; deinde si volens propter hec; tercium autem si firme et inmutabiliter habens, operatur." "Caste" means temperately.

temperance as "holding to the mean in our actions by removing excess and deficiency."[102] For is not another name for temperance *moderation*, whose root is *modus* or "mean"? Philip clearly recognized that by defining the essence of temperance as "attaining the mean," he so *universalized* temperance that it became part of every virtuous action, as a general "act" present in every specific, virtuous action.

Aristotle's last condition was also obscure. He seems to have meant that virtuous actions must come from a pre-existing habit, but the Chancellor fixed on Aristotle's phrase *firme et immobiliter*. "*Firme* (resolutely)" is but another way of saying "courageously," and so the Chancellor saw yet another cardinal virtue, which Bernard, on Philip's reading of him, defined as "confronting the arduous and persevering amid difficulties."[103] Courage in this sense is not limited to the battlefield, as it was for Aristotle, but is found in all virtuous actions.

Having identified three of Aristotle's conditions with three of the cardinal virtues, the Chancellor did not hesitate to connect the last virtue–justice–with Aristotle's remaining condition. Here the Latin translation of Aristotle helped Philip, by substituting for the Greek term "choosing" a more universal notion "willing." Willing actions rationally is a feature of the inner harmony Plato had conceived the inner justice of the soul to be, and Philip recognized that justice in this sense is a kind of "act" which must be part of every virtuous action.

By turning away from Aristotle's own focus on habits, and with inspiration from Bernard, the Chancellor re-read Aristotle's four conditions for virtue. In this way, they became four general "acts" universally found in each and every virtuous action: "to know, to will, to persevere amid difficulties, and to attain the mean between excess and deficiency." His peculiarly medieval approach to philosophical scholarship led the Chancellor to draw a conclusion of momentous importance for the development of the doctrine of cardinal virtues: these general acts, he said, "come from" prudence, justice, courage, and temperance respectively. If examining their objective *matter* showed the Chancellor the prominence of reason in a life led by the cardinal virtues, looking at their *form* showed him how ubiquitous they are. As Philip defined them, these four acts extend beyond the

[102] See p. 95. Though the Chancellor purported to be quoting Bernard, he was not, but gave a highly creative, scholastic condensation of what Bernard had said. Compare pp. 216-9.

[103] Philip, pp. 95-7; Bernard, pp. 217-9.

realm of specific virtuous habits to *every* morally good action. For in a concrete action, one may know the good which is a "mean," will it, and persevere in it until accomplished, without the action coming from a virtuous habit such as chastity, sobriety, or justice. If Aristotle's virtues were defined so narrowly as to be beyond the reach of most humans, Philip's cardinal virtues seem universally available to everyone, whenever they do the good with open eyes.

If Philip's first "reason" clarified the objective *matter* and *form* of the cardinal virtues, his two other "reasons" in Q. 3 cast light on their *final* cause. His second "reason" focused on the meaning of the term *cardinal*. He did not know the cosmic connotation the term had for Ambrose, but the Chancellor made use of two everyday similes from the Cistercian Isaac of Stella, who said the four virtues are "like roots or hinges (*cardines*) for all the virtues."[104] Philip elaborated: "Cardinal comes from *cardo*, the hinge on which a door turns"; but doors lead somewhere, and Scripture explains that this particular door opens to full "life" in the "kingdom of God" (*Matt.* 19:17; *Acts* 14:22). It follows that God is the *end* of the cardinal virtues. This conclusion, however, evoked a subtle distinction, since the theological virtues also have God as their end. The "cardinal virtues concern what leads *up to* our end but not *into* our end, namely, God." If the theological virtues take us all the way "into" God in heaven, the cardinal virtues only carry us along the road (*via*) toward God. Nevertheless, they do have God in sight. The pre- and post-medieval idea that the cardinal virtues have a purely secular end is nowhere present in the Chancellor's thought, nor in that of any of the sons of Ambrose.

Philip did not take up the *efficient* cause of the cardinal virtues in the questions devoted to their nature, but he had not ignored the point. The very structure of his *Summa*, which follows the *exitus* of creatures from and their *reditus* back to God, inclined him toward a certain conclusion about the *efficient* cause of the cardinal virtues. Transcendental goodness divides immediately into the "good of nature"–the ontological goodness found in all beings–and the "good of grace"–the moral goodness achieved by intellectual creatures. As the creator of nature, God is the efficient cause of ontological goodness. Should the creator of grace not also be the efficient cause of the "good of grace," that is, of virtue? By taking the "good of grace" to be coextensive with, if not simply another term for, moral goodness, Philip agreed with Lombard that both the cardinal and theological

[104] P. 89.

virtues are *infused* virtues, not distinguished "in regard to their principle from which [that is, their agent]."[105]

Theses which seem right in the abstract, however, are sometimes found wanting in the concrete. Having worked his way through the whole of the moral life, Philip backed away from this position when he took up the issue of the "connections" among the virtues, near the end of his *Summa*, and placed the cardinal virtues among the *acquired*, rather than the infused, virtues.[106] A thorough treatment of the question, "Does whoever has one virtue have them all?" covers both acquired moral virtues (*de moralibus*) and virtues infused by grace (*de gratuitis*). Philip here placed the cardinal virtues among the acquired moral virtues, which then were subdivided into Aristotelian "political" virtues and the cardinal virtues. As only "specific (*specialis*)" virtues the political virtues are unconnected to each other.

The cardinal virtues, however, are more complicated because they can be understood in two ways. Considered specifically, a cardinal virtue is taken "according to the act of the proper power and concerning the proper [objective] matter of that power, so that it does not extend analogically to the act of another power." But taken generically, "the acts of each of these [cardinal] virtues can be taken analogically about matter also taken analogically," thus widening the scope of each cardinal virtue beyond its "proper" acts and matter.[107] When the cardinal virtues are regarded as special virtues, they too are unconnected. But when the cardinal virtues are viewed in the general sense, they are necessarily unified with each other. By distinguishing two senses of cardinal virtues the Chancellor thought he had found a way to reconcile Aristotle with Plato. So enamored was he of his success that Philip attributed his distinction to Aristotle himself.

This distinction between two senses–general and specific–of the cardinal virtues was Philip's great break-through in virtue theory, for the range of the virtues could now be expanded to include treatment of the totality of good (and bad) action, thereby offering a systematically complete moral framework. He could distinguish each general cardinal virtue from its "parts," that is, from secondary virtues dependent upon it. Since the general cardinal virtues are necessary conditions for all virtue, it followed that they were "necessarily *in* the other virtues." Consequently, the secondary virtues "are reduced to these [cardinal virtues] either as *parts* or as

[105] 2: 544, 756.
[106] 2: 1069-71
[107] Pp. 101-2.

species or as their *dispositions*,"[108] that is, as what Aquinas later called integral, subjective, or potential parts.

d. Philip: The "Parts" of the Virtues

The Chancellor's success, and his consequent influence on Albert and Aquinas, cannot be over-estimated. For the first time, a philosopher managed to take a large number of virtues, much larger than the number of psychic powers, and situate them quite precisely under the general rubric of the four cardinal virtues. Among the ancients, the Stoics, Cicero, and Macrobius had tried to accomplish this task, but Philip did it far more successfully.

The Chancellor was most successful with courage. Courage at the general level is "the principal act of the power of emotion" which "is to confront the arduous" or "difficult." This object induces a passion in us, such as fear, so that courage in its wide sense "concerns *anything* difficult in the realm of the passions."[109] Understood "strictly," however, courage is "only about exterior passions inflicted on the body." This restriction allowed the Chancellor to develop a technical formula for the object of special courage: "the difficult in the realm of exterior passions which have been impressed by another."[110] To mark the difference between these two senses of courage, Philip associated Cicero with courage in the broad sense (*generaliter*) and Aristotle with courage in the most narrow sense (*specialissime*).

Cicero had identified four "parts" of courage: magnificence, confidence, patience, and perseverence. Philip, considering magnificence and confidence as outside the purview of the theologian, reduced the parts of courage to patience and perseverence.[111] These two particular virtues follow the two primary "acts" of courage: actively confronting (*aggredi*) and passively withstanding (*sustinere*) difficulties. Patience and perseverence, then, are not species of courage covering a more limited range of action than courage does, but "dispositions" of courage, that is, skills particularly needed in order to be courageous. Perseverence is skill at confronting difficulties which fill us with fear by having "the will to continue" to the end. Patience,

[108] P. 97.

[109] 2: 796.

[110] 2: 796. "Circa difficile in passionibus exterioribus et ab alio illatis est fortitudo." Cf. 1071.

[111] 2: 824.

on the other hand, is skill at "withstanding or suffering" such difficulties.[112]

Temperance likewise has general and specific senses. Generic temperance is "the principal act of the power of desire." Its range of objects is unlimited, since it is "about *any* kind of desiring and *any* kind of pleasant object." This description allowed Philip to distinguish general courage from general temperance, based on their objects: courage concerns the difficult or arduous, temperance something pleasant. Since objects engender different passions in us, the Chancellor also used such passions to distinguish the two general virtues: temperance concerns "passions in us and inborn (*innatas*) to us," such as desire and aversion, while courage concerns "passions impressed (*illatas*) by others," such as fear and confidence. But it must be said that Philip's definition of temperance, taken from its end–"to will the changeable good to exist under the highest good"–is really misleading. For the act of "willing the good" is more an act of reason governed by justice than an act of the desiring power governed by temperance. More illuminating than these definitions, however, is that taken from its subjective matter–to hold desires under the sway of reason–and that based on the form of temperance–the mean.

To distinguish specific from general temperance the Chancellor needed a differentiating note, which he found by specifying the kind of pleasures involved. While the object of general temperance concerns "*any* kind of pleasure," specific temperance is limited to "desiring *corporeal pleasures* according to the mean."[113] As with courage, Philip did not limit temperance as much as Aristotle had; but Philip did succeed in drawing a sharp line between general and special temperance, one which helped him understand the "parts" of temperance.

Since Aristotle thought of temperance as strictly a specific virtue, he had not given it parts, but Cicero had listed three: continence, clemency, and modesty. Ciceronian clemency was the virtue which helped a Roman aristocrat treat inferiors with civility, a particularly pagan virtue the Chancellor dropped, though he retained Cicero's other "parts." Philip also knew the longer list of Macrobius, a pagan contemporary of Augustine, who had said, "temperance is accompanied by modesty, shame, abstinence, chastity, honesty, moderation, lowliness, sobriety, and purity."[114] Since

[112] 2: 823.19-21; 852.110-112.

[113] 2: 1071.69-70: "circa concupiscere moderate delectationes corporales."

[114] *In somnium Scipionis* 1.8: modestia, verecundia, abstentia, castitas, honestas, moderatio, parcitas, sobrietas, puditia.

both Romans included modesty in the list, the Chancellor followed their lead. To govern nutrition and sex, Aristotle had but one virtue–temperance–and Cicero, on Philip's reading of him, only had one–continence–but Macrobius had several. The Chancellor took a middle road, choosing sobriety to cover nutrition and continence to cover sex. Finally he added two particularly Christian "parts" of temperance, virtues not in his pagan sources but long recognized as signs of an outstanding Christian life: virginity and *aureola*, the "golden crown." In this way, under general temperance, in addition to temperance understood as a special virtue, the Chancellor ranged five other "parts": modesty, sobriety, continence, virginity, and the "crown" awarded for an outstanding Christian life.

In order to show that these "parts" are actually virtues, the Chancellor turned to their matter in the sense of their objects. The *glossa ordinaria* on *Gal.* 5:23 seemed to set out an object for modesty, which is found "in words and deeds," a description corroborated by Cicero.[115] To identify the objects of sobriety and continence, the Chancellor, like Aristotle before him,[116] pointed to the external senses they govern, for "two senses pertain to our very existence, namely touch and taste." Sobriety governs the sense of taste, while continence, controlling the sense of touch, has as its act "to moderate the act of carnal knowledge, which is for the sake of generation." Only these two senses specify moral virtues, because they preserve the existence of the species and the individual. The Chancellor knew that to govern "the pleasures of both taste and touch," Aristotle, the "moral philosopher" had needed only one virtue, temperance as he understood it, while the theologians "posit two: one, namely sobriety, to govern taste, and another, namely continence, to govern touch." Philip naturally followed the theologians, but his reasoning was more Aristotelian than Aristotle himself. "In moral philosophy the Philosopher means to hand over an *art* concerned with the virtues," and as an art his ethics concerns "universals." Consequently, "moral philosophy follows a *speculative* path, while the theologian is active and attends to merit and demerit in actual deeds." Aristotle's philosophy was too speculative to "descend to singulars" in the way the practical discipline of the theologian does. In keeping with the practicality of theology, the Chancellor ended with two peculiarly Christian kinds of temperance. Virginity always signifies a kind of "incorruption," and turned the Chancellor's mind to the "golden crown," a sort of external recognition

[115] Peter Lombard, *Glossa*, PL 192: 160b; Cicero, *De officiis* 1.40.142.
[116] *Nic. Eth.* 3.10 (1117b24-1118a32).

of outstanding virtue that tradition had awarded the virgins and martyrs. Philip correlated the "crown of the martyrs" with the emotional part of the soul, making it a kind of perfection of courage, and the "crown of the virgins" with the desiring element, making it a kind of perfection of continence. To complete the picture, he added a perfection for the rational part of the soul, the "crown of the preachers," that is, his beloved Dominicans.[117] The Chancellor, then, made the "parts" of temperance more like species of general temperance than dispositions (as were the parts of courage) or integral parts.

When he came to prudence and justice, the Chancellor was without the relevant sections of the *Nicomachean Ethics*, which had not been translated. Nor did he find the "parts" Cicero had listed for them particularly helpful to his work as a theologian. So he turned away from the "philosophers" and looked to the "saints" and Scripture for help in understanding their parts.

As an intellectual virtue, prudence is different from the other cardinal virtues. Its form or act is "to discern" the difference between good and bad, which means that its subjective matter must be the power of reason. Although Philip offered no detailed explanation of how the mind works in practical reasoning, he understood that prudence has to be involved in every act of moral virtue and drew an inference from this fact, namely, that prudence cannot have its own object apart from the objects of the other cardinal virtues, because the objective matter it reasons about is precisely the matter of those other virtues. "Since it negotiates about the matters of the other virtues, it does not have its own proper and limited matter in the way the others do."[118] A further consequence follows. Matter in the objective sense is what the Chancellor had used to distinguish the various senses of temperance and courage. Without matter of its own, it would seem that prudence could not be divided into general and special senses or into "parts." There is only one sense of prudence. It is a "general" virtue because it exists "in reason" and because "the acts of the other virtues function as matter" for it.[119]

In place of "parts" like temperance and courage have, Philip turned to *Rom.* 8:6-7. To the "moral" sense of prudence known from the philosophers, he added two specifically Christian types of prudence: one is "prudence of the flesh," a kind of worldly cunning, which in the end "is death"

[117] 2: 929.70-72.
[118] 2: 769.144-5.
[119] 2: 948.35-36; 950.92-93.

and therefore not true prudence at all, but an imitation. The other is "prudence of the spirit" which is more than merely moral prudence because it gives "life and peace." These two parts, one less and one more than "moral" prudence, are distinguished from it, not by having different areas of application but by their results. The one brings damnation, the other heavenly reward. The distinction between "moral" prudence and "prudence of the spirit" seems similar to the distinction between cardinal and theological virtues. Moral prudence is not "this-worldly," concerned only with temporal matters, but has its eye on God as its final cause. Moral prudence, as the prudence of the wayfarer, moves us toward but does not achieve God, while "prudence of the spirit" does.

The Chancellor's treatment of justice, the most complicated of the cardinal virtues, is the least satisfactory. He told two inconsistent stories, based on two quite different definitions of justice he inherited from tradition. The first was a definition in the marginal gloss on *Gen.* 2:10, which describes the four rivers in Paradise. Ambrose had seen in those rivers an allegory of the cardinal virtues, and Augustine had defined justice as "the order and equity of the soul whereby the other virtues are joined together." The Chancellor understood this to mean that justice is a "general" virtue like prudence, and for the same reasons: justice, seated in the power of reason, takes its objective matter from "the acts of the other virtues," that is, temperance and courage. In this Platonizing account, justice produces an inner harmony within the individual soul, has nothing to do with neighbor, and has no "parts." Philip's second account of justice is built on a definition he found in the marginal gloss on the beatitude "Blessed are those who hunger and thirst for justice." The gloss reads: "Justice is to give to each what is his, to oneself, to neighbor, and to God," which is an elaboration of an Ambrosian definition Philip also knew: "Justice is rendering to each what is his own."[120]

In place of the many parts of justice which Cicero had ranged under the broad headings of "natural law" and "customary law,"[121] which came from the source of knowledge of the law, the Chancellor chose a trinity of parts for justice, based on the object of the obligation: worship (owed to God), reverence (owed to prelates), and obedience (owed to both).[122]

[120] Philip, *Summa*, 2: 947.137-8; 948.27-8. Ambrose, *De officiis* 1.24, PL 16: 62a.

[121] Cicero, *De inv.* 2.53.160-162, ius naturae and ius consuetudine.

[122] Worship (*latria*) and reverence (*dulia*) are taken from two different Greek words for "slave."

Just as he provided the Dominican Order with a place among the "university of masters and scholars" at Paris, so Chancellor Philip offered Albert and Thomas the intellectual materials with which to build treatises in moral theology. The Chancellor's goal was a description of the full range of the moral life. To realize this goal he organized all the virtues and vices under the seven great virtues: the theological and cardinal virtues conceived as the fundamental structure for presenting Christian morality. And to set out the structure intelligibly, the Chancellor made use of two central moral insights which are in reality the two fundamental principles of the theology of his *Summa*. First, morality must be understood in terms of the transcendental notion of goodness. Second, the sharp distinction between the two senses of the cardinal virtues is what allowed him to erect the framework for that morality: the general cardinal virtues conceived as "universal conditions" for morality; and the other virtues as "parts" somehow subordinate to the cardinal virtues.

As a thinker, however, the Chancellor was more characterized by flashing insight than thorough and profound development. First Albert, then Thomas, whose powers of synthesis went far beyond Philip's, developed his insights, in order to repay the debt their order owed the memory of the Chancellor. In this way, Philip set the foundation and erected the facade of the structure Aquinas was to complete, much as the Gothic cathedral at Chartres was rebuilt using the foundation and west facade of the smaller cathedral, which had burned in 1198.

e. Albert the Great

When Albert came to Paris he was already a mature man in his forties, but he embraced the Aristotelian learning he found there and especially the work of Philip the Chancellor.[123] His so-called *Summa Parisiensis* was writ-

[123] For Albert's life see J.A. Weisheipl, *Dictionary of the Middle Ages* 1: 126-130. For a general study of Albert's thought see A. Zimmermann, *Albert der grosse: seine Zeit, sein Werk, seine Wirkung* (Berlin: de Gruyter, 1981). Albert's ethics has drawn little attention from scholars. Alain de Libera, *Albert le Grand et la philosophie* (Paris: Vrin, 1990), passes over his ethics altogether. Albert's main works on ethics were *De bono*, part 6 of the *Summa parisiensis*, ed. Cologne 28 (written 1246-8); *In 3 Sent*, ed. Borgnet 28 (revised version by 1249); and two commentaries on Aristotle's *Ethics*: *Super ethica commentum et quaestiones* ed. Cologne 14 (written 1248-1252, when Aquinas was his student in Cologne); and *Ethica*, ed. Borgnet 7 (before 1261). On Albert's ethical doctrines consult the introductions to Cologne editions: 14.1, 28. On virtues, see J. Schneider, "Die Bestimmung des Tugendbe-

ten in six parts. Three centered on Christ (*De sacramentis*, *De incarnatione*, and *De resurrectione*), while the other three took the form of a study of the creation story: *De quattuor coaequaevis* (the four principles God first created: matter, time, the empyrean heaven, and angels), *De homine*, and *De bono*. The last was a study of transcendental goodness clearly indebted to Philip's *Summa*, even down to its title.[124] Following Philip, Albert began with goodness as a transcendental but divided it differently: "The *first* division is into the good of nature and the moral good (*bonum moris*)," the moral good then being subdivided into "the good of habit (*bonum consuetudinis*) and the good of grace." By making the good of grace a species under the moral good Albert successfully made room in his general schema for acquired virtues in addition to infused ones. This produced a more satisfactory account of the three classes of virtue than had the Chancellor's scheme. Content with Philip's work on the theological virtues, Albert could then confine his *De bono* to the four cardinal virtues and include the specific "political" virtues as their parts, since both are acquired.

Albert began Tract 1 of *De bono* with five questions devoted to transcendental goodness, and then in q. 6 raised the same three questions the Chancellor had raised about the cardinal virtues in general: their number, cardinality, and order. These general topics were followed by four more tracts, each devoted to one of the cardinal virtues, as Philip had done. Albert focused on a systematic treatment of all their "parts," that is, the virtues subordinate to the cardinal virtues. Here is where he had something new to contribute. He was still limited to Aristotle's *Ethica vetus* (now including Bk. 1), but he made more extensive use of Cicero in treating the "parts" of the cardinal virtues. Unlike Philip, Albert did not return to the topics of the "connection" and "equality" of the virtues at the end of his

---

griffes in den Schriften Alberts *De natura boni* und *Summa de bono*," in *Albertus Magnus–Doctor Universalis 1280-1980* (Mainz: Matthias-Grunewald, 1980) 295-322; J. Müller, *Natürliche Moral und philosophische Ethik bei Albertus Magnus* (Munich: Aschendorff, 2001).

[124] Philip, *Summa de bono*, 1: 40*. Though untitled by Philip himself, in the mss. his work is usually called *Summa* or *Summa quaestionum* and attributed to Philip. While not part of the titles given in the mss., *de bono* accurately describes its contents and structure. Albert's work is usually called *De bono* in the mss., and for this reason the Cologne editors refused to include *Summa* in its title. Cf. ed. Cologne 28: xiii-xiv. But in his *Summa theologiae* (ca. 1270-80) Albert himself described his early work thus: "De his tamen iamdudum facta est *summa* quae intitulatur *de bono*."

section on justice, because he never finished it. He did take up these topics, however, in his *Commentary on the Sentences*, d. 36, also written during his stay in Paris. Between these two works, then, Albert covered exactly the same ground Philip had traversed in his *Summa de bono*.[125]

f. Albert: The Nature of the Cardinal Virtues

Albert was intent on pursuing Philip's overall approach, even though treating the cardinal virtues as acquired virtues. Temperamentally disinclined to abandon the tradition of the masters completely, he did not hesitate to face the difficult question of what happens to an acquired virtue, such as prudence, in the presence of grace:

> Though it is not our present intention to dispute whether the natural order turns into the order of grace, I readily concede that a political virtue either remains alongside (*manet cum*) grace or is united to it. It seems better to say that it is united to it. For though [political virtue] is not proportioned to grace in relation to its source of generation, nonetheless it is proportioned to it in relation to its matter and its act. In this way infused [virtue] will not be useless, because it makes the deed one of grace; while natural [virtue] will not be useless, because it makes action less difficult for the agent, something grace does not do.[126]

The main issues about the cardinal virtues, however, concern their "matter and act," and here Albert could apply what Philip had said about infused cardinal virtues to cardinal virtues which are acquired. Albert began with the very same question Philip had asked: "In relation to what are the virtues taken to be four?" He recognized that no argument could be based merely on the powers of the soul, because there are three, not four such powers. He knew that "some," namely Philip, turn to the "principal *acts* of the powers" as a foundation for such an argument, and he quoted eight of Philip's arguments. But Albert found them non-demonstrative: "All these [arguments] do not prove the number of the virtues, but are mere justifications (*adaptiones*) which can easily be disproved by someone who knows something." The problem running through them was a problem Plato would have seen: an under-emphasis on the rule of reason. To be de-

[125] On Albert's doctrine of the virtues, and the cardinal virtues, and the cardinal virtues, as an "amalgam ... of different philosophical traditions," see J. Müller, esp. 141-155, 198-221.

[126] Albert, *De bono*, 240.93- 241.6.

monstrative, an argument for the cardinal virtues must incorporate the powers of the soul and their acts, but most of all it must focus on the "order" brought into the soul by acts of reason. For the essence of the virtues is that they are "perfections of the motive powers of the soul," perfections which come from "the order of reason." Consequently, from all of Philip's arguments, Albert found only the one which clarified the term *cardinal* to be demonstrative, and he paraphrased it closely in his response. The order of reason exists in the power of reason in two ways: "In one way the perfection of reason is prudence, which shows us the mean" wherein virtue resides and which *internally* governs the other two parts of the soul of the virtuous person. The *external* relations of reason, however, show that "in a second way the perfection of reason is justice which directs us to others as we ought." Philip was a reliable guide in seating temperance in desire, the "concupiscible" power, and courage in the emotions, the "irascible" power. But here again demonstration required Albert not merely to correlate power and virtue, but to look to the virtues as *perfections* of the powers: "Now the powers which are ordered are desire and emotion, in the presence of strong passions. Now those [passions] which are in desire are inborn (*innatae*) and their perfection is temperance; while those which are in the emotions are impressed (*illatae*), and their perfection is courage." Temperance involves controlling those inborn passions such as our inclinations to self-preservation, eating, drinking, and reproduction; while courage involves those passions which arise as a result of experience, such as love and hate, fear and daring. Albert thought that to be demonstrative an argument based on the powers of the soul cannot be static, but must incorporate the internal dynamism found in the acts of those powers, in so far as those acts are *affected by the rule of reason,* a theme also developed in the parallel text of his *Sentences* commentary.

In q. 6, Art. 2 of *De bono,* Albert explained the term "cardinal." He followed Philip's definition of *cardo* as the hinge "on which the door of a house turns." But where Philip had concentrated on where the door leads–to the inner room of heaven–Albert wondered about the door which hangs from the hinges. The cardinal virtues "are called cardinal because they are like a hinge for the principal acts of the motive powers of the soul, to which the acts of the other virtues are connected, as to a hinge." The door, then, consists in other, subordinate virtues, which "are reduced to" the cardinal virtues. For Albert, then, the essence of cardinality consists, not so much in having a heavenly end as in being "principal" virtues to which other, subordinate virtues are attached. The way Albert construed "cardinal," then, leads directly to two topics central to his account of the cardinal virtues: the distinction between two senses of such virtues, as seen in his explanation of the *connections* among the cardinal virtues; and his account of the "parts" of each cardinal virtue.

When Albert addressed the issue of the connection of the cardinal virtues, in his *Commentary on the Sentences*, he followed Philip's doctrine closely. He distinguished general from specific acts of the cardinal virtues and concluded that their general acts are necessarily united to each other, while their specific acts are not:

> There are certain general acts of the virtues, and in relation to these the virtues are not distinguished from each other. And there is something of each one of these in every virtue. For in each virtue there is some *object of choice*, but this object is not proper to prudence. Likewise, in each virtue there is something *difficult* to overcome, but this difficulty is not proper to courage. Rather, courage concerns difficulty covering a limited matter, namely passion impressed from without. Likewise, a *mean* between excess and deficiency is found in every virtue, but this is not proper to temperance. Rather, temperance concerns the matter of inborn passions concerned with the pleasures of taste and touch. And the *obligation* (*debitum*) found in every virtue is not the obligation justice treats; but justice concerns matter related to our neighbor, as falling under natural or positive law.[127]

Albert made use of the same doctrine in his paraphrase of Aristotle's *Nicomachean Ethics*. There he noted that there are four general attributes which are "properly in *every*" virtue. Following Philip, Albert attributed this doctrine to Cicero, who "says the four attributes which are found in the actions (*operationibus*) of the virtues argue for the four virtues. For to know (*scire*) what is required argues for prudence; the strength to act resolutely (*firmiter*) argues for courage; the mean argues for temperance; and correctness (*rectitudo*) argues for justice." Albert clearly recognized the difference between these four "general acts" and the proper acts of each virtue. The general acts are universal, as the Chancellor had said; but then Albert added something new. At the general level, the cardinal virtues do not completely ensure that an individual action is morally right. Even "if one has these general traits, one does not necessarily possess all the specific types of virtues; for these traits are not features of some specific virtue, except by being appropriated to the special area of that virtue." Courage is

[127] P. 143.

an instance. "It is not the same strength which is proper to courage and which is found in all virtuous actions, for what is proper in courage is to act against *difficult passions*, while what is common in courage is the strength to act according to virtue." When Albert viewed the cardinal virtues in terms of the acts they produce, he first saw four general, Platonic "acts" which are found in every good action. But he recognized that each of the four cardinal virtues also can produce certain specific "acts." The general virtues become specific by a process he called "appropriation."[128] Albert seems to have chosen this term because he thought of each general cardinal virtue as a kind of abstract essence that then is narrowed to its "proper" matter, much as metaphysical essences are constricted by matter within individual horses, dogs, and men.

g. Albert: The "Parts" of the Cardinal Virtues

Albert thought his particular contribution to the development of the doctrine of the cardinal virtues was staking out the specific areas for all the "parts" of each general cardinal virtue. Like Philip, Albert thought of courage and temperance as one group, because "they are developed in the passions," while prudence and justice go together, because they "are developed in reason." Albert added special virtues to Philip's list of the "parts" of temperance and courage; and where Philip had said prudence and justice are only general virtues, Albert found "parts" for them. To make his improvements on Philip's doctrine, Albert followed Philip's lead and concentrated on the "proper act" and the "matter," understood in its objective sense, of each virtue.

Albert began with courage, which "is taken in two ways" based on its "matter." When exercised about its "proper matter," courage is a "special virtue." Albert began where Philip had left off, by describing this matter as "passions impressed from without, or extrinsic passions" produced by the "difficulty" of death. Three levels of "difficulties" produce three different sub-species of courage: courage in the face of death freely accepted, such as the martyr and warrior have; courage in the face of death by disease or bad luck; and courage to face what is directly related to death, such as infirmity, war, sieges, persecution, storms, and shipwrecks. The "saints,"

[128] Albert, *In Nic. Eth.* 2. 6, ed. Cologne 14.1: 120. *In III Sent.* d. 36.1, ed. Borgnet 28: 666-7. Cf. O. Lottin, "Les vertus cardinales et leur ramifications chez les théologiens de 1230 à 1250," *Psychologie et morale aux XIIe et XIIIe siècles*, 2: 154-194.

however, added instances of courage which are not confined to facing death, such as "resisting desires of the flesh and the devil." These areas of courage show that in its broad sense, as Philip said, courage is "a *condition* of any virtue, because every virtue is about the difficult." Courage in this sense is a general or universal virtue. In addition to distinguishing general from special courage, Albert recognized that it has "parts" or specific virtues subordinate to it. Where Philip had accepted only two, Albert incorporated all four Ciceronian "parts" of courage: magnificence, confidence, patience, and perseverence.

When he came to temperance, Albert refined Philip's view even more. He adopted Philip's account of general temperance: its matter covers "all sensibles" and its act consists in attaining the "mean." But Albert narrowed the range of special temperance more than Philip had. Where Philip said temperance includes all bodily passions, Albert confined it within Aristotelian limits, to the pleasures of "touch and taste" understood to refer to eating, drinking, and sex. The "parts" of temperance, however, he expanded beyond those recognized by Philip, in order to include Macrobius's parts, as well as Cicero's.

Justice is the most complicated of the cardinal virtues. The Chancellor had refused to follow Cicero about justice, even though he made good use of his ideas concerning temperance and courage, but Albert would turn to Cicero to understand justice as well. The Roman advocate had explained justice through two legal concepts, the "law of nature (*ius naturae*)" and "customary law (*ius consuetudine*)," since in etymology and in reality *iustitia* is built on *ius*. Albert took Cicero's point and began his treatment of justice with *ius*, which he understood to be a command of the moral law, and *lex*, the same command codified in writing. Since the purpose of the law is to produce goodness in humans, *ius* leads quite directly to general justice, about which Albert recognized two distinct conceptions. The general justice of the philosophers, called by Aristotle "legal justice," Albert defined as "the genus of all the virtues." The *sancti*, however, had recognized another kind of general justice, one "about which the philosophers had said nothing." This justice is 'general' because it incorporates "rectitude in all the powers" of the soul, and it is 'justice' because it "justifies," that is, it opens sinners to a heavenly reward. Albert, then, seems to have seen both the Platonic and Aristotelian sides of the Chancellor's account of general justice, but, more consistently than Philip, Albert limited general justice to a Platonic conception of justice, understood as the totality of inner goodness and virtue in an individual, traits which lead to heaven.

Albert, however, did not completely abandon the Aristotelian conception of justice as fundamentally a political virtue, one that essentially concerns relations with others. Where Philip had thought of Aristotle's justice as a second conception of general justice, one competing with Plato's, Albert simply moved Aristotelian justice to the level of a special virtue. In this way, he realized more perfectly the Chancellor's dream that all the cardinal virtues have two tiers. He then situated Aristotle's "distributive justice," which concerns the distribution of goods by the ruler, and commutative justice or "the justice of restitution," which concerns relations between the ruler's subjects, as two sub-species of special justice. Because Bk. 6 of the *Nicomachean Ethics* still had not made its way to Paris, or perhaps simply because he ran out of time before returning to Cologne, Albert did not develop a detailed consideration of the "parts" of justice in his *De bono*. Though incomplete, it provided his student Thomas with a way of approaching justice, and with the materials for an even more thorough treatment of the subject.

Prudence had proved to be the most difficult virtue for the Philippian model of two senses or levels for each cardinal virtue. Albert did manage to distinguish two senses of prudence, a term he said is used analogously (*per prius et posterius*). In its primary sense prudence refers to "practical knowledge which is ordered to consequent voluntary action," and is for this reason "one of the political virtues." In its secondary and wider sense, prudence is "sagacity and the wit to find what is good in itself or absolutely, concerning any matter." This broader sense of prudence can extend beyond the practical realm and can even include facility at performing actions which, while good in some sense, are morally bad, as Philip had noted in referring to the "prudence of the flesh" identified in Scripture. Albert neglected to say whether these senses of prudence are general or special virtues. Even though he did not move beyond the Chancellor on this point, Albert did identify the "principal parts of prudence." They are "memory, intelligence, and foresight," as Cicero had said.

As is typical of the way he used his sources, Albert did not fundamentally alter the project he took over from Philip. He was more consistent than the Chancellor about the fact that the cardinal virtues are acquired virtues; but he did not change Philip's fundamental principle that there are two senses of the cardinal virtues, nor did he alter Philip's account of their basic nature. When he came, however, to the details, the multitude of "parts" lying under the cardinal virtues, his *De bono* shows how far Albert took Philip's vision toward its full realization. But then Albert moved back to Germany and the unfinished task of the *De bono* gave way to the even more important project of paraphrases which could bring the learning of the Greeks and Arabs to the Latins, so that scholars throughout Christendom could share the enthusiasm Albert had felt at Paris. The task of completing Philip's grand project thus passed to Albert's pupil.

h. Thomas Aquinas

Thomas Aquinas addressed the nature of the cardinal virtues three times in his writing career: in his *Commentary on the Sentences* (1252-6), *Summa of Theology 1-2* (1268-71), and his *Disputed Question on the Cardinal Virtues* (1271-3).[129] Both the cardinal virtues and the vast range of specific virtues are noticeably absent from the *Summa contra gentiles* (1260-5). Aquinas paid some attention to the specific virtues in the *Sentences* commentary and the disputed question *De malo* (1269-71), but offered no systematic treatment there. It was not until he wrote *Summa 2-2* (1271-3) that someone finally completed the task Philip and Albert had envisioned–a systematic and thorough presentation of the whole range of specific virtues and vices set out under the structure of the four cardinal virtues.[130]

[129] For the life of Aquinas, see Torrell, *Saint Thomas Aquinas* (Washington: CUA Press, 1996). The literature on Aquinas is vast; for general treatments of his ethics, see: E. Gilson, *The Christian Philosophy of St. Thomas Aquinas* (New York: Random House, 1956), "Part 3: Morality," 251-378, a still profound treatment; R. McInerny, *Ethica Thomistica* (Washington: CUA Press, 1997), a fine short introduction to the subject; M. Rhonheimer, *Natur als Grundlage der Moral* (Innsbruck: Tyrolia-Verlag, 1986), useful for its comparisons with Kantian deontology and consequentialism; and Vernon Bourke, *Ethics: A Textbook in Moral Philosophy* (New York: Macmillan, 1966), a helpful neoscholastic textbook.

[130] On the structure of the *Summa*, see: L. Elders, "La méthode suivie par saint Thomas d'Aquin dans la composition de la *Somme de théologie*," *Nova et Vetera* 66 (1991) 178-192; W. Metz, *Die Architektonik der Summa theologiae des Thomas von Aquin* (Hamburg: Meiner, 1998); and A. Patfoort, *La Somme de saint Thomas et la logique du dessein de Dieu* (Paris: Cerf, 1997). On the virtues in Aquinas, P. Geach, *The Virtues* (Cambridge: CUP, 1977) offered an analytic-Thomistic study before the revival of virtue theory brought on by A. MacIntyre. For MacIntyre, see *After Virtue* (Notre Dame: University of Notre Dame Press, 1981), a critique of the eclipse of the virtues by deontology and consequentialism; *Three Rival Versions of Moral Enquiry* (Notre Dame: University of Notre Dame Press, 1988), setting out his version of Thomistic virtue theory; *Dependent Rational Animals: why human beings need the virtues* (Chicago: Open Court, 1999). Jean Porter, *Moral Action and Christian Ethics* (Cambridge: CUP, 1995) and *Natural and Divine Law: Reclaiming the Tradition for Christian Ethics* (Grand Rapids, MI: Eerdmans, 2000) tries to use Thomistic prin-

Aquinas's account of the basic nature of the cardinal virtues and their "parts" shows the deep and abiding influence of the Chancellor and Albert. In treating the moral virtues in general in *Summa 1-2*, he followed their approach of using the four causes to understand virtue. Since a virtue is "an operative habit," its proximate *end* is "operation itself" and its remote *end* is happiness. Humans are the *efficient* causes of "acquired" virtue, while God is the efficient cause of "infused" virtues.[131] When he turned to *form*, Aquinas recognized two meanings: ontological form, which excludes matter and is called "the form of the part"; and definitional form, which is but another word for essence, and is called "the form of the whole." The latter helps define the universal essence of virtue: "Now the formal cause of a virtue, like the formal cause of anything, is taken from its genus and difference." On this model of definition, the four cardinal virtues are like genera, while other virtues are like species. Since species of a common genus are distinguished from each other by differentiating notes, understanding each special virtue involves isolating its *differentia*. To do so Aquinas turned to matter, which has three senses. Matter "out of which (*ex qua*)" refers to the material components of a substance, and is therefore irrelevant to the virtues, which are "accidents." Matter "in which (*in qua*)," however, is the "subject" of some accident, and in the case of the virtues this kind of matter is a power of the soul, as Philip and Albert had said. Since more than one habit can exist in each part of the soul, matter "in which" does not distinguish specific virtues from each other, though it does provide evidence for the four *general* cardinal virtues. Finally, "matter about which (*circa quam*) is the *object*" that "determines a virtue as to its species," by providing that differentiating note.

Based on this causal account of virtue as such, Aquinas then turned to the seven fundamental virtues. He used both *matter* and *form* to argue for the nature of the cardinal (*1-2*, q. 61) and theological (q. 62) virtues. He then sharply separated acquired from infused virtues based on their *efficient* causes (q. 63), followed by a discussion of the "mean" as *formal* cause of virtue (q.64). Aquinas could then find a logical place for the connections

---

ciples to draw some un-Thomistic conclusions. Characteristic of European emphasis on re-connecting Aquinas's account of the virtues with religious spirituality is H. Dörnemann, *Freundschaft als Paradigma der Erlösung: eine Reflexion auf die Verbindung von Gnadenlehre, Tugendlehre und Christologie in der Summa theologiae de Thomas von Aquin* (Würzburg: Echter, 1997).

[131] *ST* 1-2.55.4.

(q. 65) and equality (q. 66) of the virtues, by conceiving of them as *properties* in the technical, Aristotelian sense of attributes flowing from the essences of the virtues. Finally he capped the whole treatment with the *end* of both cardinal and theological virtues, that is, their status in heaven (q. 67). At long last, someone finally achieved a fully integrated treatment of the *general* nature of the seven fundamental moral virtues.

The way Aquinas dealt with the nature of the cardinal virtues in *Summa 1-2* required that he take the detailed treatment of the "parts" of the cardinal virtues, which Philip and Albert had directly appended to consideration of their nature, and put it into another whole treatise, *Summa 2-2* (1271-3). There Aquinas developed a virtue theory more elaborate in its details than anything found in the ancient authors or in earlier medieval authors.[132] While writing *Summa 2-2*, Aquinas seems to have kept his eye on the contours of the whole by offering a series of disputed questions *On the Virtues*, one of which is the *Disputed Question on the Cardinal Virtues*.[133] There, in four magisterial articles, he set out his final and most integrated presentation of the cardinal virtues, in a kind of 'short course' on their basic nature.

i. Aquinas: The Nature of the Cardinal Virtues

Br. Thomas wasted no time. He set up the problematic for the whole disputation with the very first objection in Art. 1 and set out the fundamental principle guiding his argument in his reply to that objection. On the authority of Pope Gregory the Great, the objector lays out a Platonic view of cardinal virtues so strongly connected with each other that it seems they

[132] See S. Pinckaers, *The Sources of Christian Ethics* 230-2, on how Catholic theologians later lost sight of the cardinal virtues in ethics.

[133] The whole set includes: *De virtutibus in communi, De caritate, De correctione fraterna, De spe, De virtutibus cardinalibus*. Cf. G. Emery, "Brief Catalogue," in Torrell, *Saint Thomas Aquinas*, 1: 336. The treatise *De virtutibus cardinalibus* has been little studied, see: R. McInerny, introduction to Thomas Aquinas, *Disputed Questions on Virtue*, tr. R.M. McInerny (South Bend, IN: St. Augustine's Press, 1999); D. Oderburg, "On the Cardinality of the Cardinal Virtues," *International Journal of Philosophical Studies* 7 (1999) 305-322, focusing on the concept of cardinality rather than this particular text; R.E. Houser, "The Cardinal Virtues: Aquinas and the Fathers," in *Les philosophies morales et politiques au Moyen Âge* (Ottawa: LEGAS, 1995) 2: 699-708; "The *De virtutibus cardinalibus* and Aquinas' doctrine of happiness," *Atti del IX Congresso tomistico internazionale* (Vatican City: Libreria Editrice Vaticana, 1991) 3: 250-9.

"ought not be called *four* cardinal virtues" at all. Rather than simply take the opposing side by invoking the name of Aristotle,[134] Aquinas takes the opportunity to set out *both* senses of the cardinal virtues. Far from taking sides, he accepted both kinds of cardinal virtues as each in its own way absolutely essential to a comprehensive understanding of their nature. To explain the distinction between the two senses of cardinal virtues, Aquinas turned to formal and material causality.

Form opens up the cardinal virtues in their "general" sense, because they are four "different formal aspects (*rationes formales*)" of any virtue. Each and every specific virtue has four general attributes which constitute a set of necessary conditions for the existence of virtue itself, and Aquinas offers brief, formulaic descriptions of them: Prudence in the broad sense refers to "*all* rational direction" of human action; justice includes "*all* correctness producing equity among human actions"; temperance extends to "*all* moderation restraining human appetites from worldly goods"; and courage incorporates "*all* resoluteness of mind steadying a human in the good and against the assaults of all sorts of evils." These formulae succinctly distinguish the two senses of the cardinal virtues, at least verbally. "Moderation," for instance, has a broader extension than "temperance." The cardinal virtues in this broad sense Aquinas quite rightly attributed to Augustine. He then offered Aristotle as representative of the opposing view, where *matter* in its objective sense is used to understand the cardinal virtues "in so far as they are special virtues limited to their proper matters." In his reply to Obj. 1 Aquinas did not describe their "matters" precisely but posited the distinction sufficiently to use it as the point of departure for his three arguments in the *responsio*.

As presented thus far, Br. Thomas simply followed the general contours of the distinction as Philip and Albert had developed it. He realized, however, that their way of making the distinction, based on the difference between general and special "acts," was faulty. Acts are not habits, so that if the special cardinal virtues are essentially acts, they cannot essentially be habits. Aristotle was correct to say that *special* virtues are essentially habits. Consequently, Aquinas noted that "virtue is taken in two ways, properly and broadly. Taken properly, a virtue is a kind of perfection ... based on *habit*.... Taken broadly, however, *everthing* that is good and praiseworthy in human actions or passions is called virtue."[135] Broadly considered, the

[134] As Albert had done, see pp. 129-30.

[135] *ST* 2-2.144.1c.

cardinal virtues are "general *modes* of the virtues," while cardinal virtues in the narrow sense are "special virtues." In Aquinas's scholastic terminology, "mode (*modus*)" signifies an internal or intrinsic subdivision of a broader notion, in this case, the notion of virtue. Here he envisioned, it would seem, two modes of the cardinal virtues: 'general modes' which are aspects of any virtue or virtuous action, and 'special modes,' which are the cardinal virtues, as limited by their objective matter to narrowly defined areas of moral life. The notion of 'mode,' then, was a notion supple enough to include the general virtues as acts or attributes but not full blown habits, and the special virtues as habits in the Aristotelian sense of the term. The point, however, is not just one of terminology, as can be seen through its parallel with one of Aquinas's central metaphysical doctrines.

Under the inspiration of Philip and Albert, in the first article of his disputed questions *On Truth* (1256-9), Aquinas had explained the nature of truth by situating it under the widest of all notions, that of being (*ens*). Being has two modes: the "general modes of being" include its three transcendental attributes: unity, truth, and goodness. While each individual thing in the universe has some specific nature, it also has these four universal attributes. Each exists (*ens*), is an individual distinct from others while internally whole (*unum*), and can be an object of cognition (*verum*) and desire (*bonum*). The second set of modes Aquinas called, after Avicenna, the "special modes of being." They are made up of the ten Aristotelian categories and all their subdivisions, which determine the specific nature of each individual thing in the universe. Every individual being, then, has a specific nature which falls under the "special modes" of being, as well as certain transcendental or universal attributes which fall under the "general modes" of being. Far different from Aristotle, whose metaphysics focused on substance, one of the *special* modes of being, the fundamental focus of Thomistic metaphysics is on the transcendentals, the *general* modes of being. The reason Aquinas refocused metaphysics is because the transcendentals constitute a set of universal conditions for the very existence of individual beings, universal conditions found even in God.

The terminological parallels are striking, but even more so are the parallels in doctrine. As the general modes of being form a set of universal conditions for the actual existence of any real being, the general cardinal virtues constitute a set of "universal conditions," as Philip called them, for all virtue and for all virtuous actions. For this reason, it is only when the cardinal virtues are taken in their general sense "that the other virtues are contained under them," in the structure elaborated in *Summa 2-2*.[136] And as each individual being has a specific nature that is describable under the special modes of being, so too every individual virtue, even each individual virtuous action, is describable as falling under one of the "special virtues." The terminology of 'modes,' therefore, opens up the three arguments of the *responsio* of Art. 1.

Those three arguments were designed to defend the traditional doctrine of four cardinal virtues by uncovering their true nature. Each argument develops themes set out by Philip the Chancellor and Albert; they move well beyond Aquinas's illustrious predecessors in width of vision and demonstrative character; and they even move beyond Aquinas's parallel treatment in *Summa 1-2*. The third and last argument is based on the "matter in which" or "subject" of the cardinal virtues. So brief it may not seem like an argument at all, merely a simple-minded example of medieval concordism, it was called by no less an interpreter of Aquinas than Jean Poinsot "quite unsound (*multo magis infirma*)."[137] When taken in historical light, however, the argument appears more impressive. For here at last someone dealt deftly with the problem which had baffled Philip and Albert, who had found it impossible to argue directly for four cardinal virtues based on the powers of the soul. Aquinas's elegant solution was simplicity itself: he moved beyond the Platonic assumption of a tripartite soul and added a fourth power to the faculties of the soul, a free will different from intellect, emotions, and desire.

In *On the Cardinal Virtues* Aquinas did not argue for this signal innovation in philosophical psychology, but he had done so earlier.[138] Human action involves both a passive, cognitive side and an active side, by which we initiate movement toward things. Consequently, cognitive powers are different from appetitive powers. Sense cognition concerns individuals, while intellectual cognition involves universals. It follows that the cognitive powers of sensation are different from those of intellect. Since appetite presupposes cognition, there must be a corresponding distinction among appetitive powers. Consequently, sense appetite, the power which produces inclinations based on what is known through sense cognition, is different from intellectual appetite or will, the power to make choices based on

[136] *ST* 1-2.61.3c.

[137] John of St. Thomas (Jean Poinsot), *In Iam-Iae de virtutibus*, ed. A Mathieu and H. Gagné (Laval: 1952), sec. 1074, p. 330.

[138] *ST* 1.80.1-2; 1.81.2.

intellectual knowledge. The ultimate reason why these powers are different from each other lies in the fact that they have different *objects*. On this basis, Aquinas concluded that the will is different from the intellect, as well as from emotion and desire. The ontological difference between intellect and will had not been properly recognized by Philip or Albert, nor by Plato, nor even by Aristotle. For Aquinas, then, emotion and desire are sense appetites because the other animals have them, while only human animals have free will or intellectual appetite. Sense perception is a prerequisite of moral choice, but not part of the activity of choosing itself. Consequently, there are four and only four powers involved in making choices: intellect, will, emotion, and desire.

In *On the Cardinal Virtues*, Art. 1, Aquinas presupposed this psychology and correlated the four parts of the soul with the four cardinal virtues. For the virtues to be cardinal, they must cover the whole range of human powers relevant to virtuous action, neither leaving any power out, nor situating two virtues in a single power. Aquinas followed Philip and Albert in saying that prudence is found in the intellect, courage in the emotions, and temperance in the power of desire. Having isolated the will as a power distinct from intellect, it was quite natural for him to situate justice in the will. In this way, a philosopher finally succeeded in finding a home for Platonic justice; and this home was appropriate. For the will is the power to make internal moral choices, which in turn are the starting point for external actions, deeds that necessarily affect other people and consequently fall within the domain of justice. Aquinas's argument has seemed unimpressive to those who assume the cardinal virtues are *only* special virtues of the Aristotelian sort. But in fact the argument, as Aquinas actually presented it, is directed at the four cardinal virtues, understood as *general* modes of virtue. Once it is seen in this way, the argument takes on a different and more persuasive appearance. It is true, however, that this argument, "taken from the power of the soul which is the subject for each virtue," achieves its full import only when the cardinal virtues to which it concludes are understood as defined by the formulae for the *general* virtues, as presented in the reply to Obj. 1 and elucidated in the first argument of the *responsio* to Art. 1.

As we have seen, Albert thought the only demonstrative argument for the four cardinal virtues is the argument based on the dominion of the "order of reason" over all the functions of the various powers of the soul. In *Summa* 1-2.61.2, Aquinas adopted Albert's argument, with one emendation, that the will is a power distinct from the intellect.[139] For Aquinas, as for Albert, in *this* argument the primary function of the cardinal virtues is to bring human actions and passions under the dominion of reason. What is not nearly so clear, however, is which virtues perform this function. Did Aquinas have in mind prudence, justice, courage, and temperance in their *specific*, limited operation as "special virtues," or was he thinking of them in broad terms, as general virtues? Aristotelianizing interpreters of Aquinas, which includes most commentators over the centuries, have been less than satisfied with this argument, precisely because they have taken these terms as Aristotle would.[140] Br. Thomas himself, however, seems to have realized how his argument could be misunderstood, and in the disputed question *On the Cardinal Virtues* he did two things to sharpen the argument. First, he avoided ambiguity by using different terms for the general and special senses of the cardinal virtues, as Philip had done. The four general cardinal virtues are described as "rational direction, correctness, resolution, and moderation," which "are required for *any* virtuous act." Such care with terms cannot be happenstance, but seems self-consciously designed to emphasize the difference between the general and special senses of the cardinal virtues. Second, for the first and only time in his writing career, and in his own name as a theologian, Aquinas gave his own interpretation of the Aristotelian text which had initiated the thirteenth-century development of the doctrine of the cardinal virtues.

To highlight the fact that he was arguing for cardinal virtues in their general sense, Aquinas described this argument as "taken from the *modes* a virtue exhibits." Such modes are "like its formal aspects (*formales rationes*)," where the term *formal* means that these four features are a set of four attributes essential to virtue as such. The argument first sets out the four attributes, then shows how they are found in the text of Aristotle. To describe unambiguously the *general* cardinal attributes of all good actions,

[139] The argument in 1-2.61.2 is: (a) The order reason brings to moral life is guided by the "formal principle of virtue," which is "the good as discerned by reason (*bonum rationis*)." (b) This good is manifested in "operations" and "passions." (c) Prudence is simply this good "as it consists in the very consideration of reason." (d) Justice is the order of reason put "into operations" which affect others. Both (e) temperance and (f) courage put "the order of reason into the passions."

[140] Jean Poinsot, to turn to the same commentator, found both arguments in 1-2.61.2 incomplete and in need of being supplemented by the argument of Art. 3, which he thought demonstrative precisely because it is concerned with the cardinal virtues understood as special virtues.

Aquinas chose extremely abstract terms. Philip the Chancellor was correct to say the 'temperate' feature of all virtuous actions is 'attaining the mean.' To signify this notion Aquinas used the term "modification (*modi-ficatio*)," which in its etymology means 'to produce (*facere*) the mean (*modus*).' Both Philip and Aristotle had said that virtuous action must be based on knowledge, but to emphasize that such knowledge is practical, that is, geared to action, Aquinas used the term "rational direction (*ratio dirigens*)" to show that its 'prudential' feature is the direction the mind gives to all good action. Aquinas took his term for general courage from Aristotle and called it "resoluteness (*firmitas*)." Only for justice did neither the Chancellor nor Aristotle have an appropriate term for its general sense. The baffling problem about justice which Philip and Albert had failed adequately to resolve was whether in its general sense justice signifies some kind of Platonic inner harmony within the individual soul or is a purely political virtue limited to external relations with others, as Aristotle had held. More decisive than his teachers, Aquinas opted for the Aristotelian conception and called the Platonic view merely "metaphorical."[141] All justice, even in its most general sense, requires that action "be proportioned in the right way toward *something extrinsic* as its *end*." Justice, then, is a virtue governing our interaction with the outside world, and justice as a general virtue subordinates the individual to an extrinsic end, the community or the ruler of the community. Consequently, Aquinas chose the abstract term "correctness (*rectitudo*)" to incorporate the notion of moral obligation involved in acting "in the right way (*debito modo*)" toward the community.

Aquinas understood justice teleologically because the "formal principle" of the general cardinal virtues, namely, "the good discerned by reason," he also understood teleologically. The most essential feature of human action is that it is purposeful, which means that through actions we try to realize our goals, using free choice guided by reason.[142] Aquinas thought that throughout nature one finds end-directed actions, but what distinguishes human teleology from the rest of nature is self-conscious awareness of our goals. Every purposeful human action, therefore, necessarily involves four factors:

[141] *ST* 2-2.58.2c.

[142] Cf. *ST* 1-2.61.2c: "the formal principle (*principium formale*) of the virtues of which we now speak is the good discerned by reason (*rationis bonum*)." Here "good" signifies the end the will intends, and implies the set of will acts needed to attain the end, while "reason" signifies the intellectual acts producing a human action. Thus, *rationis bonum* is a convenient formula for the teleology of human action, which involves both intellect and will.

We must *know* our goal and the means we are taking to achieve it; we must actually *choose* what we do to attain our goal; we must be *resolute* in overcoming obstacles on the way to our goal, and to keep our attention on our goal we must *moderate* inclinations leading us away from it. These are the four cardinal features of all human actions, features which flow from its goal-oriented character. If human action is teleological in this way, the first stand ard for *good* action is success in achieving a goal. One *acts well* in a minimal way when one achieves the goal intended. This aspect of his doctrine of the cardinal virtues is completely teleological, and Aquinas found it in Aristotle, when read through the lenses of Philip the Chancellor. One *acts better* when one's successful action is moral. For an action to be good in either of these two senses, it must exhibit the four *general* cardinal virtues.[143]

The first and third arguments of Aquinas's *responsio* in *On the Cardinal Virtues*, Art. 1, are meant to complement each other: one concerning the internal source of the action and the other the action itself. Both arguments concern the cardinal virtues conceived as *general* virtues. They set out two universal requirements for good action: all four parts of the soul must be involved in such an action and the action itself must exhibit the four 'cardinal traits' of rationality, moderation, resoluteness, and correctness toward the community.

j. Aquinas: The Special Cardinal Virtues and the "Parts" of the Cardinal Virtues

If the two arguments considered thus far show the four virtues are *cardinal*, are they *virtues* in the full, Aristotelian sense of the term? Aquinas's second argument in the *responsio* is where he "appropriates" the broad formal attributes which make up the essence of each general cardinal virtue to specific and limited areas of action governed by each "special" cardinal virtue. He does so by identifying "certain specific matters and acts" for each special cardinal virtue. They serve to distinguish each special cardinal virtue from the general cardinal virtue standing over it. In *On the Cardinal Virtues* Aquinas also made selective use of the "parts" of each cardinal virtue, that is, those other specific virtues which also fall under each general cardinal virtue. He did so because these "parts," which are delineated more fully in *Summa 2-2*, help differentiate the special cardinal virtue from the other special virtues which are allied to it. To understand each *special* cardinal virtue, then, Aquinas viewed it in relation to two other things: the

[143] Precursors of this argument are in Philip, p. 94, and Albert, p. 122.

general cardinal virtue standing over it like a genus, and the *other specific virtues* which constitute the "parts" of that general virtue.

Prudence: Prudence is particularly difficult to understand, and Philip the Chancellor had gone to the extreme of abandoning his own model for the cardinal virtues when he said that prudence is only a general virtue and has no special sense, because its "matter" is determined by the matter of the other virtues. Rather than give up so easily, to isolate "special prudence" Aquinas turned away from its matter to its "acts." There are three intellectual acts involved in the reasoning process. Humans use their minds to deliberate, that is, to reason from premisses, and to make judgments, that is, to draw conclusions, but neither of these intellectual acts distinguishes theoretical from practical thought, and so cannot be used to distinguish prudence, as a practical virtue, from other intellectual virtues. Where theory and practice do diverge is that in practical matters we actually perform actions, which requires "forethought about things to be done (*praemeditari de agendis*)." As described thus far, however, the area prudence governs is no narrower than that covered by "rational direction," which is how Aquinas described prudence in its *general* sense. To proceed all the way to special prudence, Aquinas turned to Aristotle's list of lesser practical and intellectual virtues: "*eubulia* (deliberating well)," which governs the act of deliberation, and "*synesis* (understanding)" and "*gnome* (judgment)," which govern the act of judgment. These three virtues are different from prudence, but allied to it as its "potential parts," because they do not govern the "principal act" of practical reason, which is "to apply precepts (*praecipere*)."[144] The reason why Aquinas introduces them here is to point out that there is another virtue, namely, prudence understood as a special virtue, through which "reason comes to apply precepts well (*per prudentiam fit ratio bene praeceptiva*)." In this deceptively dense description Aquinas set out three criteria for distinguishing special from general prudence.

First, special prudence is a virtue in the true sense of the word, that is, prudence is a habit. This seems to be the reason why Aquinas introduced the "potential parts" of prudence, which as intellectual virtues must be fully developed habits, while *general* prudence need not be. Second, prudence "applies precepts" or, more literally, is "preceptive." The function of prudence is not to draw up abstract rules or precepts, but to apply previously understood precepts to individual cases by engendering real, physical ac-

[144] *ST* 2-2.48.un.c.

tions. Such actions proceed from two correlative acts, which Aquinas calls the intellectual act of "command *(imperium)*" and the will act of "use (*usus*)."[145] Aquinas here uses the term "preceptive" in order to indicate that the function of prudence is to *prescribe* how we ought to act in the concrete and to *initiate* such prescribed actions. While prudence in the general sense is broad enough to include knowledge which is not directly practical, when taken as a "special virtue" prudence is always and necessarily practical.[146] Third, and most importantly, prudence applies precepts "well (*bene*)," a term added to "preceptive" in order to indicate that the actions produced by prudence, when conceived as a special virtue, are *morally good actions*. Consequently, while general prudence is wide enough to include actions good in some non-moral sense, special prudence is strictly limited to actions which are habitual, practical, and morally good.

Aquinas elaborated the different senses of prudence when considering "whether prudence can exist in sinners" in a part of the *Summa* written about the same time as *On the Cardinal Virtues*.[147] Philip had found that in addition to the "moral prudence" recognized by the philosophers, there are two other kinds: "prudence of the flesh" and "prudence of the spirit." Aquinas developed Philip's point, arguing that there are three senses of prudence, two of which, even though they describe a real kind of prudence, just as clearly fall beyond the moral realm. The best of these three is *true and perfect* prudence. A virtue in the full sense of a morally good habit, such prudence makes a person morally good by producing all three kinds of intellectual acts governed by prudence–acts of deliberation, judgment, and applying precepts–and by causing such intellectual acts as produce *morally good actions*. The reason why these actions are morally good is because they contribute "to a good end for a whole life."[148] Prudence in this sense is a "special virtue."

The next kind of prudence Aquinas called *true but imperfect*, due to falling off from the premier sort of prudence. One sort of imperfect prudence still concerns *moral* goodness, because it "pertains to a whole life," but is deficient because the intellectual acts of prudence are not 'carried to term.' There is "deficiency in the principal act of prudence," namely, in applying precepts to produce real actions. This sort of prudence still falls

[145] *ST* 1-2.11-17.
[146] Cf. *ST* 2-2.48.un.c; 47.2 ad 2m.
[147] *ST* 2-2.47.13.
[148] Cf. p. 174 below.

under the special virtue of prudence, because it still concerns the moral good, though incompletely realized.

A second sort of *true but imperfect* prudence is quite different from the first. Here the action is complete because it reaches its end, but the end in question is *not* the moral end, properly speaking. "The good which it takes for its end is *not* the common end of a whole human life, but some special endeavor." The 'prudential' acts which realize that end are not properly moral, even when they are successful. Aquinas's examples are helpful. A prudent businessperson and a prudent sailor are successful at their trade, but not necessarily morally good. This sense of prudence clearly fits within the broad range of the *general* virtue of prudence, but just as clearly lies outside the narrow range of *special* prudence.

The last kind of prudence mentioned in the *Summa* is furthest removed from the ideal of special prudence. Aquinas initially calls it "false" prudence, but this description can be misunderstood, since even this sense of prudence possesses certain features of the ideal, albeit in a minimal way. So he adds that it "is called prudence owing to some likeness (*per similitudinem*)." On Aquinas's teleological account, a person who has *true and perfect* prudence "rightly disposes what should be done for the sake of some [morally] good end, while one who, for the sake of a [morally] bad end disposes things congruent with that end has *false prudence*, in so far as he takes as his end what is not good truly, but only owing to some likeness." This trait is really "prudence" because it succeeds in achieving the end, but it is "false" because the end achieved is immoral. Philip's "prudence of the flesh" is one sort of "false prudence," and Aquinas says it is exemplified by the "good" or "prudent robber." This example, and false prudence generally, fit within the broad range of prudence taken as a general virtue, because the good robber is the robber who succeeds; but since theft is contrary to the moral law, such prudence clearly falls outside the narrow range of special prudence. The distinction between special and general prudence is well illustrated in the way Aquinas explained how even sinners can be prudent in the general sense of the term.

To round out Aquinas's treatment of prudence in its proper and narrow sense, it remains to consider its other "parts." His predecessors had listed a number of parts Aquinas described as "integral parts," the kind of components which are combined to produce prudence, as walls and roof produce a house. Trying to be as accommodating to his sources as possible, Aquinas recognized the following integral parts: memory, intelligence, docility, quick-wit, reasoning, foresight, circumspection, and caution. The "subjective parts" of a virtue are the "species" which fall under the general virtue conceived as a "genus." Prudence taken as a "special virtue" is prudence governing one person–ourselves. The other species are taken from the groups they govern: "military prudence" governing armies, "economic prudence" concerning family households, and "political prudence" covering the political community. Aquinas's argument in *On the Cardinal Virtues*, Art. 1, accounts for the many senses of prudence in a way none of his predecessors had done.

Justice: Aquinas's doctrine of prudence went well beyond Philip and Albert, but his most brilliant innovations concerned the other cardinal virtue which had given them trouble: the virtue of justice. Aquinas rejected the Platonic conception of inner justice and followed Aristotle in limiting justice to transitive actions, those proceeding outward from an agent and affecting others. All such actions necessarily involve a relation whose subject is the active agent and whose term is some 'other' affected by that agent. The fact that individual humans live in communities sets up a triangle of three different relations: the relation of an individual to his community, that of community to individual, and of one individual to another individual. The first of these relations is quite different from the other two, because the community (or its ruler) is its term. This relation concerns how individual actions affect the community, that is, how individuals affect, and effect, the common good. General (or legal) justice is based on this relation, and it consists in the actions of individuals benefitting the common good. Two features of Aquinas's conception of general justice are of paramount importance. First, the good of the community (and its ruler) are by nature the "end" for the sake of which individuals do and ought to act. Membership in a community necessarily obliges the individual to act for the sake of the good of that community. Second, the good of the community is not seen as being at odds with the good of the individual. General justice will normally be produced in the course of performing actions which are also just at the "specific" level.[149]

In *On the Cardinal Virtues* Aquinas did not fully elaborate his conception of justice as a "special virtue," but did say enough to distinguish general from special justice. Justice in the special sense is that "through which

[149] M. Lutz-Bachman, "The Discovery of a Normative Theory of Justice in Medieval Philosophy: On the Reception and Further Development of Aristotle's Theory of Justice by St. Thomas Aquinas," *Medieval Philosophy and Theology* 9 (2000) 9-10.

a human in the right way joins together in equity with others with whom he has to act in common." This dense definition includes a number of features central to special justice: humans are by nature communitarian; equity or equal treatment is the fundamental principle of justice; special justice is a *moral* virtue; and the principle of equity describes *moral* obligations. Most important for distinguishing special from general justice, however, are the subject and term of the justice relation. The *term* of special justice is "others," that is, other individuals. Thus, the distinction between the two levels of justice is made as sharply as possible. The term of general justice is the community or its ruler, while the term of special justice is the individual; general justice is for the sake of the common good, while special justice is for the sake of the individual good.

Special justice is further divided into two "subjective parts," based on the subject of the justice relation, rather than its term. Commutative justice runs from one individual to another, while distributive justice proceeds from the community (or its ruler) to an individual. In both cases an individual benefits from a just action, the difference between them consisting in the agent performing the action. In this way Aquinas could incorporate the two most prominent features of Aristotle's theory of justice, and in so doing he put the lie to the view that one could somehow be good to neighbor while undermining the broader community: for being truly just to neighbor feeds into the common good.[150]

There are other "parts" of special justice, as well. Its *integral* parts are taken from the first principle of practical reason, 'do good and avoid evil' by adding the qualification '*to others*.' What is really quite astonishing is the influence of Cicero on Aquinas's thought. If Aristotle's two divisions became the "subjective parts" of justice, when he came to consider the "potential parts" of justice, that is, those lesser communitarian virtues allied to justice, he followed Cicero. Consequently, the "potential parts" of justice consist in religion, piety, observance, gratitude (*gratia*), punishment (*vindicatio*), and friendliness, all taken from Cicero, along with liberality and equity, taken from Aristotle. So much was Aquinas a Ciceronian that topics that we would situate under justice, most notably war and other forms of discord, he placed under charity rather than justice. What all of these virtues have in common is that they contribute directly to the good of other individuals within the community, and thereby indirectly aid the community.

[150] *ST* 2-2.61.1.

The fact that Br. Thomas had access to the whole of Aristotle's *Nicomachean Ethics*, where Philip and Albert had only the *Ethica nova*, cannot completely explain the great strides he took beyond his predecessors. His real genius lay in taking the basic structure of the two senses of the cardinal virtues and developing it consistently, by adding the multitude of details he took from Cicero as well as Aristotle.

Temperance: If Philip and Albert offered Aquinas little help with prudence and justice, they provided invaluable aid when it came to temperance and courage. These two personal and moral virtues had led Philip to his fundamental principle, that the cardinal virtues have two senses. Aquinas approached the special virtue of temperance in the same way they had, beginning with the universal, formal trait of "moderation," understood as attaining the mean. He then searched for the limited area of the *special* virtue of temperance. Philip's matter–"bodily passions"–was too broad, but Albert was right to look to the "greatest desires" for a differentia, since temperance governs desires. These are the desires for certain tactile pleasures, those connected with sex, food, and drink. These passions are so important because of their link to fundamental goods: preserving the existence of individuals and the nature of the species. The differentia, then, that sets out the object of the special virtue of temperance is "reining in" our desires in the areas of reproduction and nutrition.

Temperance has numerous "parts." Its integral parts, which help produce the virtue, he took from Macrobius's commentary on Cicero's *Dream of Scipio*. It is simply impossible to be temperate without having a sense of the difference between "honesty" and "shame (*verecundia*)," for these two internal barometers warn us beforehand when the desire for pleasure is on the verge of getting out of hand. Its subjective parts are sub-species of temperance conceived as a "special virtue." "Abstinence" governs the desire for food and "sobriety" that for drink, virtues Aquinas drew from his master Albert, who took them from Philip and Macrobius. "Chastity," "virginity," and "purity (*puditia*)," also taken from Macrobius and Philip by way of Albert, are the sub-species of temperance governing sex.

The "potential parts" of temperance apply the generic, formal trait of 'moderation' to other specific areas, beyond the realm of nutrition and sex. To identify these virtues Aquinas combed carefully through Cicero, Macrobius, Andronicus, Philip, and Albert, since Aristotle had surprisingly little to offer. The list Aquinas developed is quite long, and since most of these predecessors offered little more than terms, he was at his most creative in developing his account of these virtues allied to temperance. The first and most important is "continence," by which Aquinas did not mean the virtue of "abstaining from sexual pleasure," as Philip, Albert, and the Fathers had used the term, but continence in the Aristotelian sense: that ability "to resist vehement evil desires." This ability is not a full-blown virtue, but concerns "when we take the term virtue broadly for any principle of praiseworthy deeds." The other potential parts of temperance produce moderation in our mode of living: "clemency" and "meekness (*mansuetudo*)," "modesty" and its sub-species, "humility" (whose importance the friar clearly downgraded from the lofty place it had for the monks, who had thought it an eighth principal virtue, along with the seven cardinal and theological virtues), "studiousness" (clearly a Dominican virtue), and modesty in behavior and dress. To Aquinas's mind, such parts of temperance as these showed clearly the benefit of extending the range of temperance beyond the narrow, though important, area of virtues connected with the sense of touch, as Aristotle had confined it.

Courage: Courage was perhaps the easiest of the cardinal virtues for Aquinas to set out its "special" sense, because Aristotle had dealt with it, and both Philip and Albert had been most successful in setting out its "parts." "Resoluteness" in facing any "difficulty," the general sense of the virtue, had to be limited in scope, based on the kind of difficulty an obstacle presents. As he had done with temperance, Philip looked to the difference between mind and matter in choosing "exterior passions inflicted on the body" as the object for special courage. Albert had seen, however, that this area was still too broad, and followed the advice of Aristotle: death is clearly the greatest obstacle humans face. Aquinas agreed with his teacher and said that "facing the dangers of death" is the *matter* of special courage. Both Dominicans refused to go quite so far as Aristotle, who had limited courage even further, to facing death in battle for one's country, although both followed the spirit of Aristotle in saying that the prime instance of courage is the courage of that kind of Christian soldier who is a martyr for God.

When he took up the "parts" of courage, Br. Thomas noted that, unlike the other three cardinal virtues, there are no sub-species or "subjective parts" of courage, presumably because death, the object of special courage, is already so narrow in extension. Philip, followed by Albert, had adopted the four parts of courage Cicero had first identified: magnificence, confidence (*fidentia*), patience, and perseverence. As good as were their accounts, however, and as much as they seemed to agree, there were problems with what they said. For all three ignored the premier Aristotelian virtue–magnanimity–and there was some confusion among magnanimity, magnificence, and confidence. Aquinas solved these confusions in an exceedingly clever way. For each of these virtues he distinguished its objective matter from its formal character. When taken in terms of their matter, these four become the "potential parts" of courage, four virtues like courage in overcoming difficulties, but virtues that deal with different difficulties than death. They are magnificence, dealing with the difficulties suffered by patrons of "great works"; magnanimity, that "greatness of soul" honored by the community; patience which gives us the strength to face the difficulties connected with the sorrows of life; and perseverence, whereby one overcomes the difficulties associated with long labors for the good. On the other hand, the "integral parts" of courage are analogous traits not limited in scope by special difficulties. They are respectively "accomplishment (*executio*)," "confidence," "endurance (*sustenentia*)," and "constancy." These are four components of courage, both in its narrow and its wide sense, traits which must be present for one to be courageous at all.

A clear sign of the difference between general and special virtues is the way they are connected to one another. In Art. 2 of *Of the Cardinal Virtues* Aquinas dealt with this issue, as a way of further clarifying this distinction so fundamental to the project begun by Philip the Chancellor. Since general virtues are conditions necessary for any virtuous act, they are unified in a Platonic way: "Without *all* the conditions dovetailing together, one of the conditions by itself is insufficient to produce what is truly a virtue." By contrast, each specific virtue functions independently of other specific moral virtues, depending only upon prudence: "No moral virtue can exist without prudence, nor can one who lacks moral virtue possess prudence. On the other hand, if we consider the four cardinal virtues as signifying the general conditions for virtue, in this respect they are connected in this way, that the presence of just one of these conditions, without fulfilling all four, is not sufficient to produce a virtuous act."

For Aquinas, the project of setting out a systematically complete, Christian vision of moral and immoral behavior focused on human virtues and vices. He understood, as every Platonist does, that virtue, not vice, is what makes that behavior intelligible. In this respect, *Summa 2-2* and *On the Cardinal Virtues* far surpass *De malo*, which had taken the seven deadly sins as its architectonic principle. To understand virtue one needs a map which shows how the various virtues (and vices) are related. The seven fundamental virtues are essential to reading the map rightly. For the part of the map concerned with the cardinal virtues, the overstated moral rigorism which had plagued philosophy almost since its inception can be avoided, once one grasps, as had Philip and Albert, this central principle of ethics:

the cardinal virtues function on two levels. The general cardinal virtues are necessarily united in every good or virtuous deed, no matter how minimal its sense of goodness. But the life of *moral* virtue, which is the one *reditus* taking men all the way back to God, requires special virtues, both infused and acquired. Contrary to the ancients, these virtues are within reach of 'everyman,' but not without a lifetime of effort.

Philip the Chancellor

Summa on the Good

[ca. 1225-1228]

On the Four Cardinal Virtues [1]

Our tract concerning the four cardinal virtues asks: First, what is the basis for taking the division and number of the cardinal virtues? Second, what is the reason for their order, since different thinkers take different positions. And third, why are they called cardinal virtues and, since they are infused virtues, can they be called divine virtues? And fourth, we look at each virtue.

Q. 1. CONCERNING THEIR DIVISION AND NUMBER

About the first question, namely, *What is the basis for taking their division and number?* there are the following

Objections [*against the four cardinal virtues*:]

1. Since virtue *is* a perfection of the rational soul based on its powers, as grace is a perfection of the soul based on its essence, it seems that the number of perfections should be taken from the number of powers which are perfected. If so, then since there are three powers in the rational soul, there should only be three cardinal virtues.

2. There are only three theological virtues: faith, hope, and charity, which perfect the three powers of the soul, each in its own way. For the same reason there should only be three cardinal virtues.

3. One might respond that a fourth virtue is assigned, one which pertains to all the powers, namely, justice, as the gloss says about *Genesis* 2, where it treats the four rivers, where justice is compared to the Euphrates, which is not assigned a land it circles: "Justice pertains to all the parts of the soul, because it is the order and equity in the soul, through which are united the other virtues: prudence, temperance, and courage. For one is just in so far as his soul is prudent in contemplating truth, temperate in restraining desire, and brave in withstanding adversity."[2]

On the contrary, by the same argument a fourth virtue should be found for the three theological virtues, one which also encompasses all the pow-

[1] *Summa de bono*, ed. N. Wicki (Bern: Editiones Francke, 1985) 2: 744-756.

[2] *Glossa marg.* 1: 72D, taken from Augustine, *De Gen. contra Manich.* 2.10.14, PL 34: 204, on *Gen.* 2:10-14.

ers. For just as faith perfects the reasoning power and charity the desires and hope the emotions, each in its own way, so likewise prudence perfects the reasoning power and temperance the desires and courage the emotions. Therefore, why is a fourth virtue assigned in one case and not in the other?

4. If it is true that 'one is just in so far as his soul is prudent, etc.,'[3] so it is also true to say that one is just in so far as he believes in God by adhering to the first truth through faith, hopes by facing what is arduous through hope, and loves by adhering to the first good through charity. Therefore, there will exist some virtue pertaining to the three theological virtues, an argument that it is a theological virtue. For just as the fourth virtue, which puts order into the three human virtues, is a human virtue, so likewise what puts order into the three theological virtues must be a theological virtue, which makes four theological virtues.

5. Motive powers agree in respect of making motion to exist. But motion exists as related to something else. Now this only happens in three ways: for there is motion toward another for its own sake, or toward another for the sake of removing that from something else, or toward another for the sake of adding it to something else. If the motion toward another is for its own sake, then that sort of thing will be good, because the good is that toward which we are moved for its own sake, as is said in *On the Soul*.[4] If the motion toward another is for the sake of removing it from something else, then that sort of thing is what accompanies; it is not enjoyable, and in the *Sophistical Refutations* this is called expedient evil.[5] For in this way sometimes we are freely moved to what is bad, in order to remove what is worse, as happens in arguments which are reductions to absurdity, which we use to remove falsity. But if there is motion toward another for the sake of adding it to something, that thing is called enjoyable, and this term is used when choosing the expedient good. Therefore, since there are three types of objects, that is, the good, what accompanies, and the enjoyable, as is said in the *Topics*, there are only three pleasures, that is, there are only three things it is licit to will.[6] Since according to this reasoning there are three powers–reason, desire, and emotion–there are also three virtues. For the first there is prudence in the reasoning part, which concerns the good; for the second there is courage in the emotions, which

[3] Cf. Obj. 3, p. 86.

[4] Aristotle, *On the Soul* 1.3 (406b9).

[5] Aristotle, *Sophistical Refutations* 4 (165b34ff.).

[6] Aristotle, *Topics* 1.13 (105a28ff.).

withstands evil because it accompanies avoiding more evil; and for the third there is temperance in the desires, which concerns enjoyment. For temporal good, which temperance makes moderate use of, is not enjoyable in itself and for its own sake, but to the extent that it is a way to and a cloak covering what is good for its own sake or absolutely.

[*Replies to the objections*:]

Reply to Obj. 1. The number of the virtues is not taken from the number of the powers but from their principal acts. Since the virtues are perfections of the powers, their perfections are compared to their acts. Therefore, temperance is based on an act of desire (*concupisciblis*) as it is subject to the order of reason, that is, to restrain our cupidities. Courage is based on an act of the emotions (*irascibilis*) which has been ordered, that is, to confront what produces fear. Both prudence and justice are based on acts of reason, because prudence is taken from the act of distinguishing good from bad, which is an absolute act concerning ourselves, while justice, which orders us in relation to neighbor through rendering what is due to him, is based on an act of reason, namely ordering, which concerns others.[7]

Reply to Obj. 2. Every virtue is a perfection of the rational soul, in relation to one of its powers. But there are two kinds of perfection, perfection in relation to the superior part of reason and perfection in relation to its inferior part. The kind of perfection which concerns the superior part of reason comes about through the three theological virtues, for the soul is the image of the one and triune God only in its superior part, as St. Augustine explains in commenting on *1 Cor.* 11:7 "the man is the image of God, not the woman."[8] Therefore, this part has to be perfected and reformed by these three virtues.

By contrast, the perfection of the rational soul in its inferior part, which is not the image of God, comes about, not through this number of virtues, but through the next number, the number four, because in accord with the three theological virtues the soul is ordered to contemplating eternal matters, but in accord with the four cardinal and human virtues it is directed to arrange temporal and physical things. And just as after the number three comes the number four, so after eternal matters come temporal matters. The one area is related to the three virtues, the other to the four virtues, and therefore there is a greater number of cardinal and human virtues than

[7] Cf. Albert, *De bono* 6.1, arg. 1 on the contrary, pp. 120-21 below.

[8] Augustine, *De trinitate* 12.7, PL 42: 1003.

theological and divine virtues, virtues which fall away more from simplicity and which are less abstract.

The three theological virtues are distinguished by enjoyment, while the four cardinal virtues are distinguished by use; for we enjoy eternal things, while we make use of temporal things; we enjoy our end, while we make use of what leads to the end. Consequently, in his book *On 83 questions* Augustine says: "All perverse human order consists in either enjoying what should be used or using what should be enjoyed; correct order, however, consists in enjoying what should be enjoyed and using what should be used."[9] The three theological virtues are designed for enjoying what should be enjoyed, because there are three things we enjoy, that is, as Augustine says in his book *On the Customs of the Catholic Church*: to know God through faith, to love God through charity, and to have or hold onto God through hope.[10] God is known as truth, is loved as charity, is held or had as eternity. The four cardinal virtues are designed for using what should be used, and this in relation to creatures. For whatever pertains to us either pertains by reason of our soul or by reason of our body, by reason of the soul in two ways and by reason of the body in two ways. If by reason of the soul, then either in relation to self or in relation to neighbor; and if in relation to self, then prudence, if in relation to neighbor, then justice. If in relation to the body, then either in respect of what is interior, which gives temperance, or in respect of what is exterior, which gives courage.

Reply to Obj. 3: To the objection about justice, that it pertains to all the powers, my reply is that the gloss is true in its own way of speaking, but one ought not say that justice is in all the powers as in a subject, but is in the power of reason, as prudence is.

Reply to Obj. 4: To the objection that 'if it is true that one is just in so far as his soul is prudent in contemplating truth, etc., so it is also true to say that one is just in so far as the soul is faithful by adhering to the first truth through faith, etc.,' I reply: The claim is true, but is not the basis for positing along with the three other virtues another theological virtue. The reason is that when one says 'just in so far as the soul is faithful, etc.' this is said in relation to general justice, which applies commonly to God and neighbor. This is not a theological virtue, but as it orders us to neighbor it can be called a human virtue, and as it orders us to God it can be called a divine or theological virtue.

[9] Augustine, *De div. quaest. lxxxiii*, q. 30, PL 40: 19.
[10] Augustine, *De mor. ecc.* 1.3-14.

Reply to Obj. 5. To the objection concerning the three objects of the virtues, my reply is that these virtues are not determined based on the number of their objects, especially since they do not concern our end, as the three theological virtues do, but concern what is for the sake of that end. As has been said, justice is determined by the act of reason which is to order, that is, to render to each what is his, and it has the same object as prudence, but is taken in another respect. For prudence concerns distinguishing the good from the bad and choosing the good, while justice concerns rendering the good to whomever it belongs, that is, to whom it is due, and does not consider in the good the very nature of goodness, as does prudence which chooses, but considers the aspect of whose good it is.

[*Arguments from authorities in favor of the four cardinal virtues*:]

1. The point can be proven by arguments. For there is temporal good and temporal evil. Temporal good is divided in two, and two virtues are found in this way; and temporal evil is likewise divided in two, and two virtues are found in this way, thereby resulting in exactly four virtues. Now temporal goods are either apparent goods, and in this respect deceptive, or they are excessive goods, and in this way corruptive. Contrary to the first, which deceives, there is prudence, which directs us; thus betrayal is evil and to be avoided, though it appears good. Consequently, about *Matt.* 15: 38, "those who ate were 4,000 men," the gloss says: "4,000 because of the four virtues by which we live rightly: prudence, temperance, courage, and justice, the first of which is knowledge of things to be sought and avoided."[11] And Augustine in his book *On the Customs of the Catholic Church* says: "Prudence is love wisely preferring what aids it over what impedes it." Against the second, that is, excessive good which corrupts, there is temperance, which is what preserves us. Consequently, about *Matt.* 15:13 the gloss reads: "Temperance is reining in desire." And Augustine, in *On the Customs of the Catholic Church* says: "Temperance is love giving itself wholly to what is loved." This wholeness is contrary to corruption.

Likewise, there is adverse evil and perverse evil; perverse evil is called the evil of guilt, while adverse evil is the evil of pain. Perverse evil perverts the soul, for it is disordered, and therefore destroys the beauty of the soul, and makes it ugly. Contrary to it is the virtue of justice, which introduces order in the soul, which is beauty in the soul. Augustine speaks of it in his

[11] *Glossa margin.* 5: 271B, taken from Augustine, *De div. quaest. lxxxiii*, q. 61 n. 4, PL 40: 51.

book *On the Customs of the Catholic Church*: "Justice is love serving the beloved alone, and ruling rightly for the sake of the beloved."[12] This correctness is for the sake of a man being subordinate to God alone and other things being subordinate to him; and this subordination is beauty in the soul. And its justice is called beauty in Augustine's gloss on *Psalm* 44 "thy form and thy beauty," where he says "form and beauty refer to the same thing, to the justice of God." And after "thy form and thy beauty" the gloss reads "that is, out of thy justice by which thou art formed and beautiful."[13] Adverse evil, that is, the evil of pain, saddens the soul. Contrary to this is the virtue of courage, which endures it, and for the sake of what it loves delights in enduring evil. Consequently, in his book *On the Customs of the Catholic Church* Augustine says: "Courage is love easily enduring everything for the sake of what is loved."

Isaac of Stella in his book *On Spirit and Soul*, which follows Augustine, says: "All sensibility in the soul originates from the power of reason (*rationabilitate*), while all affections originate from the other powers, that is, from desire (*concupiscibilitate*) or from emotion (*irascibilitate*). Four kinds of affections come to exist, when concerning what we love either we presently enjoy it or we hope for it in the future or we hate what is now giving us sorrow or we fear the sorrowful. For this reason, in the power of desire originate *joy* and *hope*, while in the emotions originate *sorrow* and *fear*. Now these four affections of the soul are like the elements and common materials for all the vices and virtues, for "the affection imposes its name on every deed."[14] Since virtue is a habit in a mind which has been correctly instructed, the affections of the mind should be instructed and combined and ordered by reason for the sake of that which is right and in the right manner, so that they can produce virtues, for otherwise they easily sink into vices. Therefore, when love and hate are instructed prudently, modestly, bravely, and justly, they grow into the virtues of prudence, temperance, courage, and justice, which are said to be like roots or hinges (*cardines*) for all the virtues."[15] For, as St. Augustine says in his book *On the Customs of the Catholic Church*: "that which is called four-fold virtue

[12] Augustine, *De mor. ecc.* 1.15, PL 32: 1322, for all four definitions of the virtues.

[13] Augustine, *Enarr. in Psalmos* 4, n. 14, PL 36: 502.

[14] Cf. Ambrose, *De officiis* 1.30.147, PL 16: 66A.

[15] Isaac of Stella, *Epistola de anima*, PL 194: 1878D, in *De spiritu et anima* 4, PL 40: 782.

is formed from various affections of love ... so that temperance is love giving itself wholly and incorruptibly to God, courage is love readily enduring all things for God, justice is love serving the beloved alone and for this reason rightly ruling all its subjects, and prudence is love rightly distinguishing what helps us get to God from those things which impede us from him."[16]

[*Response*:]

Now all this should be understood in the following way: There is either good which we desire or evil which we hate (hate is used rather than detest, for hate belongs to the power of desire, as does love, while detesting belongs to the emotions). If something is good, either it is present, and then we feel *joy* about it, or it is not present but expected, and then we feel *hope* about it. Or the thing is bad, and then if present we feel *sorrow* about it, and if not present we feel *fear*. Now these sorts of affections, that is, those belonging to desire or emotion, should be ruled by reason, and then they are worthy of praise. Otherwise, if they are disordered, they are contemptible; and this is why the affection puts its name on the deed, whether for good or evil. Now love, when ordered, mounts up to virtue; for when ordered, it loves what should be loved and how it should be loved. Therefore, it loves prudently, so that no appearance of seeming good deceives it. And this is what Augustine says: "Prudence is love wisely preferring what aids, etc.," as was said above. It loves sweetly and pleasantly, so that it is not abducted from its delight by anything illicit, and this is what Augustine says: "Temperance is love giving itself wholly to what is loved." It loves resolutely, so that it is not averted from the beloved by any adversity, and this is also what Augustine says: "Courage is love readily enduring everything for what is loved." And love is for the sake of the right end, and this too is what Augustine says: "Justice is love serving the beloved alone, and ruling rightly for the sake of the beloved."[17]

[*Additional arguments for distinguishing the cardinal virtues*:]

1. The distinction among the aforesaid virtues can also be based on the three-fold law. For there is the law of reason, following which there is free choice, and there is the law of indigent nature, and there is the natural law

[16] An extremely free rendering of Augustine, *De mor. ecc.* 1.15, PL 32: 1322.

[17] Cf. Albert, *De bono* 6.1, resp., pp. 122-3 below. Definitions from Augustine, *De mor. ecc.* 1.15, PL 32: 1322.

of reason. The law of reason is found in choosing what is useful, which concerns prudence. The law of indigent nature is found in making use of good and evil. Using temporal goods to sustain life concerns temperance; while using bad things for experience or to cure ourselves concerns courage. And the natural law of reason concerns distributing goods, that is, to our neighbor who is our confederate by nature, according what it says in *Tobit* 4:16 "Do to no one what you would not want done to you." *Matt.* 7:12 and *Luke* 6:31 also say: "And as you wish that men would do to you, do so to them." And in his book *On Soul and Spirit* Augustine says: "Prudence is found in choice, temperance in use, courage in endurance, and justice in distribution."[18]

2. Another way of distinguishing among these virtues is based on principle and end, because every human virtue perfects the soul, either in its actions or in its passions. We can look at actions either regarding ourselves, and then the virtue is prudence, or with regard to others, and then the virtue is justice. This distinction is based on the end. We can look at passions which come from us, and then the virtue is temperance, or which come from others, and then the virtue is courage, and this distinction is based on their principle.[19]

3. There is another basis for the distinction among these virtues according to Augustine.[20] The soul has four virtues by which it is armed against vice and instructed about its operations. In its operations it is instructed either in relation to us, and then we have prudence, or in relation to neighbor, and then we have justice. And it is armed against vice, either in regard to prosperity, and then we have temperance, or in regard to adversity, and then we have courage. Now this division is based on the following reason: Since virtue is perfection of the soul in regard to being a rational creature, this comes about either in relation to neighbor or for some other reason. If for some other reason, it will concern the rational motive power or the motive power of desire or the motive power of emotion. Now prudence concerns the rational motive power, temperance the motive power of desire, and courage the motive power of emotion; and if in relation to neighbor, then the virtue is justice.[21]

[18] Cf. Albert, *De bono* 6.1, arg. 4 on the contrary, p. 121 below. Augustine, *De spiritu et anima*, c. 20; PL 40: 794.

[19] Cf. Albert, *De bono* 6.1, arg. 5 to the contrary, p. 121 below.

[20] Augustine, *De spiritu et anima*, c. 20, PL 40: 794.

[21] Cf. Albert, *De bono* 6.1, arg. 3 on the contrary, p. 121 below.

4. There is another basis for the distinction among these virtues according to Augustine.[22] The function of prudence is to know what is possible, that of courage is to do what is possible, that of temperance is not to presume to do what is not possible, and that of justice is to will what is possible. Now this division is based on what is necessary for virtue, namely, to know, which requires prudence, to will, which requires justice, to do, which requires courage, and the mode of acting, which requires temperance.

5. Finally, according to this same doctor there is yet another basis for the distinction.[23] The function of prudence is to desire nothing regretful, that of courage is to fear nothing but what is base, that of temperance is to repress earthly desires and completely to forget them, and that of justice is to direct every motion in the soul to God alone. Now this division is based on interior appetite, exterior deed, order to our end, and not letting stand an impediment on the way to our end. Consequently, the function of prudence is to rule the beginning we desire, that of temperance is to rule over the means which is the deed, that of courage is to remove impediments, and that of justice is to order us to our end.[24]

Q. 2. Concerning the Order [of the Cardinal Virtues]

It follows in second place that we look at the order of the aforesaid virtues, which is found to be different in different authorities.

[*Different orders for the cardinal virtues*:]

1. One order is found in which prudence comes first, then temperance, courage third and justice fourth. This order is found in the gloss on *Matt.* 15:38 "those who ate were 4,000 men," which runs: "By 4,000 men [is signified] the four virtues by which one lives correctly: prudence, temperance, courage, justice."[25]

2. The same order is found in the gloss on *Genesis* 2, where it speaks of four rivers, as was said above.[26]

3. A different order is found in the book *On the Customs of the Catholic*

[22] Augustine, *De spiritu et anima*, c. 20, PL 40: 794.
[23] Augustine, *De spiritu et anima*, c. 20, PL 40: 794.
[24] Cf. Albert, p. 122, Aquinas, pp. 163-64 below.
[25] *Glossa margin*. 5: 271B, cf. n. 11 above.
[26] P. 86 above.

Church, where temperance is listed first, then courage, third justice, and then prudence, where it reads: "Temperance is love giving itself wholly, etc." These are almost the same words Isaac of Stella uses in his book *On Spirit and Soul*.[27]

4. Another order is found in the book of *Wisdom* 8:7, where temperance is listed first, then prudence, third justice, and fourth courage. For it says: "sobriety," that is, temperance, "and prudence she teaches, justice and virtue," that is, courage, "than which in life nothing is more useful to men." This is said by way of a sign, for in this way wisdom teaches that these virtues are for what we use, not what we are to enjoy.

5. A different order is given by Aristotle in his *Ethics*, where he first takes up courage, then chastity, third prudence, and fourth justice.[28]

6. Cicero gives a different order in his *De Officiis*: first prudence, then justice, third temperance, fourth courage.[29]

Consequently, the question does arise: What is the reason for these differences?

To which I respond:

There is an order based on worth. For that power of the rational soul is worthier by which a human is separated from the brute animals. The other powers are common to us and to the brutes, except in so far as they are ordered to reason. Also, desire and emotion receive order from the rational power, not the other way round, which is why the rational power is finer. Therefore, prudence and justice, since they exist in the rational power, are prior by reason of the worth of their subject. Consequently, in prudence should be seen the worth and priority of the subject and the act of bringing order, that is, the power of reasoning, in comparison with the other two powers, that is, desire and emotion, and for this reason it takes precedence over temperance and courage, but also over justice to the extent that its act concerns others. For justice we do not look at the priority of the dignity of the subject, because in this respect it would seem to be placed before prudence, since it is present in the same subject as prudence, and it orders prudence and the other virtues to our end. But we look to the

[27] Augustine, *De mor. ecc.* 1.15, PL 32: 1322; Isaac of Stella, *Epistola de anima*, PL 194: 1879B.

[28] Aristotle, *Nic. Eth.* 3.9 (courage); 3.13 (temperance); 5.1 (justice); 6.5 (prudence).

[29] Cicero, *De officiis* 1.6-42, nn. 18-151.

fact that justice is nearer our end and that the other powers and their acts are like materials in relation to it. Therefore, the others come first, and justice after all the others. For a similar reason temperance takes second place, behind prudence and before courage, because its act concerns us, while the act of courage concerns others, and the absolute is prior to the relative.

[*Replies to the objections*:][30]

Reply to Obj. 3. In the book *On the Customs of the Catholic Church* the four virtues are defined through love. The reason for this is that the definitions are based on what is needed to negotiate life, which is Augustine's topic, that is, to pursue happiness, that is, the highest good. Therefore, he defines them in relation to their motive cause, which is taken in relation to their end, that is, the end which moves the efficient cause; and therefore he places love in all their definitions. Consequently, the order of the definitions and the order of the virtues is here set down based on how love is related to them. Therefore, since absolutely speaking love is in the desires, the definition first set out is that of temperance, which exists in the desires (*concupiscibili*); then that of courage, which exists in the emotions (*irascibili*), for both desire and emotion pertain to the affections, and all affections come from them. And since only in a secondary way is love in the power of reason, which is a motive power as well as a cognitive power, the definitions set out afterwards are those of justice and prudence. And because prudence comes more from the cognitive than the motive part of the soul, and because of the meaning of the term prudence, and because justice comes more from the motive part, and for this reason seems to partake less of the nature of love, prudence is the last virtue set out.

Reply to Obj. 4. In the book of *Wisdom* 8:7 is recognized an order between sobriety and prudence, as preparatory for what follows. For sobriety prepares us to receive prudence, so that *Dan.* 1:16-17 speaks first about abstinence in youths, afterwards about wisdom: "So the steward took away their rich food and the wine they were to drink, and gave them vegetables," that is, sobriety. And next it says: "God gave the youths learning and skill in all letters and wisdom, etc.," that is, prudence. Next in order after prudence is justice, because, since it is the function of justice to render to each what is his, one first has to know what is his. After justice in order comes

[30] Since Philip agrees with the order found in the first two objections, he does not reply to them.

courage, because justice concerns action in relation to neighbor, while courage concerns passions, and action is prior to passion.

Reply to Obj. 5. In his *Ethics* Aristotle treats courage before chastity, because he treats civil courage, which concerns the kind of fearful things which threaten death. Since chastity pertains to the good of the individual subject, while courage concerns the common benefit, which is preferred to the private, he sets courage before chastity. And he puts prudence before justice, because it is the function of prudence to know what belongs to each, and the function of justice to render it so. The act of discerning what belongs to each is prior to rendering to each his own.

Reply to Obj. 6. In his book *On Duties* Cicero orders things so that first come prudence and justice, because each is in the reasoning power, but prudence comes first because it concerns us, while justice concerns the other. Prudence is in the reasoning power principally, and prudence knows first what belongs to whom, which is the function of justice. He puts temperance before courage, because temperance concerns good we should make use of, while courage concerns evils we should withstand.

Q. 3. Why are the virtues called cardinal?

It follows that in third place we consider: *Why are they called cardinal?*

[*Objection*:]

Since the other virtues have their own proper acts different from the acts of these virtues, it seems that they similarly ought and can be called cardinal virtues, as these are.

To which I respond:

These virtues are called cardinal virtues for three reasons (*triplici rationi*): the first is taken from their conditions, the second from the meaning of the term, and the third from their acts.

The first reason comes from their conditions. As St. Bernard says in his book *On Consideration to Pope Eugenius*,[31] where he offers a significant treatise on these virtues: For the existence (*esse*) of virtue four things are required: to know, to will, to persevere amid difficulties, and to attain the mean between excess and deficiency. But to know comes from prudence,

[31] Bernard, *De consid.* 1.7-8, nn. 8-11, 3: 402-407.

to will from justice, to persevere from courage, and to attain the mean between excess and deficiency from temperance. Therefore, since some universal condition is touched upon there in each of these [virtues], they are rightly called cardinal, that is, principal.

But are not these conditions also present in the other virtues? They are always present, because, as it says in the *Ethics*,[32] for the existence of virtue are required to know, to will, etc.

To this question I respond: Although these conditions are present in other virtues they are named from these virtues, as prudence is named from producing (*prodendo*) because it makes judgments and produces knowledge, etc. Again, the other virtues are reduced to these virtues, either as their parts or as their species or as their dispositions, as will be made clear below. Therefore, the other virtues ought not be called cardinal virtues, but only these virtues are called cardinal, that is, principal or initiating virtues. Consequently Harold,[33] in *On Rest for the Mind*, compares them to the elements when he compares the health of the soul to the health of the body, which comes from the concurrence of the elements, and he says: "health of the body is found in equilibrium and the concurrence of the members without lesions," and likewise where he says "the health of the soul is a virtue of the animal or spiritual members, a harmonious agreement." And afterward he says: "As there are four elements for the health of the body so are found four bases for the virtues of the soul."

The second reason comes from the meaning of the term "cardinal." For cardinal comes from *cardo*, the hinge on which a door turns. Now there are two things by means of which we enter into life: actions and passions. What is said in *Matt.* 19:17 concerns actions: "If you would enter life, keep the commandments," that is, act according to the commandments; and *Acts* 14:22 concerns passions: "through many tribulations we must enter the kingdom of God." Two virtues are taken based on actions: prudence with regard to actions as they concern us, justice with regard to actions as they concern our neighbor. Two other virtues are taken based on passions: concerning passions in us and natural to us is temperance, concerning passions introduced by others is courage.

The third reason comes from their acts. The acts of these virtues are principal because they are acts of the three primary motive powers in relation to those things which lead to our end (*ad finem*). For the act of reasoning

[32] Aristotle, *Nic. Eth.* 2.4 (1105a31ff.)

[33] An author whose works have never been found.

is to distinguish between the good which leads to that end and the bad which leads away from that end, or between two goods, to distinguish which of them leads more to the end, or between two bad things, which of them leads more away from that end. Also, the principal act of the power of desire in relation to those things which lead to our end is to will the changeable good to exist under the highest good, which pertains to temperance. Also, the principal act of the power of emotion in relation to those things which lead to our end is to confront the arduous, which is frightening to confront and difficult to withstand, and this pertains to courage. But the act of justice is to order all these to our proximate end, and this is an act in relation to all the powers, not just one. Therefore, for this reason they are called cardinal or principal, because they are the primary acts of the powers acting in those things which lead to our end, namely, God.

Objection:

Since pride is the primary vice, according to *Eccles.* 10:15 "Pride is the beginning of all sin," it seems that humility is the first of the virtues, and consequently humility is a principal virtue and a cardinal virtue.

To which I reply:

In one way pride is said to be love of one's own excellence, and this love is in the power of the emotions, and in this respect is not the beginning of all sin. Consequently, the kind of humility opposed to it will not be a principal virtue. In another way pride is love of one's own good, and in this respect is the beginning of all sin; or as it is said to be contempt for the commandments, and likewise in this way it is the beginning of all sin. In a similar way, love of the highest good is the beginning of every cardinal virtue. Consequently, Augustine defines them through love in his book *On the Customs of the Catholic Church*, where he says: "Temperance is love giving itself wholly to that which is loved."[34]

[Q. 4.] THE NEXT QUESTION IS WHETHER THE AFORESAID CARDINAL VIRTUES CAN BE CALLED DIVINE VIRTUES.

1. *It seems they can,* since they are infused virtues, different from the political virtues, according to the theologian.

[34] Augustine, *De mor. ecc.* 1.15, PL 32: 1322.

To which I reply: They cannot be called divine because this denomination comes not in relation to the principle "from which" something comes, but in relation to the term "to which" something leads. Since these cardinal virtues concern what leads up to our end (*ad finem*), but not into our end (*in finem*), namely God, they should not be called divine. Justice, however, which orders things to our end holds a middle place, and therefore can be called both human and divine, since it orders things to our end.

2. Again, that act is more a principal act which arrives at our end than one which concerns what leads to our end. Therefore, it seems that the three virtues–faith, hope, charity–should be called cardinal, that is, principal, rather than the four virtues–prudence, justice, temperance, and courage.

To which I reply: These virtues are not called cardinal in relation to the theological virtues, but in relation to other virtues. The [three] virtues ought not be called cardinal, but from their finer end they are called theological virtues.

[*On Virtue in General: Continuation*]

[Q. 1.] DOES WHOEVER HAS ONE VIRTUE HAVE THEM ALL?

[Art. 1.] *About the moral virtues*

This question is whether whoever has one virtue has them all, and it has two parts, one about virtues coming from grace and the other about moral virtues. The first asks about the moral virtues, since it seems less true about them.

[*Objections in favor of the unity of the virtues*:]

That it is true, however, can be taken on the *authority of philosophers*:

1. Seneca says that "All that happens well happens justly and bravely and prudently and temperately."[1]

2. In the *Tusculan Disputations* Cicero says: "If you lose one of your Corinthians, you can say that the rest of the vases are safe with you. But if you lose one of your virtues, you must necessarily confess that you no longer have any virtue,"[2] explaining the matter by reference to "Corinthians," that is, Corinthian vases.

3. And St. Bernard in the first part of his book to Pope Eugenius says the same thing: "What is temperance but holding to the mean in our actions by removing excess and deficiency? And what is courage but confronting the arduous and persevering amid difficulties? And what is justice but rendering to each what is his due? And what is prudence but in our choices distinguishing good from bad?" And in the same text he says: "The mean is where there is the whole internal power and the very core of all the virtues, and where all are so united that all seem one virtue. This is especially true since they do not communicate by somehow participating in the mean, but each of them wholly and integrally possesses it."[3]

But this means that whoever has one virtue has all. For there is no virtue of justice without discerning the difference between choosing to distribute goods and not, or choice of him to whom to distribute, or distin-

[1] Seneca, *Ep.* 66, n. 5.
[2] Cicero, *Tuscul. Disp.* 2.14.32.
[3] Bernard, *De con.* 1.8.9-11, 3: 404-6.

guishing him from one who receives no distribution. Therefore, there is no justice without the operation of prudence. Likewise, there is no justice without confronting what is arduous, for the task of each virtue is arduous and extremely difficult, according to that maxim of moral philosophy: "Art and virtue concern very difficult matters."[4] The consequence is that since confronting the arduous task and persevering in the most difficult task are necessary, courage is necessary. For it is true that whoever is just so behaves equitably that he would save the pauper from a malevolent king or from any other evil person, and would treat others likewise. It is likewise true that whoever is just must hold to the mean in all actions, rendering neither more nor less than is necessary. From this it is clear that whoever possesses justice has all the virtues; and the same argument can be made for the other virtues.

The same thing can be proven through argument:

4. As the Philosopher says, "virtue is the ultimate end of a potency for something,"[5] and he explains that courage is defined in terms of the ultimate end of which it is capable, while debility is defined in terms of how little it is capable. Therefore, a virtue of the rational soul can be defined in terms of its ultimate end. Now this ultimate end is not found in distinguishing when we choose, for more is involved, nor in confronting the arduous, for more is involved, nor in giving each what is owed, for more is involved. Therefore, justice is not a virtue without prudence, and conversely neither is it a virtue without the others.

5. The same conclusion is reached from a second definition of virtue: "virtue is the disposition of a perfected [subject] in relation to its optimum state,"[6] and the Philosopher explains this as one circle compared with the greatest circle. The consequence is that goodness in the rational soul will be a virtue only when there is goodness in every act. Therefore, none of these is a virtue without the others.

6. The soul is a simple essence. But contraries cannot exist in a simple essence. Now good and bad, absent any further determination, are contraries. Therefore they cannot exist in something at the same time. Now virtue follows on the species of virtue. Therefore, in one and the same soul evil cannot exist along with some species of virtue.

[4] Aristotle, *Nic. Eth.* 2.2 (1105a9).
[5] Aristotle, *De caelo* 1.16 (281a14-15).
[6] Aristotle, *Phy.* 7.3 (246b8).

To the contrary [*arguments against the unity of the moral virtues*]:

1. Its genus follows on each species of virtue. Therefore, when a species exists in some subject it follows that its genus exists in that subject. In a similar way, the genus of vice follows on any species of vice. But chastity, prudence, and fear are not inconsistent with each other. Therefore, both virtue and malice can exist in someone. Therefore, whoever has one virtue need not have all.

2. One can also argue that virtue and evil can exist together from the definition of virtue. For virtue is a habit making its deed good, while vice is a habit making its deed bad. But a habit making its deed good and a habit making its deed bad can both exist together in someone.

Response to the foregoing arguments:

Virtue can be taken in one way, as *political virtue*, and in this respect whoever has one political virtue need not have every such virtue. For a special political virtue can be attained, for example, chastity which concerns touch or taste, and even though one has this virtue one does not necessarily have others. For a human can act well in one deed and not act well in another deed, as the arguments to the contrary said, in a way similar to what happens with the bodily senses.[7] The Philosopher defines virtue as "a habit making the deed good and the one who has it good."[8]

About the *cardinal virtues*, however, a distinction must be made. For justice or another cardinal virtue can be taken in two ways: It can be taken as one considers it according to the act of its proper power and concerning the proper matter of that power, so that it does not extend analogically to the act of another power; for example, prudence as concerned with making distinctions, and temperance as concerned with desiring corporeal pleasures moderately, and similarly courage as concerned with confronting and enduring what is fearful, where we mean not everything fearful but what is physically fearful. In this way it is not necessary that when one has one virtue one has all, because the act of a power in this sense does not extend beyond its proper power or beyond its matter. And it can happen that a

[7] Philip refers to the two arguments to the contrary which immediately precede his response. In his original text there seem to have been two more arguments, based on an analogy between the virtues and the senses, for he refers to the analogy here, and replies to two arguments to the contrary not found in the extant text.

[8] Aristotle, *Nic. Eth.* 2.6 (1106a22-4).

power be well ordered about its proper act and its proper matter while another power is not so related.

It is also possible that the acts of each of these powers be taken analogically and be taken about their matter taken analogically, for example, the acts of the powers falling universally (*circumincidentes*). For while desiring is the proper act of our power of desire (*concupiscibilis*), nonetheless each of them has its own desire in relation to what is pleasant to it. Therefore, the act of desiring is said to be taken analogically about a power other than the power of desire, and the same thing is true about the matter of the pleasant.

An example: By nature the pleasant pertains to the power of desire, but it extends analogically to the matter of other powers, so that each power has its own pleasurable object and what appears proper to it, yet this is determined by its proper nature. For example, the true is said to pertain to the power of reason, while the arduous or difficult is what pertains to the emotions. The same thing is clear about the act of "confronting" and about the matter of "the difficult," which are proper to the emotions, yet the act of "confronting" falls universally and can be taken analogically, and likewise the matter of "the difficult," because each has its own mode of "confronting" its own "difficult" objects.

Following these distinctions, if one takes temperance about any kind of desiring and any kind of pleasant object, and courage about any kind of confronting and any kind of difficult object, in this respect it is true that whoever has one virtue has all. In this way what Seneca says is true: "All that happens well happens justly and bravely and prudently and temperately," and also what Cicero says in his book *Tusculan Disputations*: "If you lose one of your Corinthians, etc." and also what Bernard says: "What is temperance, etc."[9]

But the virtues are taken in the other way by Aristotle in his *Ethics*, where he descends to the special acts of the virtues. Cicero does the same in his book *On Duties*, for he speaks about the proper acts of the virtues, not taking them analogically, and also in his book of *Paradoxes*. Note, however, that in the *Paradoxes* he takes the other side and seems to follow the view of the philosophers who said that whoever has one virtue has all.

Now I consider how to respond to the definitions of virtue given above. The first definition is "virtue is the ultimate end of a potency for some-

[9] Obj. 1 - 3, p. 101 above.

thing." The second definition is "virtue is the disposition of a perfected [subject] in relation to its optimum state."

About the first definition, in which potency comes into the definition of virtue, the ultimate end of a potency is said to be the optimum end for that potency in relation to its principal act. Now this can be taken in different ways: in relation to some determinate matter or not. Examples of being taken in relation to some determinate matter are the act of desire about pleasures of the flesh and the act of the emotions about getting angry over evil or confronting the physically fearful. In this respect chastity is said to be a virtue, but not because it is the ultimate end of a power concerning the act of that power about some determinate matter, but the matter which can be more or less determined, more when it concerns the objects of touch, so that it either does not or does include taste. In the first sense, chastity is the same as continence, but in the second sense it also contains sobriety. In a similar manner, courage is a virtue speaking specifically, because it is the ultimate end of a power with regard to a determinate matter. When virtues are taken in this way it is clear that it is not true that whoever has one virtue has all. For a power can have a good habit in relation to one determinate matter and not in relation to another.

Again, virtue can be called the ultimate end of a power in such a way that this ultimate end of a power is an act covering every matter pertaining to that power, where neither matter nor act are taken analogically. In this case chastity is called a virtue only when united with the other habits of the power of desire. This is because the optimum end of the power of desire does not concern chastity, but its optimum end is called temperance. Here chastity is only a virtue relatively speaking, not absolutely. And temperance, absolutely speaking, is the virtue of desire as virtue is understood under the notion that it is said to be the virtue of the power of desire, a habit of the desiring power for correctly ordering the objects of desire in relation to that power.

Now it is still clear that it does not follow that whoever has one virtue has all, for there are many powers and each one has its own ultimate end and optimum end, which can exist without the ultimate end or optimum end of another.

Therefore, to the objection[10] that the virtue of the rational soul should be defined through the ultimate end it is capable of, but that the ultimate does not concern confronting difficulties, for it is capable of more than that,

[10] Obj. 3 , p. 101.

nor does it concern moderation concerning pleasure, because reason is capable of more than that, I reply:

If we are talking about power in general terms, the argument is true, because the ultimate end of power does not reside determinately in this or that thing. But if power is construed determinately, as the power of desire or the power of emotion, then the argument is not true. For the ultimate and optimum end of a given power, for example, desire, is moderation concerning what that power enjoys. And the same thing holds true for the emotions.

However, if one takes the act of any power analogically, its matter will also be taken analogically, and in this way desiring includes every power and also every enjoyable object, and the same thing holds about the act of "confronting" and the matter of the "difficult." Now when taken in this way, it is true that whoever has one virtue has all.

About the second definition, that is, that "virtue is a disposition of the perfected [subject] in relation to its optimum state," I reply:

This definition is not given in relation to power, as was the first, but in relation to the subject, that is, the soul in which powers reside. This definition can be taken in different ways. For virtue can be taken as the disposition of a subject concerning the act of a certain power, such as the power of desire or similar powers, in regard to some determinate matter. In this case virtue will be a disposition of the perfected [subject] concerning the act of a certain power, such as the power of desire, for the optimum state about a determinate matter. In this way chastity is called a specific virtue and courage is called a virtue at the specific level. Virtue also can be taken as the disposition of a subject concerning the act of a certain power taken generally, about every matter of that power, such as temperance concerning corporeal or sensible pleasure, and other things of this sort. And virtue also can be taken as the disposition of a subject considered generally with regard to every act and every matter.

If virtue is taken in the first two ways, then it is not true that whoever has one virtue has them all. If virtue is taken in the third way, then nothing would be called a virtue except a habit through which the subject is perfected to the optimum degree, which is beatitude. In this sense, chastity would not be called a virtue of the soul, nor would temperance, and the same for all the virtues, unless we are speaking in a certain respect; but the habit through which the soul is rightly related to every act would be called a virtue, and thus there would only be one virtue for this one subject. Nevertheless, in a way each virtue could be called a virtue, as it is coordinated and united to another virtue, as chastity or temperance, when coordinated with other virtues, is called a virtue, or to the extent that act and matter are taken analogically, as said above. In this respect it would be true that whoever has one virtue has them all. Taken in the prior way, however, there would only be one virtue.

To the objection[11] that good and bad are contraries, and therefore they cannot exist at the same time in a simple essence, and therefore, if there is virtue present, there cannot be any evil in the soul or it has a virtue which is not good. I reply: Good and bad can be taken in relation to subject, power, or act. If they are taken in relation to their subject, it will not be called, at the same time and speaking absolutely, good and bad, but good in one respect and bad in another. If one asks how that subject is in one way good and in another bad, since it is a simple being, I reply that simplicity of essence does not prevent it from having several powers. If considered in relation to power, I reply similarly that different acts of different virtues can exist in one and the same power, and the power can be well ordered in relation to one act but not in relation to another, as one can be continent but not sober. However, if good and bad are taken in relation to the act of something the same in species, then it is clear that good and bad cannot exist together in it at the same time. For example, one cannot be chaste and incontinent together, for these virtues refer to an act the same in species.

And the following argument is invalid: Absolutely speaking, justice is a type of goodness, or chastity is, etc.; therefore, whoever possesses chastity is good, absolutely speaking, or whoever is absolutely chaste is absolutely good. For we first note the comparison of species to its genus, and the converse; only afterwards do we note the comparison of accident to its subject, and this is a secondary relation. Nevertheless, one should note that some accidents are taken analogously and some are not. When accident is not taken analogously, it does not follow that since chastity is a type of goodness, therefore whoever has chastity or is chaste is also good. For when one says "a human is good," without any added determination, one understands it absolutely, that is, with respect to every act. However, when one says "chastity is [a type of] goodness," we understand a determinate act, that is, chastity, and therefore "good" cannot be added in an absolute way. However, if "chaste" is taken analogously, then it does follow: "he is chaste, therefore, he is good," in so far as chastity or temperance is taken

[11] Obj. 6, p. 102 above.

about desiring *every* pleasure, not about the pleasures of only one power. For in this respect whoever has one virtue has them all.

[*Replies to the arguments to the contrary*:]

Therefore, to the understanding of the philosophers who said "whoever has one, etc.," I reply to the arguments to the contrary as follows:

Reply to Arg. 1 to the Contrary, which said that "to a species of virtue there follows its genus, therefore to a species existing in a subject there follows the existence of its genus in that subject, and the same is true of vice, and so in the same thing at the same time there will exist both virtue and vice." I reply: This is true, and the subject will be good in some way and bad in some way, as was said. But there is no contradiction here, because the philosopher understands how accidents are taken analogously. Those who make this objection do not take the terms analogously, and consequently there will be something rendering the deed good in one respect and not doing so in another respect.

Reply to Arg. 2 to the Contrary: The same kind of response works for the second argument, based on the definition of virtue. Virtue is a habit rendering its deed good, as concerns one act but not the other, because good is not taken analogically.

[*Replies to two missing arguments to the contrary*:]

Reply to Arg. 3 to the Contrary: The same kind of response works for the argument about the senses, that "someone can be well disposed in one sense and not in another," because the same thing is true in this case about the virtues, if act and matter are not taken analogously.

Reply to Arg. 4 to the Contrary: To the fourth argument, concerning the connection of the senses, a similar reply can be made. For the acts of the senses cannot be taken analogously, as the acts of the powers and the virtues can. Consequently, while it is said that "prudence is brave, etc.," and the converse is true as well, one cannot say "vision is hearing" or the converse.

[Art 2.] *About virtues which come from grace*

What follows concerns virtue coming from grace. About this topic the question is: [Part 1:] Does whoever has one virtue have them all, and if he does, what is the reason for this? [Part 2:] And is some one virtue enough to make a human worthy of eternal life, even without possessing the other virtues, that is, if the others are not possessed?

[Part 1: *Does whoever has one virtue have them all?*]

That whoever has one has all:

1. Proof through the authority of Jerome in commenting on *Ez.* 1:11, "The two wings are joined to each other." Here the gloss says: "He said the four virtues are joined to each other so that whoever lacks one lacks all." And a little before in the same gloss it says: "We can say the same thing is true about the virtues of the mind and about the movement of the seasons and about the mixture of the elements."[12]

2. On *Isaiah* 16:11 "my groaning for Moab," the gloss says: "As a lyre does not emit its complex sound if one of its strings is broken, so if one string of the virtues is absent it will not resonate sweetly." And later it says: "The opinion of the philosophers is that the virtues stick together. And James says: Whoever lacks one lacks all, an explanation of the scripture: Whoever fails in one point, etc."[13]

3. In his *Moralia* Gregory says: "None is truly a virtue if not mixed with the other virtues."[14]

4. To the extent that one virtue is joined to another are good deeds more enkindled.[15]

5. Whoever fails in one point destroys many good deeds and puts himself outside charity and any other virtue.[16] But this could not happen if the virtues were not connected. Therefore, the virtues are connected.

6. In the beginning, through sin were the powers of humans wounded. But the Lord is a physician who heals no one in part, but wholly. Now healing comes through the virtues. Therefore, all the virtues are infused together.

7. If grace makes a human worthy of glory, a human becomes graced before God through virtue given by grace. But God is good to the highest degree. Therefore, there will be no commerce with Belial in one and the same soul. Therefore, a human will not be graced before God unless possessing the habits of all the virtues; otherwise there would be commerce between Christ and Belial in one and the same soul.

8. Grace makes a human worthy of glory, where glory is remuneration and complete happiness. Therefore, when grace makes one worthy of mer-

[12] *Glossa marg.*, 4: 1073C, 1076C.

[13] *Glossa marg.*, 4: 181B.

[14] Gregory, *Moralia* 1.32.45, PL75: 547C; also 22.1.2, PL 76: 211.

[15] Gregory, *Moralia* 1.32.48, PL75: 548.

[16] Cf. *Jas.* 2:10; *Glossa marg.*, 6: 1277B.

it, free will is infused with the virtues. For how could desire be worthy of eternity if it did not have meritorious habit, and emotion, and reason as well? From this it is clear that whoever has one virtue has all.

9. Nothing can be reformed through grace except in the part which is made in the image of God. When reformation comes about, it is measured by what reforms it; and so the created trinity is measured by the uncreated Trinity. Therefore, in the trinity of powers [in the soul] nothing is left behind lacking reformation, something which happens only by receiving the fulness of all the virtues. Consequently, concerning *Eph.* 4:30 "And do not grieve the Holy Spirit in whom you were sealed," the gloss says: "by the image of God which remains in you like a waxen seal, that is, the form of new [life]."[17]

10. A virtue without grace and a mortal sin are the kinds of things that can be immediately present in the rational soul. Nonetheless, a virtue of this sort and a mortal sin of this sort are not immediately present together, because if one does not possess the continence which comes from grace it does not follow that he possesses the opposing incontinence, for he can lose the virtue due to another vice, such as avarice. Hence it follows that if one has one vice one is without virtue. But why is this so? Not from a connection among the vices, since it does not follow that whoever has one vice has all the vices. Therefore, it must come from the connection of the virtues.

To the contrary:

1. In something attributed to him which I have not found, Augustine says: "As one can possess one virtue more than another, so one can possess one virtue but not another."

2. Augustine says that the opinion that whoever has one has all was the opinion of great men, but only men.[18] But why did he want to note this, except that this opinion which proceeded from man was false? Therefore, etc.

3. Augustine says: "As our body climbing out of a pit is not illuminated all at once, so our soul climbing out of sin is not illuminated all at once." Therefore, the soul comes to have one virtue earlier, another later. I have not found this text either.

4. About *Mark* 8:24, which concerns the blind man who did not see all

[17] Peter Lombard, *Glossa*, PL 192: 208A.

[18] Augustine, *Ep.* 167 (to Jerome) 3.10, CSEL 44: 596.

at once, but first saw men who looked like trees walking, the gloss says: "Though he could cure him with one word all at once, he cured him gradually, in order to show the magnitude of human blindness, which with difficulty, as though step by step returns to the light."[19] Therefore, all the virtues are infused successively and not at once.

5. On *Job* 38:24 "through what way is the light dispersed?" the gloss reads: "Say by what way, that is, by what order do I infuse justice, with now this and now that virtue I complete [it]."[20] Therefore, it seems that they are not given at once.

6. If the virtues coming from grace are connected, this must come from some one cause existing with them. For they are not unified through effects, since we see that virtuous deeds are disconnected. If someone says that they are united through this common effect, that is, making one worthy of eternal life, I reply to the contrary: By the same argument the vices are united because they make us worthy of eternal death. Therefore, they must be united by something prior. But this cannot be their efficient cause, namely God, who is the one cause. For if this were true, then all things would exist at once, and all the gifts of grace would exist at once, since it says: "To one is given the utterance of knowledge, to another the utterance of wisdom, etc."[21]

7. Nor is it through charity which is called the form of all the virtues, for just as charity is one specific kind of virtue, so are the others. But how can one [virtue] which is never divided from another be perfected by that other?

Virtue is defined thus: virtue is a good quality of mind which God produces in us without our help.[22] Neither the first nor the second part of this definition posit some respect in which one virtue has to be connected with another. Therefore, the connection of one virtue with another is not necessary.

Charity in one way has one meaning or definition, whether it is a virtue coming from grace or a political virtue, and even as it signifies that love which is an intellectual virtue mentioned by the ethical philosopher. For everywhere there is love of God and love of neighbor, and both of these above all else. For it is natural to reason to know that the highest good

[19] *Glossa marg.* 5: 566D.
[20] *Glossa marg.* 3: 357B.
[21] *1 Cor.* 12:8.
[22] Peter Lombard, *Sent.* 2. d. 27. 1.1, 2: 480.

exists and is highest. But that in virtue of which there should be a connection among the virtues must be proper to the virtue which comes from grace, as coming from grace. Therefore, charity as charity is not the cause why the virtues are connected, since it is not found in political virtue. Nonetheless, since in a way they have one meaning, [their connection] is due to the disposition of grace.

8. Each act of each virtue given by grace is that by which free will merits eternal life. But for such an act nothing falling under the genus of habit is necessary except that virtue alone by means of which the act is elicited, for, since it is a virtue, it can elicit its own act. Therefore, even if every other virtue were subtracted, that act would be elicited; and the reason for that act is meriting eternal life. Therefore, the nature of merit does not require that whoever has one virtue has all.

Response to these arguments:

What they intend to prove about virtues coming from grace, namely, that whoever has one has all, we readily concede. This is more manifest in virtues coming from grace than in political virtues, not owing to some analogy among the virtues, as happens among political virtues, but arguments appropriate to their nature will show this below.

Replies to the arguments to the contrary:

Reply to argument to the contrary 1: I reply in order and first to the point of Augustine, where he says that "someone has more of one virtue than another": One is said to have more of that virtue of which one makes more use.

Reply to argument to the contrary 2: To Augustine's claim that that is the opinion of men I reply: Here Augustine made a distinction: There are some things in theology with which human reason agrees, and through the footprint of God that is reason we can come to know, while there are other things [in theology] which we cannot know, about which it is written: "Unless you believe you shall not understand." He understood this cognition to be the first sort, and therefore he said "of men," as though to say that it was not merely divine, but the kind to which one can come through the footprint of God that is reason.

Reply to argument to the contrary 3: To the next argument about climbing out of the pit, I reply: Just as one part [of the body] is illuminated earlier in time than another, so likewise the rational soul is illuminated in the intellect before the affections, but this is a priority in nature, not in time.

Or one can reply: The point can be understood about the use of the virtues, since one does make use of one virtue before another.

Reply to argument to the contrary 4: About the passage from *Mark*, I reply in the same way: For [Christ] is said to cure gradually in relation to the full effect of sight. Nonetheless, his physical cure was absolutely immediate, yet his sight was still not completely co-ordinated, as happens in a child whose seeing is not immediately distinct. Likewise, whoever leaves darkness does not immediately see distinctly and fully, but with confusion. His spiritual cure is understood to be perfect, through infusion of the virtues, yet certain remnants of sin remain, for example, in our memory and such powers, and even certain impediments [to virtue] remain, for which reason he is said not to see fully.

Reply to argument to the contrary 5: About the passage "through which way" from *Job,* I reply: The gloss which reads "with now this and now that virtue I complete [it]" should be interpreted to mean with now this and now that *use* of virtue.

Reply to argument to the contrary 6: To the objection concerning connection, I reply: In reality it is true, as is said in the argument that whoever has one virtue has no vice, so likewise, whoever has one vice has no virtue, not because of a connection among the vices but because of a connection among the virtues. The connection among the virtues, as the objection says, is not owing to their efficient cause, nor is it owing to some common effect, like making us worthy of eternal life. Rather, it comes from an intrinsic cause existing in the virtues themselves, as will be shown.

Reply to argument to the contrary 7: To the argument which asks whether this connection comes from charity, I reply: Charity can be taken in two ways. In the first way, what is called charity is a specific virtue, and in this respect it divides the genus of virtue along with the other virtues. Since one species of virtue is not the reason for or cause of another, in this respect charity is not the cause, the reason for the other virtues, nor is it the immediate cause of the connection among the virtues. Nevertheless, without charity there would be no connection.

Second, what is called charity is general love, which is not some determinate virtue, but is the reason for and cause of every virtue, as Augustine says in his book *On the Customs of the Catholic Church*. There he defines every species of virtue by means of love, and consequently says about prudence: "Prudence is love wisely preferring what aids it over what impedes it." And he defines the other virtues similarly. One should note that general love would not exist if the special love called charity, strictly speaking, did not exist. For because one loves God or the highest good above all things for himself alone, one also loves every good which is a way to him. Specific charity is different from general charity, because specific love has the same thing for its matter and its end, since it loves the highest good for its own sake. General love, however, has one thing for its matter and another for its end; it has some good which is a way to God for its matter, but God himself, who is the highest good, for its end. Consequently, there is the following order: first one must consider grace, since it comes from grace that one loves the highest good for its own sake, and the greater the grace the more one loves, etc.; and from the fact that one loves God above all things and for his own sake, it follows that one loves, as I said, every good which is a way to him. Therefore, since discerning good from bad choices and distributing to each his own and making moderate use of pleasures and dealing with terrors bravely and with perseverence are goods which lead to him, therefore one loves these. Consequently, without this love prudence would not be a virtue, nor would justice nor anything else. Therefore [general love] is called the reason for and immediate cause of every virtue. For the same thing can be said of faith and hope. Charity, however, as love, agrees with general love, but it differs, however, as was said, because it has a different matter from general love, that is, God. They also agree in having the same end, namely, God, and because there would be no general love if there were no specific love, this union in their end comes from specific love. Therefore, from what has been said it is clear that, though there are different matters for these virtues, and different acts, nevertheless they are immediately united in general love, and from this union it follows immediately that whoever has one virtue has all.

[*Objections to the foregoing reply*:]

[*a*.] But one can raise the following question: Even if all the virtues are united in general love, since they concern different matters, it does not seem to follow that whoever has one virtue has all. For whoever loves to distribute to each his own does not for this reason love to moderate his love of pleasure, nor does he have other loves, just as, when things are united in one genus, they can also be essentially separate and disconnected from each other.

[*b*.] Likewise, all vices and sins are united through evil love, which is called lust, yet whoever has one vice need not have all.

Reply [*to arg. a*]: They are united, not just in general love, but also by having one end, which is the highest good, and general love has this from charity, and in this respect general love agrees with charity. For, as has been said, there would be no general love if there were no specific love. And since specific love, that is, charity, loves God above all things and for his own sake, love of each sort of good for the sake of the same end follows charity, and thereby connects and associates every love of every sort of good. This is why *Col.* 3:15 says "above all these put on love, which is the bond of perfection," and the gloss says: "Charity connects all the others, so they are not missing."[23] This is why whoever has one virtue, since he does not have it without charity, and love of every good follows on charity, as a consequence he has love of every good and so has every virtue. For the same reason it follows that no vice, since if it has love of rendering to each what is his own, lacks its opposite vice; and in the same way, whoever has love of moderation lacks the opposing vice. But whoever has one love, since he has it together with charity, has every love. Therefore, he must necessarily lack every opposed vice.

[*Reply to arg. b*]: To the objection about the vices, I reply: This is not true of the vices, because even if they agree in lust, which is a kind of general love, they are not unified in one end. Rather, each and every deadly vice is separated from the one and same end which is the highest good, in relation to which they are like one privation, that is, the privation of one thing, while in respect of their different matters and acts they are different privations. Consequently, just as for the virtues there is one and the same end, so there is one and the same source or efficient cause, and one origin, because they are infused at one time, by one, and for the sake of one. But the different vices are acquired, not at one but at different times, through different acts concerning different matters, and they agree only in being separated from the one end, and, since they are privations, everything they possess pertains to the nature of difference, and nothing properly and correctly pertains to the nature of union.

Reply to argument to the contrary 8: To the argument about merit, I reply: Although by an act of one virtue one can merit eternal life, yet based on one virtue alone one cannot be worthy of eternal life, which one can achieve, even without any meritorious act, as in the case of children. Also, even though one actually can gain merit by one virtue without the rest, one cannot be worthy of eternal life without being worthy of the other virtue. Consequently, the connection of the virtues is not based on merit but rather on worthiness.

[23] *Glossa interlin.* 6: 630; Peter Lombard, *Glossa*, PL 192: 283D.

[Part 2: *Is one virtue enough to make a human worthy of eternal life?*]

The next question is whether charity alone is enough to possess eternal life, or to make one worthy of God and able to resist all sin.

[*Argument pro*:]

Since charity prefers God to every other object of love, it prefers God to that object of love which is sin. Therefore, whoever has charity does not adhere to sin through love. For love of sin is not compatible with love of God, and beyond this "charity loves God more than lust loves thousands of gold and silver pieces."[24] Therefore, since this love is greater than any other, and is intrinsically repugnant to love [of sin], it is intrinsically able to resist [sin] and in its proper act to resist [sin]. Therefore, solely by the resistance of charity does one resist every sort of sin.

Response:

I respond by means of the previously mentioned distinction among kinds of charity, namely, general and special charity. In one way, each and every virtue is love, or the completion of each and every virtue is love, though in another way this is not true. This is why charity is said in different ways. Therefore, there is no question of seeking whether charity alone can suffice, because if we are speaking about charity, in so far as it is general love, as has been said, general love cannot exist without the specific love which is charity. And the love of every good has to follow this [charity], and so does every virtue, and so it cannot exist alone.

One should note, however, why it is said that the greatest merit follows charity and not faith, which is first and the foundation of the virtues. I reply that, even though faith is the foundation of all the virtues, the actions faith produces are not the foundation for the actions of the other virtues, in the way the actions of charity are. Consequently, even though the virtues are separate in their operations, and the motion of one does not complete the motion of another, nonetheless, it is true only of charity that it completes the motion of every other virtue. For charity is like a universal mover and every other virtue is like a particular mover, just as the sun is by nature a common mover, while human or plant or other such things are specific movers. Consequently, one should note that there are two powers, as far as merit is concerned: The universal power to acquire merit is based on charity, which is the reason why we are capable of any meritorious action;

[24] Augustine, *Enarrat. in Ps. 118*, 17.10, PL 37: 1550.

while there is also a particular power by which we are capable of particular merit, through the other virtues. The case is similar to the sun, which is a power involved in all generation and destruction, while a human or plant is capable of specific kinds of generation and destruction.

Another reason for their connection can be taken from their end, which is glory. For glory is a kind of likeness of the highest good, in every power and in every essential act of that power. Therefore, something completely corresponding to the highest good must in all respects be its likeness, as this is possible for wayfarers. In this way the perfection of grace during the time of wayfaring corresponds to the perfection of glory in our heavenly homeland. But this could not happen if there were no perfection of grace in all the powers of the soul, just as there will be perfection of glory in all of them.

Albert the Great

Parisian Summa

[ca. 1243-1248]

[Part Six: *On the Good*]
Tr.1: *On the Good in General*

Q. 6. On the Division and Sufficiency of the Virtues

This question concerns the division and sufficiency of the virtues, and three questions are raised. First, what is the basis for taking the virtues to be four? Second, why are these virtues called cardinal? And third, about their order.

Art. 1. *What is the basis for taking the virtues to be four?*

We proceed to the first issue thus:

1. Virtue is the perfection of the motive powers of the soul. Now perfections differ based on what is perfected. Therefore, there are as many perfections as there are things perfected. But the motive powers, as was shown above,[1] do not extend to more than three. Therefore, it seems that this should be the number of cardinal virtues.[2]

2. At the end of *Nic. Eth.* 1 Aristotle divides the powers of the soul, which are the subjects of the political virtues, into the rational and the irrational. The irrational he divides into those which participate somehow in reason, such as emotion and desire, and into those which do not participate in reason, such as nutritive power.[3] Now the subjects of virtue are only reason, and emotion and desire, which somehow participate in reason. Therefore, it seems that there are only three political virtues.

To the contrary:

1. Some[4] say that the political virtues are divided based on the "principal acts of the powers" and not in relation to the powers themselves. Now temperance is taken in relation to the acts of desire, as they are ordered by

[1] Albert, *Summa Parisiensis, De homine* 68.2.

[2] Cf. Philip, *Summa on the Good*, "On the Four Cardinal Virtues," q. 1, obj. 1; p. 86 above.

[3] Aristotle, *Nic. Eth.* 1.13 (1102a28, b13-31).

[4] Philip, q. 1, Reply to obj. 1; p. 88 above.

reason as curbing desires. Courage is taken in relation to acts of the emotions which are ordered to confronting what is arduous. Prudence is taken in relation to the acts of reason itself in distinguishing what is good and bad for us. And justice is taken in relation to the act of reason in relation to others, through discerning and rendering what we ought.

2. Secondly, they say that these four virtues order us with regard to good and bad. Good which lacks order is of two kinds: the apparent good, which is deceptive, and excessive good, which is corruptive. Prudence works against the first by discerning what is good, while temperance works against the second by restraining us. Likewise, there are two kinds of evil: perverse evil is evil which produces guilt, while adverse evil is evil which produces pain. Against the first justice produces order, while courage confronts the second to keep us from harm.[5]

3. In a third way they say that the four virtues are based on the four affections of the soul. These are joy and hope, sadness and fear, which are the seed-beds of the virtues and vices, because the root of all these affections is love. Now Augustine says that every virtue is a kind of love: "Prudence is love wisely preferring what aids it over what impedes it. Courage is love readily enduring adversities for the sake of the beloved. Temperance is love giving itself wholly to what is loved. Justice is love serving the beloved alone and ruling rightly for the sake of the beloved."[6]

4. In a fourth way they say that the distinction of the virtues is based on distinctions among laws, for there is the law of reason and the law of nature. Now the law of reason consists in distinguishing good from bad, and this is the basis for prudence. The law of nature concerns either what we make use of for ourselves or give to our neighbor. Concerning the latter there is justice, according to *Luke* 6:31: "Do unto others as you would have them do unto you." Concerning the former, either it is a matter of attaining good, which concerns temperance, or of avoiding evil, which concerns courage.[7]

5. In a fifth way they say that virtue puts order into our actions or our passions. In our actions the order either concerns us and thus involves prudence, or it concerns our neighbor and thus involves justice. In our passions the order either concerns those which are inborn and thus involves

[5] Philip, q. 1, arg. from authority 1; p. 90 above.

[6] Philip, q. 1, response; p. 92 above. Cf. Augustine, *De moribus ecclesiae* 1.15.25.

[7] Philip, q. 1, add. arg. 1; p. 92-93 above.

temperance, or it concerns those which are impressed and thus involves courage.[8]

6. In a sixth way they say that the virtues arm us against the vices. Therefore we are armed for ourselves through prudence and are armed against our neighbor through justice, against prosperity through temperance, and against adversity through courage. For a man enters battle with himself and his neighbor, with the wealthy and his adversaries.[9]

7. In a seventh way they say that the four virtues are found in a virtuous deed: in the deed itself, to discern which belongs to prudence; and clothed with the right circumstances, and to attend to this belongs to justice; and the difficulties virtue involves, which belongs to courage; and the pleasant good, which is a sign of generation, as was said above,[10] belongs to temperance.

8. In an eighth way they say that in a virtuous deed there are four features: its beginning, means, end, and removing impediments which arise due to difficulty. Now to mark out a beginning belongs to prudence; to posit a means belongs to temperance; to direct something to its end belongs to justice; and to remove impediments belongs to courage.[11]

Now none of these [arguments] demonstrate the number of the virtues, but are merely accommodations to that number which can easily be disproved by anyone who knows something.

Therefore, I respond otherwise:

Virtues are perfections of the motive powers of the soul. Now one kind of power in the soul *orders*, while another is *ordered*. Since the order of that which orders exists in what is ordered, the power which orders does not need any matter beyond the matter in the powers which are subject to its order. Now the power which orders is reason, while the powers which are ordered are emotion (*irascibilis*) and desire (*concupiscibilis*), as was proven above in the questions on the soul.[12] Now the order of reason, which in moral issues is determined in relation to the notion of the good and acts for

[8] Philip, q. 1, add. arg. 2; p. 93 above.

[9] Philip, q. 1, add. arg. 3; p. 93 above.

[10] Albert, *De bono,* Tr. 1, q. 4, ed. Cologne 28, n.78: 50.5-10, quoting Aristotle, *Nic. Eth.* 2.2 (1104b4-6).

[11] Philip, q. 1, add. arg. 5; p. 94 above, Aquinas, pp. 163-64 below.

[12] Albert, *Summa Parisiensis, De homine,* 68.2c.

the sake of what is best, can only exist in relation to the mean which is found in actions and passions, or in relation to another [person] toward whom action and passion are related. In the first way the perfection of reason consists in prudence which manifests the mean. In the second way its perfection consists in justice, which directs us to others as we ought. Now the powers which are ordered are desire and emotion, in the presence of strong passions. Now those [passions] which are in desire are inborn (*innata*) and their perfection is temperance; while those which are in the emotions are impressed (*illata*) and their perfection is courage.

In this way the solution to all the objections is manifest.

Art. 2. *Why are these virtues called cardinal or political?*

The second question is why these virtues are called cardinal or political.

[*Arguments against the four cardinal virtues*:]

1. A hinge (*cardo*) is that on which the door of a house turns. Therefore if virtues are called cardinal due to being like the hinge in a house, they will be the virtues on which the complete activity of the soul turns. But it seems that not all the virtues can be reduced to these virtues, for example, faith, hope and charity.

2. To one place there is only one door. Therefore, since happiness is one thing, there will only be entrance to it through one door. Consequently, there will be only one cardinal virtue, because there is only one hinge for the one door.

If someone says that the cardinal virtues are the principal virtues, and since these four are the principal virtues they are therefore also called cardinal, *to the contrary*: the theological virtues–faith, hope, and charity–have more right to be called principal virtues, yet they are not called cardinal virtues.

Response:

These four [virtues] are called cardinal because they are like a hinge for the principal acts of the motive powers of the soul, to which the acts of the other virtues are connected, as to a hinge. For the principal act of reason is to distinguish good from bad in actions and passions and to follow what is right in putting order into our actions and passions as they affect others. This is how prudence and justice are present in reason. Now the hinges of all the passions are those inborn passions which involve touch, which are the concern of temperance, and those impressed passions which involve touch, which are the concern of courage.[13] For it was proven above in the questions on the soul that pleasure and pain are present absolutely speaking in touch, but are present only relatively in the other senses.

These virtues are called principal virtues because other virtues, which are present in actions and passions and consist in a mean, are reduced to these virtues. And they are called political (meaning civil) virtues because in them and in their activities the government (res publica) achieves perfection by achieving the best condition for its citizens. A sign of this is that all legislation is designed to produce some of these virtues.

Reply to Obj. 1. To what is objected to the contrary I reply: Faith, hope, and charity are not virtues which concern means but rather direct us into our end (*in finem*), and therefore they are not reduced to the cardinal virtues.

Reply to Obj. 2. Happiness does not consist in just one thing and consequently there is no entrance to it through one thing. For happiness is an act involving every perfected virtue in the mind.

There are those[14] who say that these four virtues are called cardinal because they determine four conditions which are present in every virtue. These conditions are to know, to will, to persevere in difficulties, and moderation, which concerns the mean. And they say that prudence determines knowing, and justice willing, and courage persevering in difficulties.

This view seems to have come from the text of Bernard, in *On Consideration* 2, where he says: "Observe that there is a certain beautiful harmony and connection among the virtues, and that one depends on another. So you see that prudence is the mother of courage, and no daring deed is courage, but rashness, which was not born from prudence. This is she who sits like a judge between pleasures and necessities, and sets the boundaries on both sides within certain limits, to one assigning and offering what is enough, to others madly offering what is excessive, and then from both forming a third virtue, which is called temperance." "About justice, which is one of the four, is it not true that consideration precedes the mind being formed by her? For it must first think about itself in order of itself to

[13] "Inborn" translates *innatae*–passions generated from within the person; "impressed" translates *illatae*–passions introduced from without. Albert's clever linguistic opposition focuses on the *cause* of the passion: interior cause for *innata*, exterior for *illata*. "Innate," meaning present from birth, is not what Albert means by *innata*.

[14] Philip, q. 3, resp; pp. 97-9 above.

produce the norm of justice: do not unto another what one would not have done unto self, and do not deny to another what one would have done unto self. In these two are manifest the complete body of justice."[15]

Art. 3. *Concerning the internal order among these virtues.*

The third question concerns the order among these virtues.

1. Prudence seems to be first. For choosing actions comes before performing actions. Now prudence teaches us to choose among possible actions, as Augustine says,[16] but the other virtues only concern actual actions. Therefore, prudence is first.

2. But justice seems to be first. For the gloss on *Genesis* 2.13-14 says that justice includes all the virtues, and consequently is symbolized by the Euphrates River,[17] whose source and mouth the text omits. Therefore, it seems that justice is more general than the other virtues. Since what is general comes before what is specific, it seems that justice is the first virtue.

Since it is easy to get into disputes about this issue,

I respond:

Each of the virtues can be first, according to various arguments:

If one refers to the powers in which the virtues exist, since reason is first among the powers, the virtues present in it–prudence and justice–will be prior. Next comes temperance, which is found in inborn passions, and last comes courage, which is found in impressed passions, because the natural is prior to what comes to be impressed.

If one refers to actions, then what is prior is choosing among possible actions, which belongs to prudence; second comes holding ourselves between excess and deficiency, which belongs to temperance; then comes resisting what is difficult, which belongs to courage; and finally comes ordering ourselves in relation to others, which belongs to justice.

If one considers what is good but difficult, as far as habitual virtue is concerned first comes courage, which concerns what is good and most difficult; then comes temperance, which involves what is good but more difficult; third comes justice; and last comes prudence. In his *Ethics* Aristotle seems to have followed this order.

[15] Bernard of Clairvaux, *De consid.*, 1.8.9-10, 3: 404-5.

[16] Augustine, *De moribus ecclesiae* 1.24.45; 1.25.46; *De libero arbitrio* 1.13.27.

[17] *Glossa ord.* on *Gen.* 2:13-14, which comes from Ambrose, *De paradiso* 3.14-18.

If one considers the power from which a habitual virtue is generated, then the first virtue is temperance, which is where habits begin to develop; second comes courage; third justice; and last comes prudence, because prudence is generated more from experience and teaching than from habit.

One can find other ways of ordering the virtues, some of which are found in the objections.[18]

[18] In the detailed treatment of the cardinal virtues in *On the Good*, Albert followed yet another order, the reverse of the order in his response based on the soul's powers: courage, temperance, prudence, justice.

Albert the Great

Commentary on the Sentences of Peter Lombard

[ca. 1243-1249]

Book Three, Dist. 33[1]
On the Cardinal Virtues

Here we shall ask about these four virtues:
First, about their number and whether it is sufficient.
Second, why are they called cardinal virtues?
Third, about the definitions of them which the Master posits.
Fourth, will they remain with us in our heavenly homeland, or not?

Art. 1. *About the number of the cardinal virtues.*

About the first issue there are the following objections:

1. Augustine says that "virtue is the order of love or ordered love." But there is only one ordered love. Therefore, it seems that there is only one virtue.

2. If one thing in nature suffices, nature herself does not require many, because it is better to work through one finer thing than through many. But charity is sufficient for every good. Therefore, it seems that other habits are superfluous.

3. There are only two sorts of things: our end (*finis*) and what leads to our end (*ad finem*). Therefore, based on these two there should be only two virtues.

4. In the area of technical skill we see that for a given product there is not one art for teaching and another for executing the product, but one and the same art both teaches and executes the product. Since virtue is even finer than manual art, it seems there should not be one art which teaches and others which execute the deed. Therefore, it seems that prudence is not a virtue.

5. There are only three motive powers which can be perfected for action: the rational, appetitive, and emotional powers. Therefore, there should only be three habits which perfect them, and consequently there should only be three virtues.

6. It seems the number of virtues is too small. For we have a virtue which orders us with regard to inborn pleasures, and this is temperance;

[1] Albert, *In 3 Sent.*, d. 33, ed. Borgnet 28: 604-613.

and we have one which concerns difficult passions externally impressed, and this is courage. There are many other virtues, however, which order a human with respect to himself, as these do. Therefore, it seems we should admit virtues in areas such as the pleasure we take from knowledge, or the pleasure we take from honor, etc. Therefore, the number of virtues is too small.

7. According to the philosophy of Aristotle, the virtue which he calls chastity concerns only the pleasure of touch. Since the other senses have their own pleasures, as touch does, it seems they ought to have their own virtues which produce order. That this is truly what Aristotle intended and said is clear from his own words in *Ethics* 4: "But the other animals seem to make little or no use of taste. For taste judges flavor, which is what wine-tasters and gourmands do. But they are not concerned with these things (and the incontinent are not) but only with use, which happens wholly through touch, in the case of food and drink and sex and other acts."[2] Therefore, what was said is clear; and the Commentator explains this the same way.

8. According to the same Philosopher courage only concerns evil fear which is impressed, not by every sort of death, but by that found in war for a good cause. Since there are many other difficult things in life, such as confession, illness, poverty, it seems we ought to have virtues directing us in these matters, as well. But we do not. Therefore, it seems the number of virtues is too small.

9. A human can be ordered to his neighbor in many ways which go beyond the notion of what is required. Therefore, there should be virtues for these ways. Therefore, the number of the virtues is too small.

10. It seems the cardinal virtues are not the four the Master posits here. For on *Mark* 8:9, "And those who ate were about 4,000," the gloss says: "By 4,000 is signified the four virtues: namely, prudence, temperance, courage, and the fourth, which is diffused through them all, love of God and neighbor." Therefore, it seems that love of God and neighbor is one of the cardinal virtues.

11. Likewise, about *Matt.* 5:6, "Blessed are those who hunger and thirst for justice," the gloss reads: "To hunger and thirst for justice is to have love of the good." Therefore, it seems that either charity is one of the cardinal virtues or charity is the same as justice."

[2] Aristotle, *Nic. Eth.* 3.10 (1118a26-32).

Response:

Four virtues are cardinal virtues. Here many thinkers have put forward a number of reasons for this, but one is substantial. It is agreed that civic virtue is what pertains to the good condition of the city. Now for good condition in the citizens two things are required: The first is a habit (*habitus*) which determines through reason what is right about our deeds, and this habit is an operative habit, because speculative understanding is of little or no importance here. This habit is *prudence*, which is why Augustine says that prudence "wisely chooses what aids over what impedes."[3] The second thing required is to act well in difficult and important matters which are the concern of all the virtues, since a human has no need of a habit to govern easy topics, because there he is self-sufficient. Now acting well happens when one acts toward self and others according to the order of right reason. In relation to others one should follow the notion of obligation (*debitum*), because any other way of relating oneself to others does not follow the order set out by law. The habit which governs this is *justice*. In relation to self, acting well involves two kinds of difficulties. The first concerns what is inbornly pleasurable about our present life, that in the domain of touch, for example, taste as a kind of touch, and sex. The habit governing these matters is *temperance*. The other kind of difficulty is impressed from outside of us, for example, danger in war which seeks to subvert the good of the citizens, goods such as justice, faith, or liberty, or things like these. Now the habit which governs these matters is *courage*. This is the way the virtues are multiplied, according to philosophical consideration.

[*Replies to the Objections*:]

Reply to Obj. 1: Some thinkers say that the love which falls within the definition of virtue is not the habit of charity, but rather is general love, by which everything which exists loves its own perfection.[4] Others mean to say that it is charity, and then the claim is true only of well-formed virtue, not of unformed virtue. Charity is then in the virtues as a general form. For just as the good, absolutely speaking, is found in this or that good thing, likewise the love of the good, absolutely speaking, is found in the love of this or that good, as was said in the preceding distinction. But this does not exclude the existence of a plurality of virtues, as was also said there.

[3] *De mor. ecc.* 1.15, PL 32: 1322.

[4] Philip the Chancellor, pp. 113-4 above.

Reply to Obj. 2: One thing does not suffice for all acts, in so far as they are actual deeds of a specific type, but one thing does suffice as a general mover and agent. This is how heat is related to our senses and the heat of the sun is related to generation. And how this should be understood you saw before.

Reply to Obj. 3: It is true that, speaking generally, there are two types of things [ends and means], but each of these has its own special differentia. Therefore, the three theological virtues are determined based on our end, and their definitions were given above.

Based on what leads to our end, the cardinal virtues are determined as follows: What leads to our end either follows that reason which orders us to our end and to the good, or it somehow reflects the goodness of our end by following the definition of what is essentially morally good, which is the only concern of virtue. In the first way, that kind of reason is considered *prudence*, because the kind of reason which helps us perform a good deed is different from the kind of reason which impedes us. But if the goodness of our end is reflected in the virtue, either it follows the relation of one person to another and in this way is *justice*, or it concerns each person alone. The latter case concerns either what is inborn or impressed, and the first is *temperance*, the second is *courage*.

Reply to Obj. 4: A technical skill which employs instruments induces the form which is in the agent into the matter which is external to the agent. Therefore, preparation, preparatory skill, and skill which produces the form, all must exist external to the wood or stone. But in ethical matters habits are generated inside the agent. Therefore, it must be true that habits follow actions as to kind. Therefore, what suffices for developing knowledge is not sufficient to develop virtue. If, however, a technical skill produced the form [of the artifact] in the craftsman himself, then the proposed similarity would hold, just as a virtuous deed produces its form in the person who acts in accordance with virtue.

Reply to Obj. 5 and 6: Although there are only three powers [in the soul], one, namely reason, involves two relations: as ruling other powers, and in this way prudence is found there; and as ordering us in relation to other persons, and in this respect justice is found there. In the power of desire is found temperance, and in the power of emotion is found courage. This is how these three powers factor into their four virtues.

Reply to Obj. 7 and 8: Aristotle treats virtue differently from Cicero in his *Rhetoric* and his book *On Duty*. Aristotle accepts as a virtue only what is difficult and most important in the matter the virtue covers. Therefore, he does not admit there are virtues to cover love of learning or love of honor. Other thinkers, however, posit virtues for those areas and reduce them to temperance.[5] But even though Aristotle holds that a virtue is found in one area where it achieves its highest state and which is the basis for its definition, it can be used rightly in another area. For example, he discusses the courageous man who is not concerned with every sort of difficulty which fortune brings or with difficulty which involves danger from natural death, but who uses his courage rightly in these cases, and through the same habit by which we face its proper dangers.[6] And we ourselves, following the lead of Aristotle, can say that temperance, considered in its maximum area and power, is found in pleasures of touch concerning nutrition and sex; but it is also rightly exercised about other inborn pleasures, and through the same habit. This view is consonant with what Aristotle says in many places in his *Ethics*, as is clear to those who take time to look at this book carefully.

The same argument gives a clear reply to the objection about courage.

Reply to Obj. 9: It is true that there are many ways we are ordered toward others; but the order which falls under the notion of civil society is the order which includes law and obligation. For in the other ways we happen to relate (or not relate) ourselves to our neighbor fall *outside* the purview of the legislator. Therefore, these relations do not determine civic virtue, nor can they. The species of justice, which the objector perhaps has in mind, are determined according to special features of obligation, features which are multiplied based on the notion of nature, as happens in natural justice, or on the notion of contracts, or on the notion of status or benefit or condition. This is how the Philosopher determines the multiple senses of justice in the *Ethics*, in the book devoted to justice; and it is how Cicero posits numerous species of natural and positive justice.[7]

Reply to Obj. 10: These two virtues, that is, justice and love of God and neighbor, are not two civic virtues which are different from each other and are not cardinal virtues. And the gloss on *Mark* does not mean that charity is a civic virtue, but rather that charity gives justice an order to neighbor and God, so that one will do out of love what one was required to do out of duty.

[5] Philip, *Summa de bono*, 2: 823-4.

[6] Aristotle, *Nic. Eth.* 3.6 (1115a35-b6).

[7] Aristotle, *Nic. Eth.*5.1-11; Cicero, *De inv.* 2.53.160-54.162.

Reply to Obj. 11: The gloss means that justice, when meritorious, is moved by love; it does not mean that love is a civic virtue. One should note, however, that Aristotle seems to hold a different view, because he seems to mean that there are three virtues which concern the individual and are acquired: one concerns difficulties arising from inborn pleasure, which chastity (or temperance) governs; the second concerns difficulties which are impressed from without, where courage governs us; and the third concerns difficulties about our possessions which we use and which sustain our way of life, and the virtue which governs these matters he calls magnificence, and devotes a special treatise to it. Intellectual virtue, as he says, does not have a mean in the way moral virtue does, but right reason is present in a moral virtue through the mean, for example, prudence along with its parts which he says are *phronesis*, knowledge, understanding, etc. Now justice, since it is not predicated absolutely, belongs to another order; for it falls under the order of the civil law, that is, statutes and votes, and its cases vary. Therefore, it concerns the order of the common state, an order Aristotle seems to follow in his *Ethics*, as is clear in the new translation.

Art. 2. *Why are these virtues called cardinal virtues?*

The second question is: Why are these virtues called cardinal virtues? In the text of Master Lombard, Jerome seems to give the following reason for this: because "by them in this mortal life one lives well and afterward arrives at eternal beatitude."[8]

[*Objections*:]

This argument seems incorrect, for the following reasons:

1. Many authors have written about the cardinal virtues without making any mention of eternal beatitude, authors such as Aristotle, Cicero, Macrobius, and other philosophers.

2. In his "Homily on the Beginning of the Book of *Proverbs*," Basil says that many who are outside [Christianity] have written about the four virtues that are called cardinal.[9]

[8] Lombard, *Sent.* 3. d. 33. 1.3, 2: 188, quoting Jerome, *Ep. 66 (ad Pammachium)*, n. 3, CSEL 54: 649.

[9] Basil, *Homilia in Prin. Proverb.* 7, PG 31: 402c. "For those sages who are outside say much about justice, though in their probable arguments they commit fallacies."

3. Many have possessed these virtues even though they did not have faith, such as Cicero, and Scipio Africanus, and certain other Stoics, whose biographies were written by philosophers. Therefore, it seems the reason given by Jerome is not consistent with this.

4. By the theological virtues in this mortal life one lives well and afterward arrives at eternal beatitude. Therefore, the theological virtues are the cardinal virtues. Therefore, the argument Jerome gives does not hold.

5. If one argues that they are called cardinal because all the other virtues, including civic virtues, revolve on them, as on hinges, then it seems that on this argument only charity is a cardinal virtue. For charity alone, as has been frequently said, seems to make all that is found in human life good.

6. One virtue seems more to be cardinal than the rest. For about prudence Bernard says: "it is not so much a virtue as the charioteer (*auriga*) of the virtues."[10] Therefore, the others seem to hinge on it.

And there is a second question here: *Why are virtues called principal, why civic or political?*

Response:

I reply without prejudice that Jerome does not even touch on the general sense of cause, but only treats the cause of these virtues in their optimal state. And they have this optimal state only when they are "infused" and are "well-formed." Then they are called cardinal in relation to those [virtues] which are present in actions done for the sake of our end and allied to consideration of man; but they are not called cardinal in relation to the theological [virtues].

[*Replies to the Objections*:]

The solution to the first four objections is manifest from the *Response*. Other thinkers, however, such as the philosophers, call them cardinal because they are a hinge on which human life turns, at least concerning the civil state and the kind of goodness found there. This is their proper and usual definition in Cicero and the other philosophers who speak about them.

Reply to Obj. 5: To the objection about charity, I reply: Charity is not a hinge to whose nature the other particular virtues are reduced, in the way that sobriety is reduced to temperance because sobriety tempers us with

[10] Bernard, *Super cantica, sermo* 49.3.5, 2: 76.9ff. Cf. Philip, 2: 772.230.

regard to certain inborn pleasures, or in the way that continence and parsimony and similar virtues recognized by Cicero and Macrobius work, or in the way that piety and mercy and religion are reduced to justice. For all these virtues concern particular aspects of obligation. But human life is related to charity as to a general mover, and to a certain form, and to an end, but not as to a hinge, as has been said.

Reply to Obj. 6: None of these virtues is more a cardinal virtue than another, though one has more wide-spread matter than another. On this issue one should note that every political virtue adds some special aspect to its matter. For example, *courage* adds the aspect of arduous and resolute for the sake of the good; and *continence* (or *temperance*) adds the aspect of beauty to the restriction pleasures of the flesh and especially the sense of touch, because, as Avicenna argues, in touch alone pleasure is found fully and absolutely. This is why temperance in this area is difficult. *Justice*, even though it has wider matter than the externally impressed or inborn passions, has its own special aspect, namely, the aspect of obligation ordained by natural or human law.

The widest matter among these belongs to *prudence*, however, because its matter is whatever succeeds in producing a moral deed. Nonetheless, it adds a special aspect to this matter, namely, what is worthy of choice following right reasoning about the civic good. In this way prudence is, so to speak, reason's detective and thus is a special virtue over against other special virtues. So far as prudence shows what is worthy of choice, either as a kind of act or in certain circumstances, to the other virtues, it is the "charioteer of the virtues" mentioned by St. Bernard, for as reason is related to the other motive powers so is a habit perfecting reason also related to them. For reason has its object under a specific aspect, namely, the true in relation to the good, according to which reason is practical. Now the good leads to the end of the powers of emotion and desire, following their different natures. And the same thing holds about a habit governing reason, that there is some sort of special aspect it adds to the general matter which is what is determinable to the deeds of another power.

Therefore, I reply that the cardinality of the virtues is based on the aspect they add to their matter, and their inferior virtues, which Macrobius and Cicero call their "parts," focus on this aspect, rather than their matter. And since all are equally principal virtues in having such aspects, it follows that one is no more a cardinal virtue than the other, but all are equally cardinal virtues.

To the second question raised, I reply:

The aspect of *cardinality* consists in this, that inferior virtues focus on those aspects of the cardinal virtues, as was just said. Virtues are called *principal*, however, as they consist in what is essential to that virtue, so courage concerns the greatest externally impressed difficulty and temperance concerns the object giving the greatest pleasure. This makes the other virtues secondary, for they concern matter which is near to the matter of this virtue, but is not completely the same. For example, sobriety concerns tempering what gets in the way of reason and the senses, which is not so difficult as controlling the pleasures of touch. And the same thing holds for the other virtues. Virtues are called *civic* as they produce a good state of one person with another within the order of the citizenry. And this is the same reason they are called *political*, except that one term is Greek and the other Latin.

Art. 3: *Concerning the definitions of the cardinal virtues*

The third question concerns the definitions which the Master here gives: ["Justice consists in helping the miserable, prudence in taking precautions to avoid traps, courage in enduring difficulties, and temperance in restraining depraved pleasures."][11]

[Q. 1: *Concerning the definition of justice*:]

The first question concerns this definition: "Justice consists in helping the miserable."

1. This seems to be a definition of mercy, which is part of justice according to the saints, but is not part of the cardinal virtue. Therefore, the definition seems incorrect.

2. Justice is "to render to each his own," as Augustine says, and also the Philosopher.[12] Now this can happen in a variety of ways. Therefore, assuming this is what justice is, it seems that the Master's definition incorrectly descends to a certain, limited matter.

[11] Lombard, *Sent.* 3 d.33.1.2, 2: 188. Definitions taken from Augustine, *De trin.* 14.9.12, CCSL 50a: 439.

[12] Actually Ambrose, *De officiis* 1.24, PL 16: 62a. Cf. Augustine, *De mor. ecc.* 1.15, PL 32: 1322; Aristotle, *Nic. Eth.* 5.1 (1130a3-5).

3. Helping the miserable does not seem to be "rendering to each his own," but seems to be giving of one's own. Therefore, this seems more the function of charity than justice. Therefore, the definition is incorrect.

[Q. 2: *Concerning the definition of prudence*:]

The next question concerns the second definition the Master posits: "Prudence consists in taking precautions to avoid traps."

1. As Cicero says, there are three parts of prudence: memory, understanding, and foresight.[13] Taking precautions to avoid traps applies only to foresight. Therefore, this does not apply to prudence in itself, but only to a part of it, because if it applied to prudence in itself, it would have to apply to every part.

2. What the Master says seems impossible, for traps are not necessary, since then we could not be cautious about them. Therefore, they are future contingents. But we do not know them, nor can they be known. Therefore, we cannot be cautious about them, because we are only cautious about what we know or what we know beforehand.

[Q. 3: *Concerning the definition of courage*:]

The next question concerns the third definition, which says that "courage consists in enduring difficulties."

Since virtue concerns pleasure and pain, every virtue endures the difficulties of the passions it is concerned with, and therefore this is not a special defining feature of courage.

[Q. 4: *Concerning the definition of temperance*:]

The next question concerns the fourth definition: "temperance consists in restraining depraved pleasures."

To restrain does not signify an act; but every virtue seems to be defined in terms of an act which is essential to it; therefore, this definition is incorrect.

This same objection can be made about the definition of courage.

Both of these virtues are asserted by means of definitions taken from the kind of passions which are externally impressed: courage because it endures difficulties and temperance because it restrains depraved pleasures. But passions are not the basis for merit. Therefore, since virtues are set out for the sake of merit, defining them based on the passions seems incorrect.

[13] Cicero, *De inv.* 2.53.160.

[Q.5: *Concerning the order of the virtues*:]

The next question concerns the order of the virtues. In his definitions the Master puts justice first, then prudence, courage, and temperance. But the book of *Wisdom* mentioned in the text lists: sobriety (or temperance), then prudence, then justice, and finally courage (or virtue).[14]

Reply to Q. 1 [*about justice*:]

The Master is attempting to define these virtues only in so far as they produce conformity to Christ, in whom they exist in their maximum state. Although the act of justice which is "to render to each what is his" is broader, it is not as meritorious nor does it conform us as much to Christ as that act which is only a part of justice, namely, "to help the miserable." This act makes their misery our own and what is owed to them becomes ours, just as Christ became ours in this way: through helping us who were miserable he became our redeemer.

[*Replies to objections to Q.1*:]

The replies to the first two objections are clear from the response.

Reply to Obj. 3: What we give to the miserable is both ours and theirs. It is ours by right of dominion, but it is theirs by reason of the obligation of natural law, which in times of necessity makes goods common. For according to the natural law, in times of necessity all things are common.

Replies to the objections to the definition [*of prudence, Q. 2*:]

Reply to Obj. 1: The highest degree of prudence concerns caution about traps, that is, traps against virtue and the good life. Therefore, prudence is defined by means of that act and consequently not as a general habit found in all the parts of prudence.

Reply to Obj. 2: One can take precautions against traps in general, if not in particular. Thus, prudence fortifies us against all traps which might come about.

Reply to the objection about the third definition [*concerning courage, Q. 3*:]

"Difficulties" are the principal concern of courage, for externally impressed passion is more bitter or painful than other passions, and consequently is more the principal concern of courage.

[14] *Wisdom* 8:7.

Reply to the next objection [*concerning temperance, Q. 4*:]

"To restrain" does involve an act, an interior act, namely, tempering the will. In this way the solution is clear.

Reply to the question concerning the order of the virtues [*Q. 5*:]

The virtues are considered in two different ways: in relation to their subjects and in themselves. When considered in themselves, there are two substantial features of their objects, namely, the difficult and the good. Therefore, they can be ordered based on the notion of the difficult or based on the notion of the good.

In the first way, courage comes first, temperance second, and prudence third, [with justice fourth], because it is more difficult "wisely to choose what to do" than it is "to render to each his own." Aristotle seems to follow this order in his *Ethics*. The reason for this is that "*ethikon*" in Greek is the same as "*consuetum* (habitual)" in Latin, and as virtue is more concerned with what is difficult, the more it needs the practice that produces virtue. Therefore, Aristotle arranges them based on how habitual they are.

But if they are ordered based on the goodness they contain, then, as Cicero proves by many arguments in *On Duties* 1, the goodness found in justice is better than all the others, because it moves beyond the proper exercise of the other virtues.[15] Consequently, in this respect justice will be first. And because the beautiful and the good, as Cicero says there,[16] are delimited in almost the same way, and the beautiful is especially the concern of temperance, it comes second, courage third, and prudence fourth. For prudence is somewhat similar to a craft, which does not itself contain its proper good, but its good is found in the other virtues.

If virtue is considered according to the order it has in relation to the subject in which it exists, then prudence comes first, with temperance second, courage third, and justice last. The reason for this is that there can be no correct action unless preceded by correct choice, so that prudence must be first. Likewise, one cannot be brave in adversity unless resolute in the face of pleasure, so that temperance comes before courage.

The book of *Wisdom*, however, considers yet a fourth order, namely, that some feature of temperance precedes prudence, for if our spiritual senses are not sober, our judgment will not make correct choices. For this reason, temperance is prior in act to prudence. And in act justice comes

[15] Cicero, *De officiis* 1.7.20.

[16] Cicero, *De officiis* 1.27.95.

before courage, because justice concerns the common good, which always is better than the private good.

One should note that there are many different orders among these virtues, and any number can be found which we have omitted, for otherwise there would be a very long enquiry about them in common, followed by consideration of each in particular.[17]

Art. 4: *Will the cardinal virtues remain with us in our heavenly homeland?*

The fourth question is: Will the cardinal virtues remain with us in our heavenly homeland?

[*Objections*:]

It seems they will not remain, because:

1. Faith, which is a theological virtue, and also hope will pass away. Therefore, even more so will civic virtues pass away.

2. We only employ what leads to the end (*ad finem*) for the sake of that end. Consequently, once the end is achieved it would be superfluous to maintain what leads to the end. Therefore, since these four virtues concern what leads to the end, it seems that they will not remain with us in the end, that is, in our heavenly homeland.

3. Why would they remain with us? For then there will be no traps which we must take precautions to avoid through prudence, nor will there be difficulties one must endure through courage; and the same for the other virtues. Therefore, they will not remain with us.

4. There seems to be less reason for acquired knowledge [not to remain] than political virtue, because knowledge concerns the incorruptible, while political virtue concerns particular, corruptible matter. But knowledge will be destroyed, as the Apostle says.[18] Therefore, virtue will also be destroyed.

[*On the Contrary*:]

After these arguments have been acknowledged, contrary to this is what the text of the Master says.

[17] This seems to be a reference to Albert's own mode of treating each of the cardinal virtues at length in his summa *On the Good*.

[18] *1 Cor*. 13:8.

Response:

It seems to me that the Master, using the words of the saints, debates this question well, and that he determines the question rightly, namely, that these virtues will remain but will have different acts. The reason for this is that those things which lead to some end and those which are ordered to that end are different when joined to the end than when they exist in what is ordained to that end. This is true for reason, free choice, and all other such powers, and so is also true for their habits.

Reply to Obj. 1: In agreeing with the words of the Master, I reply that the cases [of the theological and cardinal virtues] are not similar, because the reason why a virtue passes away or does not is not the same as why it is a theological or cardinal virtue. Rather, this is the reason, that imperfection in relation to its end is part of its very nature, as is the case with faith and hope, which are imperfect habits in comparison with their end. But these four virtues are not compared to our end, but are compared to what leads to that end. Therefore, when what leads to our end passes away, their imperfections will pass away, but they will remain in an act appropriate to our end, as the Master says.

In this way the replies to the second and third objections are clear.

Reply to Obj. 4: Knowledge will be destroyed only in part, in so far as it derives from sense. For then we shall not have knowledge in that way, but by means of forms bestowed by the creator, as angels possess knowledge. Therefore, as something imperfect knowledge will be destroyed. But this is not true of virtue, because in some way virtue will join our end, as a disposition which is both perfected and perfective of us. Therefore, virtue will remain, as the Master says.

One should note that there are those who take a totally opposite position; but because I think their view is unreasonable, I do not follow their opinions.

Book Three, Dist. 36[1]

Three questions come up about the first part of this distinction. The first is: Are the political virtues connected to each other? Assuming they are not connected, the second question is: Are the theological virtues necessarily connected to each other? If the theological virtues are connected to each other, the third question is: Are vices or sins connected to each other, or not?

Art. 1: *Are the political virtues connected to each other?*

1. In *On Consideration to Pope Eugene* Bernard says: "Note that there is the sweetest harmony and connection among the virtues, and that one virtue depends upon another. For example, right here you see that prudence is the mother of courage, and that daring not born of prudence is temerity, not real courage."[2] Therefore it seems the virtues are connected.

2. In the same book Bernard says that for every virtue the mean is what "justice seeks, prudence finds, courage protects, and temperance possesses."[3] Therefore, since these are necessary to every virtue, it seems the political virtues are connected.

3. Seneca says: "Everything which happens rightly, happens justly, and happens bravely, and temperately."[4] But the function of every virtue is to happen rightly. Therefore, it happens justly and bravely and temperately. Therefore, these four virtues dovetail together in every virtuous deed. But they could not dovetail in every deed unless they were connected in the acting subject. Therefore, they are connected.

4. Cicero says: "If you lose one of your Corinthian vases, you can say the rest of your belongings are safe; but if you lose one of your virtues, then you have to confess that you no longer have any virtue."[5] Therefore, if you have one, you have all; but if you lose one, you lose all.

[1] Albert, *In 3 Sent.* d. 36. 1, ed. Borgnet 28: 665-7.
[2] Bernard, *De consid.* 1.8.9.
[3] Bernard, *De consid.* 1.8.11.
[4] Seneca, *Ep. 66.* 15.
[5] Cicero, *Tusc. Disp.* 2.14.32.

5. Jerome says to Pammachius: "The Stoics say the four virtues are so closely connected to each other and mutually conjoined that whoever does not have one, lacks all."[6] And whoever does have one, has all.

6. Augustine says to Jerome: "The Stoics seem to me to make a mistake, because they deny that a man progressing in wisdom has any wisdom at all, but only when he is perfect do they say he is wise."[7] Therefore, it seems that according to Augustine, one progressing in wisdom and one perfect in wisdom are both fully wise. However, one is not fully wise, unless wise about every virtue. Therefore, he has every virtue; therefore, whoever has one has all; therefore, the virtues are connected.

Argument seems to lead to the same conclusion:

7. As one power is related to another power so one habit is related to another habit. Now the inferior powers, which are parts of the sensitive soul, such as desire and emotion, are ordered and perfected only by reason. Therefore, the habits perfecting these powers will not be perfected without habits which perfect reason. Now the habits of the inferior powers are temperance and courage, and the habits of the rational power are prudence and justice. Therefore, temperance and courage must be connected to justice and prudence.

8. Prudence is the virtue by which one wisely distinguishes what helps us from what impedes us. But prudence only makes choices concerning the matter of justice, temperance, and courage. Therefore, prudence cannot exist without the other three; and by the same argument they cannot exist without prudence. Therefore, the virtues are connected.

9. Knowing and choosing are required for every virtuous deed. But these acts belong to prudence. Therefore, prudence is required for every virtuous deed. Likewise, since the function of every virtue is to hit between excess and defect, every virtuous deed necessarily requires temperance. And since a virtuous deed is what one ought to do, justice seems required. Therefore, it seems that in each virtuous deed all the virtues must be connected to each other.

10. Every virtue concerns the difficult. But "courage protects" us from the difficult, as Bernard says.[8] Therefore, every virtuous deed requires courage.

[6] Jerome, *Ep. 66 ad Pammachium,* PL 22: 640; CSEL 54: 649; p. 210 below.

[7] Augustine, *Ep. 167* (to Jerome) 12; pp. 212-13 below.

[8] Bernard, *De consid.* 1.8.11, 3: 407. Cf. Obj. 2, p. 142.

11. Whoever is chaste has virtue. But whoever has chastity is chaste. Therefore, whoever has virtue is virtuous. Therefore, he is not vicious. Therefore, from the first premise it follows that whoever has chastity is not vicious. But someone is vicious because of just one vice. Therefore, there is no vice in the person who has chastity. Therefore, the opposites of the vices, that is, each one of the virtues, are in him. Therefore, whoever has chastity has all the virtues. Therefore, the virtues are connected.

On the contrary: [*arguments against the connection of virtues*]

1. Augustine says to Jerome that it is not revealed doctrine where it says: whoever possesses one virtue possesses all. Therefore, it seems that this view is not necessarily true.[9]

2. The political virtues are generated by actions. But actions are different from each other, and exist as so divided off from each other. Therefore, the habits produced from them should also be different. Therefore, it seems that it is not necessary that the virtues exist together.

3. In deeds performed, someone can be chaste yet greedy. But from similar actions similar habits result. Therefore, habits of both chastity and greed will arise in this person. But liberality cannot be present together with the habit of greed. Therefore, someone who has chastity does not necessarily have liberality. Therefore, it is not true that whoever possesses one virtue possesses all.

Response:

There were many disagreements among the philosophers about this matter.[10] For some of them said that actions do not generate virtues but only produce a disposition for receiving virtues. Virtues are actually given by substances which, by reason of the perfection of their wisdom, are separate and above the four natural affections, namely, fear, hope, joy, and sadness (or perturbation). And they said that the first three affections remain ordered in the unified virtue of the sage, but not perturbation (or sadness), which does not even befall the sage. This was the opinion of the Stoics.

They took their notion of virtue from its real or potential ultimate end. And they said that someone who is prudent in some limited way is not

[9] Augustine, *Ep. 167* (to Jerome) 10; p. 212 below.

[10] matter] Lat. *malitiam* (Borgnet ed.).

prudent unless universally prudent about the acts of all the virtues. Therefore, they said that whoever has one virtue has all the virtues.

Their strongest argument was this: Every virtue either exists in reason or comes from reason. Therefore, every virtue perfects reason in some way. And perfect reason, such as is found in the sage, which orders but is not ordered, is found only where it is perfect both in itself and in relation to its subordinate virtues. Now this cannot happen through one virtue, but through all the virtues. Therefore, they said that the perfection of the sage requires the presence of every virtue. Now whoever is not a sage but performs some virtuous deed, they say is in disposition to virtue but does not have virtue. For actions do not generate virtue, but virtue comes from intelligences that are separate substances. This account is taken from the words of Augustine given above,[11] where he says that the Stoics denied that someone progressing toward virtue has virtue at all, but admitted only perfect virtue.

Since Augustine disapproves of this opinion, one should follow Aristotle's view in the *Ethics*. Political virtues, which are based on patterns of behavior, are generated by deeds, while the intellectual virtues come with experience and age. Because the things producing these virtues are not connected with each other, therefore these virtues themselves have no connection.

[*Replies to objections*:]

In reply to objections 1 - 6 coming from authorities there is one solution, namely, that there are certain general acts of the virtues, and in relation to these acts the virtues are not distinguished from each other. And there is something of each one of these in every virtue. For in each virtue there is some *object of choice*, but this object is not proper to prudence. Likewise, in each virtue there is something *difficult*, but this difficulty is not proper to courage. Rather, courage concerns difficulty covering a limited matter, namely passion introduced from without.[12] Likewise, a *mean* between excess and deficiency is found in every virtue, but this is not proper to temperance. Rather, temperance concerns the matter of natural passions concerning the pleasures of taste and touch. And the *obligation* (*debitum*) found in every virtue is not the obligation justice treats. Rather, justice concerns matter related to neighbor, according to natural or positive law.

[11] P. 143 above.

[12] from without] Lat. *secundum sensum tactus* (Borgnet ed.).

Therefore, I reply: The virtues are connected, with regard to what in a general way encompasses every deed. But even if this is attained, one does not necessarily have all the specific types of virtues. For this is not a feature of some specific virtue, except through adaptation. But it is a disposition of the matter [of the virtues] in general, in which later this virtue or that achieves its proper nature.

Replies to the objections based on arguments:

Reply to Obj. 7: It is true that the habit of reason rules the habits of desire and emotion, as the power of reason rules the powers of desire and emotion. But it does not follow that possessing one entails possessing another, except in a limited respect. For whoever is chaste has the prudence to make the choices required for chastity, but he does not possess prudence absolutely speaking.[13] And sometimes the chaste person is not at all courageous in the proper sense of the term.

Reply to Obj. 8: One can be prudent in different particular matters in different ways. But being prudent in one of these ways does not necessarily make one prudent absolutely. Or another answer is that being virtuous in one way does not make one virtuous in other ways, because, on the contrary, many people act virtuously in one way and not in another.

Reply to Obj. 9 and 10: The *difficult* and the *mean* found in an act of general virtue are not proper to courage and temperance, except in a limited respect and by appropriation. Therefore, these arguments do not prove that these virtues are present absolutely, but only in a limited respect.

Reply to Obj. 11: Whoever has chastity is chaste, but it does not follow that he is virtuous. For because being virtuous signifies more than the genus of chastity, it involves a fullness which is present only in one who attains all the species of virtue. Therefore, the logical movement here is not just from species to genus, but from a specific habit to the generic habit, along with an accident which is the relation of participation in all the species of virtue. Therefore, the argument is invalid, just as the following argument is invalid: This is a human, therefore this person participates in every species of animal.

[13] Cf. Aristotle, *Nic. Eth.* 6.5 (1140a25-8).

Art. 2: *Are the theological virtues connected to each other?*

The second question is: Are the theological virtues connected to each other?

[*Objections*:]

It seems that they are connected:

1. Perfection ought to correspond to what is perfect. But what is perfect is the soul, not without its parts, its powers united in one substance. Therefore, the perfection which is grace does not exist without the virtues being united in the very nature of grace.

2. There is no accord between Christ and Belial.[14] Therefore, one cannot at the same time be a vessel of God and a vessel of the devil. But through theological virtue informed by grace one is a vessel and temple of God, and consequently not a vessel of the devil. But since every vice makes one into a vessel of the devil, [whoever is a vessel of God] has no vice. Now vices are only removed by their opposing virtues. Therefore, whoever has one [virtue] informed by grace has every virtue.

3. Augustine says that it is impious to hope for less forgiveness from God. Therefore, whoever receives forgiveness of sin through one virtue which expels sin also receives forgiveness through virtue expelling all sin. Therefore, whoever has one virtue has all. Likewise, whoever has charity has perfection in merit, and consequently has everything by which one can gain merit. But that is every virtue. Therefore, he has every single virtue.

4. On *Isaiah* [66:11] "My wind sounds to Moab, as does the lyre," the gloss says: "The lyre does not emit a composite sound if one chord has been broken. Likewise, the spirit or wind of the prophet, if one virtue is missing, will not sound as sweet as honey." Therefore, all the virtues must be present.

5. *James* 2:10 says: "Whoever keeps the whole law but fails in one point has become guilty of all of it." Therefore, arguing from the opposite: whoever has one virtue has all.

6. On the text "I made a judgment,"[15] the gloss reads: "From the part to the whole, so that whoever has one virtue has them all, and whoever lack one lacks them all."

[14] Cf. *2 Cor.* 6:13.

[15] *Ps.* 118:121.

On the contrary:

1. If someone has one virtue, he has them all. But Christ had one virtue, because he had charity. Therefore, Christ had faith, which is false. The same argument holds for the blessed who have charity but do not have faith.

2. If one said that the claim whoever has one has all the virtues should be understood as referring to the state of a pure wayfarer, then there is a counter-example, because an innocent has charity but has no penitence.

3. Likewise, someone possessing charity does not necessarily have virginity.

4. If you reply that virginity signifies a virtue along with a state, but one can have the virtue without the state, I object: The argument can be put about the kind of perseverence apart from which there is no salvation. And it is true that whoever has charity does not necessarily have perseverence.

5. We see expressly that whoever has faith and hope need not have charity. Therefore, whoever has one need not have all.

6. When charity grows, our initial fears diminish, as is proven above in Lombard's text.[16] Therefore, fear is lost. Yet fear is a virtue, if virtue is taken generally. Therefore, it is not true that whoever has one virtue has them all.

7. About every saint we read that no one was found like him. But this cannot be true about the kind of body he had or about his nature. Therefore, it refers to his virtue. Consequently, every saint has a virtue which the other saints do not have. Therefore, it is not true that whoever [has one virtue has them all].

Response:

Virtues which are both infused and well-formed are connected, so that when we have one we have all of them. But this connection falls into three types: The first and most important comes from grace, which is a potential whole in relation to the virtues. Therefore, just as the perfection of a potential whole consists in all its parts taken together and united in a whole, so also the perfection of grace consists in all the virtues taken together and united in a whole. To see how this happens, and how grace differs from virtue, consult Bk. 2.[17] Therefore, for the perfection of grace to

[16] Peter Lombard, *Sent.* 2 d. 34. 3-9, 2: 191-8.

[17] Albert, *In II Sent.* d. 26-27.

exist in the essence of the soul and in its powers every virtue must be infused by grace. The second kind of connection comes from charity, which is the form of every virtue as far as the existence of merit is concerned. In order that what is well-formed be proportioned to its form, all the virtues must be infused along with charity. And how it happens that charity is the form and end of virtue is noted in the tractate on charity given above.[18] The third kind of connection is mentioned in the objections. This is the kind of connection which is a function of the general sense of justice, which justifies us and does not permit the presence of any vice. Since vice is not formally expelled except through its opposing virtue, all the virtues must be present.

Based on this response, the replies to the objections are clear.

[*Replies to the arguments to the contrary*:]

Reply to argument to the contrary 1: Whoever has one has all the virtues in the sense of having what is essential and is part of their perfection. In this respect, Christ did have faith, because he had that knowledge which belongs to the perfection of faith, and he had it comprehensively, which is like a perfection corresponding to hope.

Reply to argument to the contrary 2: Penitence signifies a virtue which is moved to detest sin, with the additional accident that there is sorrow for sin committed. It can exist in an innocent in its essential act, which is hatred of sin as sin; but what is accidental to penitence cannot exist in an innocent person. Now the term penitence is taken from this accident. Therefore, an innocent is not said to have penitence, even though he does have the essence of the virtue of penitence.

Reply to argument to the contrary 3: Virginity signifies continence, along with the accident of a certain bodily state. Now such an accident is not part of every virtue, even though the virtue is.

Reply to argument to the contrary 4: Perseverence is said in two ways: the sense of perseverence proposed in the argument and the habit which moves us to persevere, but it is this habit which is found in every virtue.

A second reply: Perseverence is the consummation of good acts. But this happens only at the last instant of life. Therefore, this is not a virtue, but a gift given by God at the end of life. Therefore, it is not necessary to have this gift with every virtue.

[18] Peter Lombard, *Sent.* 3 d. 23.3.2, 2: 142.

Reply to argument to the contrary 5: The claim is made about well-formed virtues, not about unformed virtues. But the faith and hope which exist without charity are unformed, not well-formed virtues.

Reply to argument to the contrary 6: When charity grows the imperfection of fear decreases, but the essence of the fear of the Lord remains forever. How this happens was explained in the question on fear.[19]

Reply to argument to the contrary 7: This is said of the saints when speaking about how they make use of their virtues, but not about the habit of their virtues. Or one can say that according to some thinkers, this point concerns grace freely given, not actual grace. The first answer, however, seems better and more in accord with the writings of the saints.

Art. 3: *Are the vices also connected?* [omitted]

Art. 4: *Are well-formed virtues on a par or equal with each other?*

The next question concerns this point of the Master: "Does one possess all the virtues equally?" Two questions arise about this part of the Master's text. The first is: "Are well-formed virtues on a par or equal with each other?" The second question is: "If one virtue is intensified, is the other virtue as well?"

Objections to the first Question [art. 4]

1. The text of the Master says that the cardinal virtues are "on a par (*pares*)";[20] therefore, even more so the theological virtues must be.

2. It was said above[21] that faith, hope, charity, and action are "equal"; therefore, so are the other virtues.

3. If in the same person one virtue were stronger or better than another, then the one virtue would make him a better person and possessed of more merit than another virtue would. Therefore, the same human would be both good and better, more and less worthy of eternal life, which is incorrect. Therefore, it seems the virtues are on a par with each other.

4. All the virtues are infused together. But if they were not on a par when infused, then it would follow that the increase one has over another

[19] Cf. Peter Lombard, *Sent.* 3 d. 34.3-9, 2: 191-8.

[20] Peter Lombard, *Sent.* 3 d. 36.2.4, 2: 203.

[21] Peter Lombard, *Sent.* 3 d. 25.5.1, 2: 158.

comes either from its efficient cause or from the grace which infused it. But it is agreed that it could not come from the efficient cause, because God, who is the efficient cause of infused virtue, is related equally to all the virtues infused together. Therefore, he creates as much of one virtue as another. Likewise, if the increase came from the subject, since these virtues exist continually in the subject, they should grow continuously, which is false. And if the increase came from grace, then the same human would necessarily have more grace in one virtue than in another, and consequently would be more or less graced in different parts of the soul. But this is ridiculous, because all the parts of the soul of every human are equally graced by God.

On the contrary:

1. In distinction 35 it was said many are strong in faith but not in knowledge.[22] Now knowledge is a gift, and it is a virtue, if we take the term virtue broadly. Therefore, the virtues are not on a par or equal.

2. 1 Cor. 13:12 says: "Now there abide faith, hope, and charity, these three; but the greatest of these is charity."

Response:

The virtues are on a par in *essence* and in their *formation* by grace. They are equal in essence because simple entities are in the same genus with regard to their simplicity and there is one amount of grace in a given human. They are equal in their formation by grace because actual grace equally informs all the virtues.

But in four other respects, which are consequences of the essence of virtue, the virtues are unequal. The first concerns their worth, because charity, which nothing exceeds, is greatest and of all the virtues the most worthwhile. The second concerns the universals: form, end, and agent. In this way too charity is greatest, because charity moves us in a general way to meritorious deeds, which no other virtue does. Charity is also the form and the end of the virtues, and in this respect is greatest. The third concerns how a virtue is rooted in its subject, because a disposition becomes more rooted through actions. But the virtues are not all activated with equal frequency. Therefore, whichever one produces deeds more frequently

[22] Peter Lombard, *Sent.* 3 d. 35.1.3, 2: 199, quoting Augustine, *De trin.* 14.1.3, CCSL 50a: 423.

is also more rooted than other virtues. The fourth mode concerns use, for virtues which are equally present in essence do not have to be equally used.

[*Replies to the arguments to the contrary*:]

Reply to argument to the contrary 1: This point concerns the use of a virtue.

Reply to argument to the contrary 2: This point concerns the worth of the virtues.

[*Reply to the objections*:]

In this way the reply to all the objections is clear.

Art. 5: [Q. 1] *If one virtue is intensified are all intensified?*
[Q. 2] *And, does charity alone suffice for salvation?*

[Q.1] The second question [in this part of the distinction] is: When one virtue is intensified are all intensified?

[*Objections to Q. 1*:]

It seems that they are:

1. On the assumption that one could be intensified and another not, then the virtues would be able not to be on a par. But this is contrary to what was just proven. Therefore, when one virtue is intensified the other must be intensified.

2. Intensification of the virtues only happens through intensification of grace. But grace is in each one of the virtues. Therefore, each one of them is intensified equally.

3. Virtue is only intensified by God for the sake of merit, as was often shown above.[23] But God is related equally to all the virtues, and merit, as designed to elicit all meritorious acts, is equally present in all the virtues. Therefore, since the reasons why the virtues are intensified are related equally to all the virtues, it seems they must all be intensified equally.

4. If it is necessary that when one has one virtue one has all the virtues, owing to their connection in grace and how charity binds them together, then for the same reason it seems necessary that when one is intensified then all must be intensified.

[23] Peter Lombard, *Sent.* 3 d. 18, 2:111-114.

5. In *On the Trinity* 6 Augustine says "The virtues which exist in the human mind, though they are different when understood one by one, cannot be separated but are always equal."[24] Therefore, if one is intensified, then the others also must be intensified, because otherwise they would grow unequal.

[*Arguments to the contrary to Q. 1*:]

1. Intensification seems to come from deeds. But it does not seem that all the virtues operate equally. Therefore, the virtues are not equally intensified.

2. The reasoning which says that when one virtue is intensified another is also intensified, owing to charity informing them equally, does not seem valid. For in the physical realm we see that two equally combustible things do not heat up at the same rate when they are equally distant from the same fire. Consequently, the same thing can be true for the virtues, that one receives more from the heat of charity than from another.

3. As was said above, when charity grows, wisdom also grows and fear diminishes.[25] Therefore, fear and wisdom are unequal virtues.

4. In different people their virtues are not equal; therefore, in the same person they can also be unequal.

[Q. 2] Connected to this question is the following: Does charity alone suffice for salvation, without the other virtues?

[*Objections to Q. 2*:]

It seems charity does suffice:

1. Merit and the amount of merit are determined based on charity alone. Therefore, it seems the other virtues are superfluous, since we do not possess virtues except for the sake of merit.

2. Augustine says that "charity alone divides the children of the kingdom from the children of perdition."[26] Therefore, we have the other virtues to no purpose.

3. In the following section of this distinction it says that charity alone fulfils the law, and even if we should not succeed in accomplishing all we

[24] Augustine, *De trin.* 6.4.6, CCSL 50: 233.

[25] Peter Lombard, *Sent.* 3 d. 35.4-8, 2: 192-7.

[26] Augustine, *De trin.* 15.17.31, CCSL 50a: 507.

want, it says that we have charity, "which completes all."[27] Therefore, it seems that charity alone suffices and that the other virtues are superfluous.

Response [to Q. 1]:

To the first part of the issue I respond: In one way when one virtue is intensified all the others are as well, but in another way one virtue can be intensified without another. For if virtue is related to its efficient cause, or to how meritorious it is, or if it is considered in its substance, then one virtue cannot be intensified without another. But if it is related to how it is rooted in its subject, then one virtue can be intensified without another. For this comes from deeds in which virtues are not necessarily conjoined, but can be divided.

[*Replies to the objections to Q. 1*:]

This makes clear the reply to all the objections about q. 1, since those arguments proceed according to this distinction.

[*Replies to the arguments to the contrary to Q. 1*:]

Reply to argument to the contrary 1: In its operation a virtue is intensified only based on being rooted in its subject. This I concede, for in this way one virtue can be intensified without another being intensified.

Reply to argument to the contrary 2: The cases are not similar, because wood and other physical things are not equally receptive of fire, but the virtues, in so far as they are infused, are equally able to be formed by charity.

Reply to argument to the contrary 3: Fear does not decrease substantially as it is a gift of the Holy Spirit, but only decreases as something imperfect, as was often said elsewhere.

Reply to argument to the contrary 4: The virtues in different people do not have some connection in one person whereby they increase when he increases; but in one person they are so connected, through charity and grace. Therefore, when charity and grace are intensified, all the virtues must be intensified.

[*Response to Q. 2*:]

Charity is sufficient as a moving cause. But motion requires not only a universal mover but also a particular mover, through which an act is spe-

[27] Peter Lombard, *Sent.* 3 d. 36.3, 2: 205.20.

cified. Here there is a similarity between nature and man. For in nature the sun is a universal moving cause of generation; but for the generation of this or that thing there must also be a particular moving cause in this or that thing, for example, in the case of beans or peas. In a human, however, reason moves us in our physical activities, or will does, but the motion of foot or hand require a particular mover of the foot or hand. Likewise, in motions which involve merit, the universal mover is charity, but they require movers specifying acts as acts of faith or hope or temperance, by which we earn merit.

[*Reply to the objections to Q. 2:*]

In this way the reply to all the objections is clear, for the arguments offered draw conclusions only about the power of the universal moving cause, not about the power of a particular moving cause.

Thomas Aquinas

Disputed Question on the Cardinal Virtues

[ca. 1271-1272]

This question concerns the cardinal virtues

Art. 1. *The first issue: Are prudence, justice, courage, and temperance the four cardinal virtues?*[1]

It seems they are not:

1. For things which are not distinguished from[2] each other cannot be counted in relation to each other, since distinction is the cause of number, as John Damascene says.[3] But these virtues are not distinguished from each[4] other, as Gregory says in his *Moralia*: "That prudence is not truly prudence, which is not just and temperate and brave; nor is that temperance whole, which is not brave, just and wise; nor is that courage whole, which is not wise, temperate, and just; nor is that justice real, which is not wise, brave, and temperate."[5] Therefore, these virtues ought not be called *four* cardinal virtues.

2. It seems that virtues are called cardinal because they are principal virtues in relation to others. Consequently, the virtues some call cardinal they sometimes also call principal. This is clear from Gregory's *Moralia* 22.[6] Since the end is more a principal factor than the means, the theological virtues, which have the ultimate end as their object, seem more to be the

[1] Parallel passages: Aquinas, *In 3 Sent.* d.33. 1.1.3 ad 3m and 2.1.3; *ST* 1-2.61.1-4; *In Nic. Eth.* 2. lec. 8; *De vir. in com.* 12 ad 23-27m; Alexander of Hales, *Glossa in 3 Sent.* d.33. n.1-7, ed. Quaracchi 3: 381-392; Bonaventure, *In 3 Sent.* d.33. 1.1, 3-5, ed. Quaracchi 3: 711-712, 715-724.

[2] ab *P7,O2,V9*] ad *M.*

[3] *De fid. orth.*, ed. E. Buytaert 184.27-185.30: "The three persons of the holy Trinity are united inconfusedly, and are distinct inseparably, and are numbered, but number does *not* produce in them distinction or separation or alienation or severance." If number does not imply ontological distinction in God, $\sim(N \supset D)$, it does in creatures, $(N \supset D)$ or $(\sim D \supset \sim N)$. From Gregory, the objector adds $(CV \supset \sim D)$; therefore, $(CV \supset \sim N)$. This objection strongly unifies the cardinal virtues, and Aquinas uses it to set up the problematic for his whole treatment of the cardinal virtues, in Reply to obj. 1.

[4] ab *P7, O2,V9*] ad *M.*

[5] Gregory, *Moralia* 22.1.2, CCSL 143a: 1093.39-43.

[6] Gregory, *Moralia* 22.1.2, CCSL 143a: 1093.39-43.

principal virtues than the four virtues under consideration, which are about means. So we ought not call these four the *cardinal* virtues.

3. We should not try to coordinate[7] things which are in different genera. But prudence is one of the intellectual virtues, as is clear from *Ethics* 6;[8] while the other three virtues are moral virtues. Therefore, it is wrong to posit these four as the cardinal virtues.

4. Among the intellectual virtues, wisdom is more a principal virtue than prudence, as the Philosopher proves in *Ethics* 6.[9] For wisdom is about divine matters, prudence only about human matters.[10] If there must be an intellectual virtue[11] among the cardinal virtues, it would be better to put wisdom[12] there, since it is more a principal virtue.

5. The other virtues must be reduced to the cardinal virtues. But in *Ethics* 2 the Philosopher divides courage and temperance off from certain other virtues, like liberality, magnanimity, and similar virtues,[13] without reducing these virtues to courage and temperance.[14] Consequently, the four virtues mentioned above are not the cardinal virtues.

6. What is not a virtue should not be listed among the cardinal virtues. But temperance seems not to be a virtue; for we can lack it even while possessing the other virtues. This is clear in the case of Paul, who had all the other virtues, yet did not have temperance. For desire was still in his members, according to *Rom.* [7.23]: "I see in my members another law at war with the law of my mind." The temperate person, however, differs from the continent. Someone with temperance does not have wrong desires; while the continent person has them, but does not follow them. The Philosopher makes this clear in *Ethics* 7.[15] Therefore, the four cardinal virtues mentioned have been enumerated incorrectly.

7. Just as virtue orders each human in relation to self, it also orders each in relation to neighbor. Now there have been posited two virtues through which a human achieves order in relation to self: courage and

[7] in *P7,O2*] una *add. M,V9.*
[8] Aristotle, *Nic. Eth.* 6.3 (1139b15-17); 6.5 (1140a24-b30).
[9] Aristotle, *Nic. Eth.* 6.7 (1141a16-33).
[10] humanis *P7,O2,V9*] Si igitur *add. M.*
[11] intellectualis *P7*] poni *add. M,O2,V9.*
[12] sapientia *P7*] quasi *add. M,O2,V9.*
[13] Aristotle, *Nic. Eth.* 2.7 (1107a33-08a1).
[14] et sic ad eas *O2,V9*] quae *add. P7*; quae sic *M.*
[15] Aristotle, *Nic. Eth.* 7.9 (1151b32-52a3).

temperance. Likewise, there should be two virtues through which one achieves order in relation to neighbor, not justice alone.

8. In *On the Practices of the Catholic Church*, Augustine says that virtue is the order found in love.[16] But the love coming from grace is comprehended within two precepts, love of God and love of neighbor. Therefore, there should be only two cardinal virtues.

9. Diversity of extended matter produces only numerical diversity; but diversity of matter coupled with diverse aspects of form produces difference in genus. This is why "destructible and indestructible things differ in genus," as it says in *Met* 10.[17] Now the differences among the four virtues under consideration come from the different ways matter receives form. For the way reason works in the matter of temperance is based on reining in the passions; but in the matter of courage it is based on actively striving for a goal when passion draws us away from it. Therefore, the four virtues differ in genus, and so ought not be joined together in one order of cardinal virtues.

10. The very nature of moral virtue depends upon attaining reason, as the Philosopher makes clear in *Ethics* 2, where he defines virtue as "what is in accord with right reason."[18] But right reason is a rule in turn ruled by the first rule, which is God, the rule from which reason receives the power to rule. Therefore, the moral virtues only possess the nature of virtue because they are connected to the first rule–God. But the theological virtues, which concern God, are not called cardinal virtues. So neither should the moral virtues be called cardinal virtues.

11. Reason is the principal part of the soul. Now temperance and courage are not found in reason, but in the irrational parts of the soul, as the Philosopher says in *Ethics* 3.[19] Therefore, they should not be placed among the cardinal virtues.

12. It is more praiseworthy to give from one's own possessions than to return or[20] take another's. Now the former pertains to liberality, while the

[16] Augustine, *De mor. ecc.* 1.15, PL 32: 1322.

[17] Aristotle, *Met.* 10.10 (1058b26-9).

[18] *Nic. Eth.* 2.6 (1106b36-7a2): "Therefore virtue is (a) habitual character, (b) concerned with choice, (c) lying in the mean relative to us, (d) determined by reason, and as the prudent person determines." Cf. Aquinas, *In Nic. Eth.* 2. lec. 7, ed. Leonine 47: 98.45-99.78.

[19] Aristotle, *Nic. Eth.* 3.9-10 (1117b20-4).

[20] vel *P7*] non *add. M,O2,V9.*

latter pertains to justice. Therefore, it would be better to posit liberality among the cardinal virtues, rather than justice.

13. The "firmament"[21] of the other virtues seems to have the greatest claim to being a cardinal virtue. But humility is this kind of virtue. For Gregory says that "whoever accumulates the other virtues without humility is like one throwing chaff[22] into the wind."[23] Therefore, humility should be posited as a cardinal virtue.

14. "Virtue is a kind of completion," as is clear from the Philosopher, *Physics* 6.[24] But the epistle of *James* [1:4] says "patience produces a completed work."[25] Therefore, patience, because it is a completion, should be placed among the cardinal virtues.

15. The Philosopher says that magnanimity produces "the greatest deeds among the virtues," and is "like an ornament for the other virtues."[26]

[21] Gregory, *Hom. in Ez.* 1.8.20, CCSL 142: 112.416-420, is an allegorical interpretation of Ezechiel's vision (*Ez* 1.4-28). Ezechiel saw four animals, each with the faces of a human, lion, ox, and eagle, dragging a wheeled chariot. "And over the heads of the animals there was something like the firmament, looking like a dazzling crystal, extending down over their heads" (*Ez* 1.22; Vulgate). Above the firmament Ezechiel saw a throne, then something with "the aspect of a man." Falling down, he heard a voice.

Gregory's interpretation: The wheels of the chariot are Scripture, the four animals the four evangelists, the throne angels, the man Jesus, the voice is God the Father's. Virtue descends from God to angels to humans (1.8.19-20, 111.387-112.416). Following Gregory, the objector thinks the firmament is the cardinal virtues, conceived as Christian virtues bestowed by God. Cf. Gregory, 1.8.18, 110.339-343. Here Aquinas introduces the infused cardinal virtues.

[22] paleas *P7,O2,V9*] pulveres *M*.

[23] Gregory, *Hom. in evan.* 1.7.4, PL 76: 1103A.48-49. Cf. "So in all you do, my brothers, hold tight to humility, the root of every good work."

[24] Aristotle, *Physics* 7.3 (246b28).

[25] *James* 1.2-4: "Consider it a great joy, my brothers, when you come upon various trials, knowing that testing your faith produces patience. But patience produces a completed work, so that you might be complete and whole, deficient in no way" (Vulgate).

[26] Aristotle, *Nic. Eth.* 4.3 (1123b30; 1124a1-2). Cf. Aquinas, *In Nic. Eth.* 4. lec. 8, ed. Leonine 47: 228.202-210. The "magn-animous" man (Gr: *megalo-psychos*, Lat: *magn-animus*) has a "great-soul," and does not appear to be humble. Obj. 13 and 15 thus oppose Christian to pagan virtue.

This opposition was complicated by the way Aristotle had been translated. The opposite of *megalopsychos* is "small-souled (*mikro-psychos*)," translated "pusill-ani-

This seems especially to pertain to being a principal virtue. Therefore, magnanimity seems to be a cardinal virtue; and so the four cardinal virtues mentioned are listed incorrectly.

On the contrary:

is what Ambrose says about "Blessed are the poor in spirit" in *Luke*:[27] "We know there are four cardinal virtues: temperance, justice, prudence, courage."[28]

Response:

The term cardinal is taken from *cardo*, the hinge on which a door turns, as in *Proverbs* [26:14]: "As a door turns on its hinges, so does a sluggard on his bed." Therefore, we call those virtues cardinal on which a human way

---

mous," a way of lacking courage. *Humilitas* had a more checkered career. In the *Ethica vetus, humilis* translated *praotes*, the virtue of being "even tempered." Later translators, Robert Grosseteste and William of Moerbeke, called this virtue *mansuetudo*, gentleness. They used *humilis* to translate *tapeinos* (1124b22 and 1125a2), meaning "lacking in self-respect," a vice. Cf. *Anon. in Eth. Nic.* 4.9, ed. Mercken: 344.77-80, which joins *pusillanimitas* and *humilitas* as synonyms and vices, and Gauthier, *Magnanimité* 445n2.

Aquinas argues that magnanimity and humility are consistent with each other in two different ways: (a) First, he says there is no real opposition between them, because they concern two different areas. Magnanimity is a species of courage (*ST* 2-2.129.3c), whose opposing vice is pusillanimity–lacking the courage to pursue goods "commensurate" with one's "own potential" (2-2.133.1c). Humility falls under the cardinal virtue of temperance. Humility is moderation about wanting goods hard to obtain (*boni ardui*), while magnanimity is courage to go after such goods when that is appropriate (2-2.161.1c). (b) But Aquinas does recognize the deep conflict between antique magnanimity and Christian humility. His final answer, therefore, is to baptize magnanimity, rather than cede it to the pagans:

"In a human is found something great, which comes as *a gift of God,* and something defective, which comes from *the infirmity of nature*. Magnanimity, therefore, makes a human attain dignity for himself in great matters *in view of the gifts he possesses from God*...Humility, on the other hand, makes a human esteem himself low *in view of his own natural defects*...Thus it is clear that magnanimity and humility are not contrary to each other, though they seem to tend in contrary directions, because they concern diverse features of the human." *ST* 2-2.129.3 ad 4m. Cf. *In 3 Sent.*d.33. 2.1.4 ad 2m et 3m, 3: 1050.167-1051.170.

[27] super illud Lucae Beati pauperes spiritui *P7,O2,V9*] *om. M.*

[28] Ambrose, *Exp. evan. sec. Luc.* 5.62, CCSL 14: 156.670-2.

of life is founded, and through which as through[29] a door one proceeds.[30] But that way of life is human which is proportioned to the term[31] human being.[32] In a human, however, we find: first, a sensitive nature which is common with the brute animals; practical reason, which is proper to the human level of reality; and theoretical intellect, which is not found in a human as completely as in the angels, but according to a kind of participation. Therefore,[33] the contemplative life is not properly human, but superhuman; while the life of pleasure, which is bound up in sensible goods, is not human but bestial. Therefore, the properly human way of life is the active life, which consists in living out the moral virtues. Therefore, those virtues are properly called cardinal on which the whole moral life,[34] in a manner of speaking, turns, and on which, like a set of principles for such a life, it is founded. This is why virtues of this sort also are called the principal virtues.

One should note that about the nature of a virtuous act four features stand out: The first of these is that the substance of the action itself must be intrinsically *modified*. In this respect, an action is called good when it stands, as it were, in the right matter and[35] is clothed with the right circumstances. The second is that the action must be related to the acting subject in the right way, that is, it[36] must inhere in the acting subject *reso-*

[29] sicut per *P7,O2,V9*] in *M.*

[30] Moral deeds and virtues of the active life are like a door (*ostium*). Cf. Albert, p. 123. Its hinges (*cardines*) are the four cardinal virtues. The door is designed to lead "somewhere else," Reply to obj. 4. At *In 3 Sent.* d.33. 2.1.sol.2, 3: 1046.143-1047.145, Aquinas said that place is an Augustinian inner room, part of a contemplative, monastic life lived on earth. At *Reply obj. 4* here and *ST* 1-2.3.1,8 that place is heaven, where there is full "contemplation of wisdom" itself, that is, of God. Cf. *De vir. in com.* 12 ad 24m.

[31] nomini *P7,O2,V9*] homini *M,Am2.*

[32] In Latin, the noun *homo* and the adjective *humanus* come from the same root, unlike English *man* and *human*. Cf. C. Lewis and C. Short, *A Latin Dictionary*, 1969 imp., 859-60,869. *Oxford English Dictionary* 2 ed., 1989, 7:473; 9:284. Aquinas uses this etymological fact to make the point that a way of life (*vita*) deserves the adjective "human (*humana*)" when its activities are proportioned to the nature which the term (*nomen*) "human being (*homo*)" signifies. Translating *homo* as "man" would obscure the point.

[33] Et *P7,O2,V9*] animae *M.*

[34] tota vita *P7,O2,V9*] Vita *M.*

[35] et *P7,O2,V9*] vel *M.*

[36] id est, quod *P7,O2,V9*] ex quo *M.*

lutely. The third is that the action must be proportioned in the right way toward something extrinsic as its *end*. Now these three features come from the part of the agent which is directed by reason. The fourth feature, however, comes from the part of reason which directs the action, that is, *thought*.

Now the Philosopher touches on these four features of virtuous action in *Ethics* 2, where he says that it does not suffice for virtue that things are "done justly and temperately," which pertains to *modifications* placed on the action. But three other things are required of the agent: First, the agent must be "knowing," which pertains to *rational direction*; next, the agent should "choose and choose for this reason," that is, for the sake of the right end, which pertains to *correctness* of the action as ordered to something extrinsic; and the third is whether the agent acts "*resolutely* and immovably out of habit."[37] Now these four things–*rational direction, correctness, resolution*, and *moderation*–are required for *any* virtuous action.[38]

Nonetheless, each of these four features has a kind of primacy covering certain specific matters and acts:

In the area of practical thought three things are required: The first is deliberation, and the second is judgment about matters under deliberation, just as investigation (or enquiry) and judgment are found in theoretical reasoning. Since the practical intellect sets out precepts for avoiding or pursuing ends, which the theoretical intellect does not do, as is said in *On the Soul* 3,[39] it follows that the third thing that pertains to practical reasoning is planning before the fact about what should be done. Now this is its special feature, toward which the other two are ordered. A human is perfected in the first aspect of practical thinking through the virtue of *eu-*

[37] habeat *P7,V9,textus Aris. in Leon.*] adhaereat *M.* Aristotle, *Nic. Eth.* 2.4 (1105a28-33): "If the acts that are in accordance with the virtues have themselves a certain character it does not follow that they are done (a) justly or temperately. The agent also must be in a certain condition when he does them; in the first place he must have (b) knowledge, secondly he must (c) choose the acts, and choose them for their own sakes, and thirdly his action must proceed from a (d) firm and unchangeable character." Cf. Aquinas, *De vir. in com.* 12 ad 26m. At *In Nic. Eth.* 2. lec. 4, ed. Leonine 47: 87.37-88.86, Aquinas is oddly silent about the cardinal virtues.

[38] Cf. *In 3 Sent.* d.33. 2.1.3 sol., 3: 1047.149; *ST* 1-2.61.2c (with no reference to Aristotle); *De vir. in com.* 12 ad 26m. A different interpretation of Aristotle is given at *ST* 1-2.61.4 obj. 3. Also see pp. 94, 122 above.

[39] Aristotle, *On the Soul* 3.9 (432b26-8).

bulia, which means deliberating well. In the second, a human is perfected through *synesis* and *gnome*, by which one comes to judge well, as is said in *Ethics* 6.[40] But it is through prudence that reason comes to apply practical precepts well, as Aristotle says in the same book.[41] Consequently, it is clear that *prudence* incorporates what is special about *rational direction*. Therefore, in this particular area prudence is placed among the cardinal virtues.

Likewise, *correct action* in relation to something extrinsic has something of the nature of a good and also is praiseworthy in what pertains to one person alone, but the greatest praise is reserved for those actions done in relation to others, as, for example, when a human acts correctly, not only in matters pertaining to self, but also where he acts in common with others. For the Philosopher says in *Ethics* 5 that "the many can exercise virtue about their own affairs, but cannot when it comes to their relations with others."[42] Therefore, in this particular area, *justice*, through which a human in the right way joins together in equity with others with whom he has to act in common, is placed among the principal virtues. And this is why in everyday speech actions which are joined together in the right way are said to follow common custom.[43]

Moderation or restraint is especially praised and has the nature of a good where passion's urge is especially strong and reason needs to restrain it in order to achieve the mean which constitutes virtue. Now passion's urge is greatest in pursuit of the greatest pleasures, those connected with touch. Therefore, in this particular area of activity *temperance*, which restrains desires connected with touch, is placed among the cardinal virtues.

Resoluteness is especially praised and has the nature of a good in those things where passion most vehemently urges us to flee. This is especially true of the greatest dangers, those concerned with the danger of death. Therefore, in this particular area *courage*, through which a human faces mortal dangers,[44] is placed among the cardinal virtues.[45]

[40] Aristotle, *Nic. Eth.* 6.9-10 (1142a31-3b16).

[41] Aristotle, *Nic. Eth.* 6.10 (1143a8).

[42] Aristotle, *Nic. Eth.* 5.1 (1129b33-30a1).

[43] usitata *P7,V9*] iusta *M.* Aquinas' pun does not come through in English. Customary actions (*usitata*) are also just (*iusta*).

[44] pericula *P7,Am2,As,Ve2*] intrepide se habet *add. M.*

[45] Cf. *In 3 Sent.* d. 33. 2.1.1sol., 3: 1045.135. Arguments (1) and (3) of *CV* are used at *ST* 1-2.61.2 to establish the *general* cardinal virtues; argument (2) of *CV* is used at 1-2.61.3-4 to show that each of the *special* cardinal virtues has a specific "matter." Cf. *De vir. in com.* 12 ad 23m.

Among these four virtues, prudence exists in the faculty of reason, while justice exists in the will, courage exists in the emotional part of the soul, and temperance in the desiring element. Now these powers are the *only* ones which can be the principles of a human action, that is, of a voluntary act.[46]

Consequently, the argument for the cardinal virtues is clear: [1] the argument taken from the modes of a virtue, which are like its formal aspects; [2] the argument taken from matter, and [3] the argument taken from the subject of each virtue.

[*Replies to Objections*:]

Reply to Obj. 1: Some speak about the four cardinal virtues in two ways:[47]

Certain thinkers[48] use these four terms to signify *general modes* of the virtues. They call all rational direction prudence; they call all correctness producing equity among human acts justice; all moderation restraining human appetites from worldly goods they call temperance; all resoluteness of mind steadying a human in the good and against the assaults of all sorts of evils they call courage. This is how Augustine seems to use these terms in his book *On the Practices of the Church*. And the quote from Gregory can be understood this way, because without all the conditions mentioned above dovetailing together, one of these conditions by itself is insufficient to produce the true nature of virtue. According to this way of thinking, therefore, the four things mentioned are called four virtues, not because

[46] Cf. *In 3 Sent.* d. 33. 2.1.3 sol., 3: 1047.149; *ST* 1-2.61.2c; *De vir. in com.* 12 ad 25m.

[47] The "some" are Philip, Albert, and perhaps Bonaventure. "It should be noted that one can speak about political virtues of this sort either in relation to what is proper to them (*propria*), or in relation to what is appropriated to them (*appropria*). If we are talking about what is appropriated, then there is a connection among the cardinal virtues, because the four conditions...such as discerning and following the mean etc., are appropriated to each one of these four virtues, yet at the same time every single virtue requires them all." Bonaventure, *In 3 Sent.* d. 36. 1.4c, ed. Quaracchi 3: 798.

[48] Here Aquinas mentions only Gregory and Augustine, but he knew other Christian adherents of this view: Ambrose, Jerome, Bernard of Clairvaux. At *In Nic. Eth.* 2. lec. 8, Aquinas follows Albert in attributing this view to Cicero and Seneca. At *CV* 1c and *ST* 1-2.61.4 obj. 3, the four general aspects of virtue are attributed to Aristotle.

they are different specific habits understood in relation to different objects, but because they are different formal aspects of virtue.

Other thinkers, however, like Aristotle in his *Nicomachean Ethics*, speak about the four virtues under consideration in so far as they are *special virtues* limited to their proper matter.[49] Now the quotation from Gregory is true when interpreted this way, as well: Through a kind of overflow, these four virtues concern those areas where the four general conditions of virtue we have mentioned are pre-eminently important. In this way, therefore, courage is temperate and temperance is brave, because whoever can restrain his own appetites so as not to follow the desire for pleasures–which pertains to temperance–even more can restrain the tendency to be daring in danger. Likewise, whoever can stand resolutely against the danger of death, even more can stand resolutely against the allurements of sensual pleasure. In this way, what belongs principally to temperance is transferred to courage, and the reverse is true as well. And the same reasoning holds for the other virtues.

Reply to Obj. 2: Human desire rests when it attains its end. Therefore, the theological virtues, which concern the final end, are not principal virtues in a way comparable to a doorhinge (*cardo*), which undergoes motion, but more like a foundation or a root, which stands stable and is at rest, following *Eph.* [3:17]: "Rooted and grounded in love."

Reply to Obj. 3: According to the Philosopher in *Ethics* 6, prudence is "right reason about things to be done." "Things to be done," however, are moral deeds, as is clear from what he says there.[50] Therefore, prudence agrees with the moral virtues as far as its subject-matter is concerned. This is why it is counted along with them, even though in its own essence and its subject-power it is also[51] an intellectual virtue.

Reply to Obj. 4: Wisdom, since it is not about human but divine matters, has no subject-matter in common with the moral virtues. Therefore, it cannot be counted along with the moral virtues so as to be denominated with

[49] Aristotle never presents the cardinal virtues as an identifiable unit; but Aquinas attributes to him a doctrine of cardinal virtues as "special" virtues. Cf. *In 3 Sent.* d.33. 1.1.3 ad 3m, 3: 1023.41; *ST* 1-2.61.3-4; *De vir. in com.* 12 ad 23m.

[50] Aristotle, *Nic. Eth.* 6.5 (1140b20-1) and 6.13 (1144b22-8). This famous formula for prudence (*recta ratio agibilium*), and the corresponding one for art (*recta ratio factibilium*), while not found in the Latin Aristotle, occur in Albert. Cf. Aquinas, *In Nic. Eth.* 2. lec. 4, ed. Leonine 47: 87.44-5n.

[51] et subiectum et *P7,Am2*] et subiectum *V9*; vel subiectum *M*.

them a cardinal virtue, because the very notion of "doorhinge (*cardo*)" is inconsistent with contemplation. Contemplation[52] is not like a door, by means of which one goes somewhere else. Rather, moral deeds are the door through which one enters into the contemplation of wisdom.

Reply to Obj. 5: If the four mentioned virtues are understood as signifying the general conditions of virtue, in this respect all the special virtues the Philosopher treats in the *Ethics* are reduced to these four virtues, as species are reduced to their genera.

On the other hand, if the four virtues are understood as special virtues concerned with certain principal matters, other virtues are also reduced to them, but as what is secondary to what is principal.[53] This is the way ready-wit, which moderates the pleasures concerned with being funny, can be reduced to temperance, which moderates the pleasures of touch.[54]

Therefore, when[55] Cicero, in *Rhetoric* 2,[56] posits the other virtues as parts of these four,[57] this can be understood in two ways: In one way, following the first way of understanding the cardinal virtues, the parts are subjective parts. In the other way, when the cardinal virtues are understood in the second way, the parts are potential parts. This is the way sense is a potential part of the soul, because it does not signify all the power of the soul, but one power in it.

Reply to Obj. 6: It is not part of the nature of temperance to exclude all wrong desires, but the temperate person does not suffer such "strong and ardent desires" as do those who have not made the effort to rein in their desires. Therefore, Paul suffered desires which were inordinate due to the corrupting influence of flashes of passion, but not because they were "strong and ardent," since he made an effort to repress them, castigating

[52] quae *P7,V9*] quia *M.*

[53] principale *P7*] principales *M,V9.*

[54] Aristotle, *Nic. Eth.* 2.7 (1108a22-6): "With regard to pleasantness in the giving of amusement, the intermediate person is ready-witted and the disposition ready wit, the excess is buffoonery and the person characterized by it a buffoon, while the man who falls short is a sort of boor and his state is boorishness." Ross tr. Aristotle connected ready-wit with two other specific virtues–truthfulness and friendliness. Aquinas turns away from its specific subject-matter and connects ready-wit with the source of its formal character–temperance, because the witty person controls the ability to make clever remarks. Cf. *De vir. in com.* 12 ad 26, 2: 747.

[55] quod P7,V9] et M.

[56] Cicero, *De inv.* 2.53-4.

[57] quatuor *P7,V9*] quod *add. M.*

his body and bringing it into submission.[58] Therefore, he really was temperate.

Reply to Obj. 7: Justice, through which we attain order in relation to others, is not about our own passions, but about the operations by which we join in common with others, like buying and selling, and other such things. But temperance and courage are about our own passions. Therefore, just as a human has one appetitive power separate from passion–the will, but two appetitive powers which involve passion–desire and emotion, so there is one cardinal virtue ordering a human in relation to neighbor, but two cardinal virtues ordering a human in relation to self.

Reply to Obj. 8: Charity is called the whole of virtue, not in its essence, but as a cause, since charity is the mother of all the virtues. There is always more in the effects than in the cause. Therefore, there must be more multiplicity in the other virtues than in charity.

Reply to Obj. 9: Different modes of reception can be due to the matter which receives form in different ways,[59] which produces difference in genus; or due to the form which is received by matter in different ways. This kind of diversity produces difference in species, and is relevant here.

Reply to Obj. 10: The moral virtues are connected to reason as their proximate rule, and to God as their primary rule. But things receive their species from their proximate[60] principles, not their primary principles.

Reply to Obj. 11: The principal part of a human is the rational part of the soul. But rational is used in two ways: what is essentially rational and what is rational through participation. Just as reason itself is more a principal part of the soul than the powers participating in reason, so prudence is more a principal virtue than the other virtues.

Reply to Obj. 12: The cardinal virtues are said to be more principal virtues than all the others, not because they are more perfect than all the rest, but because the human way of life turns principally on them and the other virtues are founded on them. It is clear that the human way of life turns more on justice than on liberality; for we make use of justice in our relations to all, but are liberal only toward a few. And liberality itself is founded on justice. For a gift is not an instance of liberality[61] unless one gives from his own possessions; but it is through justice that we distinguish one's own from what belongs to others.

[58] *1 Cor.* 9:27.

[59] diversimode *V9*] in *praef. P7,Am2*; *om. M.*

[60] proxima *P7,Am2*] propria *V9*; propria et proxima *M.*

[61] liberalitas *P7,Am2*] liberalis *M,O2,V9.*

Reply to Obj. 13: Humility does fortify all the virtues, but indirectly, by removing what works against the virtues functioning rightly, thereby destroying them. The cardinal virtues, by contrast, fortify the other virtues directly.

Reply to Obj. 14: Patience is contained within courage. For the brave man has what the patient one has–not being distraught by threatening evils; but bravery adds something else–fighting as required against those threatening evils.

Reply to Obj. 15: From magnanimity being the "ornament to the other virtues," it clearly follows that it presupposes the other virtues, on which it is based. From this it is clear that the others are more the principal virtues than magnanimity.

Art. 2. *The second issue: Are the virtues so connected that whoever has one virtue has them all?*[1]

It seems not:

1. Bede, in his commentary *On Luke*, says the saints are more humbled about the virtues they do not have, than exalted about the virtues they do have.[2] Therefore, they have some virtues, but do not have others. Therefore, the virtues are not connected.

2. After penance a human is in the state of charity. But in the area where one has sinned it is still difficult to act, because of a prior pattern of behavior, as Augustine says in *Against Julian*.[3] Consequently, difficulties like these seem to arise from a habit contrary to virtue, acquired[4] through

[1] Parallel passages: Aquinas, *In 3 Sent.*d.36. 1-2, 3: 1214-1220; *In 4 Sent.*d.33. 3.2 ad 6m, ed. Vives 11: 158; *Quod.* 12.15.1, ed. Marietti 233; *In Nic.Eth.* 6. lec.10-11, ed. Leonine 47: 369-377; *ST* 1-2.65.1-2. Alexander of Hales, *Glossa in 3 Sent.* d.36. n.1-4, ed. Quaracchi 3: 445-6. Bonaventure, *In 3 Sent.* d.33. 1.2, ed. Quaracchi 3: 713-715, d.36. 1.1, 3 (ed. Quaracchi) 3: 791-793,796-799.

[2] Bede, *In Luc. evan. exp.* 4, CCSL 120: 286.2225-2236. Cf. 4, 325.1179-1192, on being "humiliated to glory."

[3] Augustine, *Contra Jul.* 2.3.5, PL 44: 675-6, where he refers to baptism, not penance. (On private confession as a medieval development, *NCE* 11.73-75): "And if you [Julian] would consider this matter attentively and without stubbornness, truly you would find in the force of habit (*consuetudo*) itself how concupiscence is remitted in its guilt and remains in its action." tr. Schumacher

[4] acquisito *P7,O2,V9*] acquisitam *M.*

a bad pattern of behavior. Now the virtue contrary to this bad habit cannot exist along with the bad habit. Therefore, one can possess one virtue–charity–and lack others.

3. Charity is present in all who have been baptized. But some of the baptized do not possess prudence. This is especially clear in the mentally retarded and in children,[5] who cannot be prudent, according to the Philosopher.[6] This is also true of some simple-minded adults, who do not really seem to be prudent, because they do not really deliberate, which is the task of prudence. Therefore, it is not the case that whoever has one virtue–charity–has all the others.

4. According to the Philosopher in *Ethics* 6, prudence is right reason about things to be done, as craftsmanship is right reason about things to be made.[7] But a human can have right reason about one kind of thing made, for example, things made with tools, and not have right reason about other things which require skill. Therefore, one also can have prudence about one kind of thing to be done, for example, just acts, yet not have it about another type, like courageous deeds. In this way one can have one virtue without the others.

5. In *Ethics* 4 the Philosopher says that not everyone who is liberal is also magnificent,[8] yet both liberality and magnificence are virtues. Likewise, he says that some have attained the mean, but do not possess greatness of soul.[9] Therefore, not everyone who has one virtue has all the virtues.

6. In *1 Cor.* the Apostle says "there are varieties of gifts," and afterwards he divides them: "To one is given through the Spirit the utterance of wisdom, to another the utterance of knowledge," which are intellectual virtues, "to another faith,"[10] which is a theological virtue. Therefore, someone can have one virtue but not another.

[5] iuvenibus *P7,O2,V9*] phreneticis *M*.

[6] Aristotle, *On the Soul* 3.4 (429a4-8). Cf. Aquinas, *In de An.* 3. lec. 6. n. 670, ed. Marietti 223.

[7] Aristotle, *Nic. Eth.* 6.4 (1140a6-10) on art; 6.5 (1140b20-21), 6.13 (1144b22-8) on prudence.

[8] Aristotle, *Nic. Eth.* 4.2 (1122a28-29).

[9] Aristotle, *Nic. Eth.* 2.7 (1107b24-30). As liberality, which concerns small amounts of wealth, is related to magnificence, which concerns great wealth, so an "unnamed" (30) moderation, which concerns small honors, is to magnanimity, which is exhibited on the field of larger, civic honors.

[10] *1 Cor.* 12:4,8,9.

7. Virginity is a kind of virtue, as St. Cyprian says.[11] But many who have not maintained virginity possess other virtues. Therefore, it is not true that whoever possesses one virtue has them all.

8. The Philosopher says in *Ethics* 6[12] that we call Anaxagoras and Thales wise, but not prudent. Now wisdom and prudence are intellectual virtues. Therefore, someone can have one virtue without the others.

9. In the same book of the *Ethics* the Philosopher says that some people have an inclination to one virtue, but not to another.[13] Therefore, it can happen that someone performs the actions of one virtue, but not the actions of another. Now some virtues are acquired through performing their operations, as the Philosopher says in *Ethics* 2.[14] Therefore, at least the acquired virtues are not connected.

10. A virtue, even if connected in regard to its inherent tendency, is not connected in regard to its complete being, as is said in *Ethics* 2.[15] It is clear that this connection is not fortuitous, because what comes by chance lies outside choice. Therefore, it remains that we acquire virtue either in the way proposed or from God. If acquired in the way proposed, one virtue can be acquired without another, because one can have an intention to acquire one virtue, but not another. And the same thing is true for virtues coming from God, because one can petition God for one virtue, but not another. Therefore, whichever way virtue is acquired, one virtue can exist without another.

11. The end in moral matters is related to virtuous moral actions as principles in demonstrations are related to conclusions. But a human can draw one conclusion without another, and therefore can have one virtue without another.

12. In a letter about the meaning of the epistle of *James* 2:10, Augustine says that "it is not revealed doctrine where it says: Whoever possesses one virtue possesses all,"[16] but a human can possess one virtue without

[11] Cyprian, *De habitu virginum* n.23, CSEL 3.1: 205, where Cyprian exhorts virgins to "summon one another to glory by emulating one another's deeds of *virtue*" (n.23; 205). At n.3, 189, virgins are "the flower of the living plant which is the Church." Cf. Aquinas, *In 4 Sent.* d.33. 3.3 obj. 2, ed. Vives 11: 158. Augustine, *De doc. chris.* 4.21.47, CSEL 32: 153-4; and 4.21.49, 156.

[12] Aristotle, *Nic. Eth.* 6.7 (1141b2-8).

[13] Aristotle, *Nic. Eth.* 6.13 (1144b4-9).

[14] Aristotle, *Nic. Eth.* 2.1 (1103a14-3b5 and b21-25).

[15] Aristotle, *Nic. Eth.* 2.1 (1103a24-6).

[16] Augustine, *Ep.* 167.3.10, CSEL 44: 596.10-1. The objector misrepresents Augustine. On the debate between Augustine and Jerome, who tried to distance Am-

another, for example, mercy without continence. Likewise, one part of a physical body can be outstanding or beautiful or healthy, while another is not. Therefore, the virtues are not connected.

13. Things are connected either by reason of their causes or their subjects or their objects. But the virtues are not connected by reason of their cause, which is God, because on this reasoning all goods which come from God would be connected. Nor are they connected by reason of their subjects, which are individual souls, because on this argument no virtuous actions performed by different people would be connected. Nor are they connected by reason of their objects; because they are distinguished through their objects, and the same thing cannot be the source of distinction and connection.[17]

14. The intellectual virtues have no connection with the moral virtues. This is most clear about understanding principles, which we can possess apart from the moral virtues. But prudence is an intellectual virtue which also is considered one of the cardinal virtues. Therefore, it has no connection with the other cardinal virtues, which are moral virtues.

15. In heaven there will be no faith or hope, but charity will exist there.[18] Therefore, even in their most complete state the virtues will not be connected.

16. The angels, who lack sensitive powers, and separated souls possess a kind of charity and justice which are everlasting and immortal. But they do not have temperance and courage, because these virtues concern the irrational parts of the soul, as is said in *Ethics* 3.[19] Therefore, the virtues are not connected.

17. Just as there are virtues of the soul, so too there are bodily virtues. But there is no connection among the bodily virtues. For example, someone who is deaf can still see. Therefore, neither is there a connection among the virtues of the soul.

18. Gregory in his *Homilies on Ezechiel* says that "no one becomes outstandingly good all of a sudden."[20] And *Psalm* 83:8 says "they go from

---

brose's doctrine of unified, Christian cardinal virtues, from the overstated unity of virtue in the Stoic sage, see Albert, pp. 143-6.

[17] connexionis *P7,O2,V9*] Ergo, etc. *add. M.*

[18] erit fides et spes non, autem *P7,V9*] non erit fides et spes, sed tantum M; non (*marg.*) erit fides et spes, erit autem *O2*.

[19] Aristotle, *Nic. Eth.* 3.10 (1117b13-4).

[20] Gregory, *Hom. in Ez.* 2.3.3, CCSL 142: 238.53. *Ez.* 40:6, "he climbed the steps," Gregory understands allegorically to refer to the levels of "the virtues" (49).

virtue to virtue." Therefore, a human does not acquire the virtues all at once, but one after another. Therefore, the virtues are not connected.

On the contrary:

1. is what Ambrose says in his *Exposition of the Gospel of Luke* and in *On Duties*: "[The virtues] are connected and chained together, so whoever has one seems to have them all."[21]

2. Gregory, in *Moralia* 22, says that "if one virtue were possessed without another, either it would not be a virtue at all, or not a complete virtue."[22] But completion is part of the very nature of virtue, for a virtue is a kind of completion, as is said in *Physics* 6.[23] Therefore, the virtues are connected.

3. The gloss on *Ezechiel* 1:11, "Two wings, each of which touched," says that the virtues are conjoined, so whoever lacks one, lacks the others.[24]

Response:

We can speak about the virtues in two ways: in one way about complete virtues and in the other way about incomplete virtues. Now complete virtues are connected to each other, while incomplete virtues are not necessarily connected.

As evidence of this one should understand that, since virtue is what renders a human good[25] and his deed good, that virtue is complete which renders a human deed completely good and so the human himself good.[26] By contrast, that virtue is incomplete which renders a human and his deed good, not absolutely, but only in some particular way.[27]

[21] Ambrose, *Exp. evan. sec. Luc.* 5.63, CCSL 14: 157.677-8. Ambrose continues: "and there accrues to the saints *one* virtue, but to that [virtue] which was more plentiful, more plentiful is the reward." Cf. *De off.* 2.9.48, PL 16: 123b, where the doctrine of the unity of the virtues is said to come "from divine Scripture, which is even older" than the sayings of philosophers.

[22] Gregory, *Moralia* 22.1.2, CCSL 143a: 1093.34-5.

[23] Aristotle, *Physics* 7.3 (246b28).

[24] *Glossa ordinaria* on *Ez.* 1:11, 3: fol.225. Cf. Jerome, *Com. in Hiez.* 1:11, CCSL 75: 16.351.

[25] bonum *P7,O2,V9*] facit *add. M.*

[26] hominem bonum *P7,O2,V9*] facit *add. M.*

[27] Aquinas adapts two distinctions from Aristotle to explain the difference between complete (*perfecta*) and incomplete (*imperfecta*) virtue:

(a) At *Nic. Eth.* 6.13 (1144b14-7) Aristotle distinguishes "principal (Gk: *kuria*, Lat: *principalis*)" virtues, which are genuine moral habits, from "natural" virtues, inborn natural inclinations. Because he already (art. 1) has called the four cardinal

Human actions are good absolutely when[28] they attain the rule guiding human actions. Now there is one rule which is, as it were, homogeneous with and proper to humans; this is right reason. But there is a second rule, which is like a primary measure, transcending all; and this is God. Now a human attains right reason through prudence, which is "right reason about things to be done," as the Philosopher says in *Ethics* 6.[29] And a human attains God through charity, according to *1 John* [4:16], "he who abides in love abides in God, and God abides in him." Consequently, there are three levels of virtue:[30]

For some virtues are altogether incomplete. These remain separated from prudence and do not attain right reason. Examples are the inclinations which some have for certain virtuous deeds, even from birth, as it says in *Job*: "From infancy compassion grew with me, and came forth from the womb with me."[31] Inclinations like this are not the same in all; but some are inclined to one thing, others to something else. These inclinations do not have the true nature of a virtue, because "no one makes wrong use of a virtue," as Augustine says.[32] But one can use such inclinations wrongfully and harmfully, when they are used without discernment. So a blind horse would be more destructive the faster it ran. For this reason, Gregory says in *Moralia* 22 that[33] the virtues, if they do not lead prudently to what they

---

virtues the "principal" virtues, Aquinas uses Gregory's terms to express Aristotle's distinction. (Cf. *To the contrary* 2.) Aristotle's "principal" virtues are Aquinas' "complete" virtues, while Aristotle's "natural" virtues Aquinas calls "incomplete."

(b) At 6.5 (1140a25-8) Aristotle distinguishes a person prudent about the good and useful "for himself," that is, "for living a whole life well," from one prudent about some particular area like health or physical strength. Aquinas calls the first prudent "absolutely (*simpliciter*)," the second prudent "about something limited (*circa aliquid determinatum*)" or "in relation to something particular (*ad aliquid particulare*)," *In Nic. Eth.* 6. lec.4, ed. Leonine 47: 345.25-38.

Aquinas uses these two Aristotelian distinctions to differentiate three kinds of virtue.

[28] humanis...quod *P7,V9*; *om. M,O2.*

[29] Aristotle, *Nic. Eth.* 6.5 (1140b20-1), 6.13 (1144b22-8).

[30] Cf. *ST* 1-2.65.1-2.

[31] *Job* 31:18 (Vulgate).

[32] Augustine, *De lib. arb.* 2.19.50, CCSL 29: 271.11. Cf. *Retrac.* 1.9.4, CCSL 57: 26.111-2. Aquinas here carefully limits himself to a genuine part of the "Augustinian" definition of virtue Peter Lombard had constructed at *Sent.* 2, d. 27, ed. Grottaferatta 1: 480.8-10.

[33] quod *P7*] ceterae *add. M,O2,V9.*

desire, "cannot be virtues at all."[34] Consequently,[35] inclinations, since they lack prudence, do not completely possess the nature of a virtue.[36]

The second level of virtues are[37] those which do attain right reason, but do not attain God himself through charity. In a way these virtues are complete, in comparison with the human good. But they are not absolutely complete, because they do not attain the first rule, which is the final end, as Augustine says in *Against Julian*.[38] Therefore, they fall short of the true nature of virtue, as moral inclinations without[39] prudence fall short of the true nature of virtue.

Third is the level of absolutely complete virtues, which are those combined with charity. For these virtues make a human action absolutely good, reaching, as it were, all the way to the highest end.

Finally, one should note that, just as the moral virtues cannot exist without prudence, for the reason given above, so prudence cannot exist without the cardinal virtues.[40] For prudence is right reason about things to be done. In every pursuit, attaining right reason requires that one make a

[34] Gregory, *Moralia* 22.1.2, CCSL 143a: 1093.34-5.

[35] et *P7,O2,V9*] ibi *M.*

[36] Aquinas weaves Scripture and two Fathers into his Aristotelian description in order to show that reason and revelation tell the same story. On their relation, E. Gilson, *Christian Philosophy: An Introduction* tr. intro. and c. 1.

[37] est *P7,Am2,O2,Ve2*; *add.* illarum *M.*

[38] Augustine, *Contra Jul.* 4.3.21, PL 44: 749. Julian of Eclanum had said that the cardinal virtues are equally good, regardless of one's purpose. Augustine replies: "You know that virtues must be distinguished from vices, not by their functions (*officia*) but by their ends...The virtues Epicurus introduced as handmaids of pleasure are such that they do whatever they do for the sake of obtaining or possessing pleasure. God forbid that true virtues serve anyone but Him to whom we say: 'Lord of virtues, convert us' (*Ps.* 79:8). Therefore, virtues which serve carnal pleasure or any temporal advantages or emoluments cannot be true. But virtues that render no service to anything are not true virtues. True virtues in men serve God, by whom they are given to men" tr. Schumacher.

[39] sine *P7,Am2,O2*] a *Ve2*; absque *M.*

[40] At *Nic. Eth.* 6.13 (1144b1-30) Aristotle had argued that prudence and moral virtue are connected in such a way that without prudence there can be no moral virtue $(\sim P \supset \sim MV)$ or $(MV \supset P)$. In c. 12 (1144a23-b1) Aristotle had argued the converse, that without moral virtue there can be no prudence $(\sim MV \supset \sim P)$ or $(P \supset MV)$, from which it follows that $(P \equiv MV)$. Aquinas then adds the correlative point about charity and the infused virtues: $(\sim IV \supset \sim Ch)$ or $(Ch \supset IV)$ and $(\sim Ch \supset IV)$ or $(IV \supset Ch)$.

correct assessment,[41] a judgment about the principles from which reason proceeds. For example, you cannot make a correct assessment[42] in geometry, unless you possess right reason about geometrical principles. About things to be done, however, the principles are ends, for they provide the reasons for doing things.[43] Now one makes a correct assessment of the end through the habit of moral virtue, because "the kind of person you are affects how the end appears to you," as the Philosopher says in *Ethics* 3.[44] So just as the good in accord with virtue seems desirable as an end to someone virtuous, so the correlative vice seems desirable to someone vicious. Taste in sick and healthy people is similar.[45] Consequently, whoever possesses prudence must necessarily also possess the moral virtues.

In a similar way, whoever has charity must necessarily have all the other virtues, as well. For there is charity in a human because of an outpouring from God, as is written in *Romans*: "God's love has been poured into our hearts through the Holy Spirit which has been given to us."[46] Now toward whatever God gives something an inclination, he also provides certain forms, which are the principles for actions and movements toward whatever those things are inclined by God. For example, God gives lightness to fire, by reason of which fire immediately and spontaneously tends upwards. Consequently, as the book of *Wisdom* says, he "orders all things well."[47]

[41] existimationem rectam *P7,O2,V9*] aestimationem et *M.*

[42] existimationem *P7,O2,V9*] aestimationem *M.*

[43] Aristotle, *Nic. Eth.* 6.12 (1144a32-3), 6.5 (1140b16-7).

[44] Aristotle, *Nic. Eth.* 3.5 (1114a32-b1), cf. 6.12 (1144a29-30,34). The quote Aquinas uses is part of an objection justifying bad actions on the subjectivist grounds that they seemed good to the agent. Aristotle replies: "If each person is in a way the cause of his own habits, each is also in a way the cause of what appears good" (b1-3). While recognizing such variations in what seems good, Aristotle is a moral absolutist who places the norm in a certain kind of person: "For the good person (Gk: *spoudaios*, Lat: *studiosus*) judges each thing rightly, and in each matter the truth appears to him. For each kind of moral habit has its own peculiar notion of the good and the pleasant, but the good person likely differs from the rest most of all in seeing the truth in each matter, being as it were a rule and measure of them" *Nic. Eth.* 3.4, 1113a29-33. The rule guiding moral action is objective, but only exists subjectively, within the prudent person.

[45] Aristotle, *On the Soul* 2.10 (422b4-10).

[46] *Rom.* 5:5.

[47] *Wis.* 8:1.

Therefore, it is also necessary that God pour into us, along with charity, forms which are like habits readily generating actions toward whatever charity inclines us. Now charity inclines us toward all virtuous acts, because, since it concerns the final end, it also involves all virtuous acts. For every art or virtue which includes the end governs those concerned with means, as military skill governs horsemanship, and horsemanship governs bridle-making, as is said in *Ethics* 1.[48] Consequently, it is in accord with divine wisdom and goodness that the habits of all the virtues be poured forth, together with charity. Therefore, *1 Cor.* says: "Love is patient, kind, etc."[49]

Therefore, if we consider the absolutely complete virtues, they are connected through charity in this way. For one cannot possess a virtue of this kind without charity, and once charity is obtained, all these virtues are obtained. And if we consider virtues which are complete, but at the second level, in relation to the human good, they are also connected in this way, but through prudence. For no moral virtue can exist without prudence, nor can one who lacks moral virtue possess prudence. On the other hand, if we consider the four cardinal virtues as signifying[50] the general conditions for virtue, in this respect they are connected in this way, that the presence of just one of these conditions, without fulfilling all four, is not sufficient to produce a virtuous act. Gregory, in *Moralia* 22,[51] seems to assign this reason for their connection.

[*Replies to Objections*:]

Reply to Obj. 1: Due to an inclination, whether from nature or grace, one has for the deeds of one virtue more than another, it does happen that someone more readily performs the actions of one virtue rather than another. This is the sense in which the saints are said to have some virtues, whose actions they more readily perform, and not to have other virtues, whose actions they less readily perform.

[48] Aristotle, *Nic. Eth.* 1.1 (1094a9-16).

[49] *1 Cor.* 13:4-8. Virtues at the third level are caused by God (infused), and they are the "end" toward which virtues at the two lower levels have an internal dynamic tendency. Far from separating infused and acquired virtues, Aquinas connects them as much as possible. Virtues at the natural level open us up to supernatural virtues, just as understanding lower levels of happiness opens the mind to a sense of beatitude reason cannot encompass. Cf. *ST* 1-2.2.1-8.

[50] important *P7,Am2*] *add.* quasdam *M,O2,V9.*

[51] Gregory, *Moralia* 22.1.2, CCSL 143a: 1093.35-43.

Reply to Obj. 2: Although a habit in its own nature produces prompt and enjoyable actions, it can be impeded by some additional factor. For example, one possessing the habit of knowledge sometimes cannot use that knowledge, due to being sleepy or drunk or some such condition. Likewise, whoever does penance obtains, along with grace, charity and the habits of all the other virtues, even though, due to tendencies remaining from earlier sinful actions, he finds it difficult to follow the virtues he has received as habits. This does not happen, however, in virtues acquired by performing actions, because such actions remove contrary tendencies at the same time that they produce habits of virtue.

Reply to Obj. 3: The person who is baptized, along with charity, also receives prudence and all the other virtues. But prudence does not guarantee that a human deliberate successfully about everything, e.g. trade or military affairs or such things, but only about what is necessary for salvation. Now no one in a state of grace lacks this knowledge, however simple-minded he might be, according to *1 Jn.* [2:27], "anointing teaches you about everything." But some of the baptized might be prevented from acting prudently, either[52] due to some physical incapacity, or[53] due to age, as in children, or due to some irregular disposition, as with the mentally retarded and the delirious.[54]

Reply to Obj. 4: Artifacts of different types have causes completely different from each other. Therefore, nothing prevents someone from having the skill to make one kind of artifact but not another. Moral principles, however, are so ordered to each other that a problem with one principle produces problems with the others. For example, if someone has a problem with the moral principle which says not to follow *all* desires, which pertains to the power of temperance, it will sometimes happen that following desires injures someone, and so violates justice. This is similar to the case where in one and the same art or science, for example geometry, error about one principle produces errors throughout the science. This is why one cannot really be prudent in the area of one virtue, without being prudent in all.

Reply to Obj. 5: One reply is that it can happen that someone is liberal but not magnificent, as far as the action is concerned. For the person own-

[52] vel *P7,O2,V9*; *om. M.*

[53] vel *P7,O2,V9*; *om. M.*

[54] Aquinas explains being delirious (*phreneticus*) as due to some physical cause disrupting the normal processes of perception. Cf. *In 2 Sent.* d.20. 2.2 ad 3m, 2: 514-5.

ing less can put what he has to use and engage in an act of liberality, but magnificence is beyond reach, even though he possesses the habit needed to engage in an act of magnificence, if he had enough money. And the same thing is true for moderation and magnanimity. This first response always holds for the infused virtues.

For virtues acquired through actions, however, a second reply is possible: Whoever has acquired the habit of liberality by putting a small amount of money to use, has not yet acquired the habit of magnificence. But through engaging in acts of liberality, he has a proximate disposition to acquire the habit of magnificence, through a bit more work. This is because whatever is near to having something seems as though it does have it. As it says in *Physics* 2: "What is lacking just a little seems as though it were lacking not at all."[55]

Reply to Obj. 6: By "wisdom" and "knowledge" the apostle Paul does not mean the intellectual virtues (which do not have to be connected, as will be shown below), nor the gifts of the Holy Spirit (which are connected in charity). Rather, he understands them as graces freely given. An example would be the person who so abounds in knowledge and wisdom as to be able to fortify others, to fortify them in faith[56] and knowledge of God, and to argue against those who contradict the faith. This is why Paul does not say "to one is given wisdom, to another science," but "to one is given *the utterance* of wisdom, to another *the utterance* of science." And this is also why Augustine says in *On the Trinity* 14 that "many of the faithful are not strong in this sort of science, though they are strong in the faith itself."[57] Faith here is not understood as the faith of the unformed believer (though some say this because the gift of faith is common to all). Rather, faith here means a kind of constancy or certainty about faith, which sometimes abounds even in sinners.

Reply to Obj. 7: According to some, virginity does not denominate a virtue, but a more complete state of virtue. But it is not necessary that everyone who has a virtue possess it in a complete way. Therefore, one can

[55] Aristotle, *Physics* 2.5 (197a29-30).

[56] fidem *P7,O2,V9*] finem *M*.

[57] Augustine, *De Trin.* 14.1.3, CCSL 50a: 424.61-2. He continues: "For it is one thing merely to know what a man must believe in order to gain the blessed life, which is none other than eternal life, but another thing to know how this may help the godly, and be defended against the godless, which the Apostle seems to call by the proper name of science." tr. Schumacher.

be chaste and have other virtues, without being a virgin.[58]

On the other hand, assuming virginity is a virtue, it will signify a habit of mind according to which a person chooses to preserve virginity for the sake of Christ. Now even those who no longer possess integrity of the flesh can have this habit, just as those without great wealth can have the habit of magnificence.

Reply to Obj. 8: The intellectual virtues are not connected to each other, for three reasons: First, because habits which concern different types of things are not ordered to each other, as was said about technical skills.[59] Second, because in the sciences principles and conclusions are not so interchangeable that whoever possesses the principles also has the conclusions; but this does happen in ethics, as has been said.[60] Third, because intellectual virtue has no relation to charity, which orders a human to his final end.

Also, virtues like these are ordered to certain particular goods. For example, geometry is ordered to making measurements about abstract quantities, physics is ordered to understanding changing things, and so on. Consequently, intellectual virtues are not connected for the same reason that incomplete virtues have been said not to be connected.

Reply to Obj. 9: There are certain virtues which direct a human concerning what commonly happens in life, such as temperance, justice, gentleness, and virtues like this. When a human performs the actions of one[61] such virtue, two things can happen: Either he performs the actions falling under the other virtues at the same time, and so acquires all the habits of such[62] virtues together, or he does well in the one and poorly in others, and then acquires a habit contrary to the virtue, and as a consequence prudence will be corrupted. But without prudence, a disposition acquired through virtuous actions is not truly a virtue, as has been said.[63]

Now once we have acquired habits of this sort about things which commonly happen in life, we already possess virtually–which is like having the appropriate disposition–certain other virtuous habits, those which govern

[58]Cf. *In 4 Sent.* d.33. 3.2c, ed. Vives 11: 157,where Aquinas says "the saints sometimes call virginity a virtue," meaning by virginity "a state of complete virtue."

[59] Reply to Obj. 4, p. 179.

[60] P. 177; Reply to Obj. 4, p. 179.

[61] unius *P7,O2,V9*] huius *M.*

[62] huiusmodi *P7,O2,V9*; *om. M.*

[63] P. 177.

actions which do not[64] happen frequently in our lives. The case here is like that of magnificence and magnanimity, already discussed.[65]

Reply to Obj. 10: Acquired virtues are brought about in the way proposed, through performing virtuous actions. So it is necessary that all these virtues be brought about at the same time in a human who proposes to acquire one virtue. He will not acquire this virtue, without at the same time acquiring prudence, which accompanies all the virtues, as was said.[66] Infused virtues, however, which are brought about by charity as though from a common root, are caused immediately by God, as has been said.[67]

Reply to Obj. 11: Principles and[68] conclusions in the speculative sciences cannot be interchanged in the way this can happen in ethics, as was said.[69] Therefore, in speculative science drawing one conclusion does not necessarily lead to another. But this would be necessary, if possessing the principles required having the conclusions as well, which is what the objector proposes.

Reply to Obj. 12: Augustine here is speaking about incomplete virtues, which are dispositions leading to virtuous actions. Augustine himself, on the other hand, shows the connections among the virtues in *On the Trinity* 6.[70]

Reply to Obj. 13: Virtues are connected by reason of their proximate cause, that is, a cause in their own genus, which is prudence or charity; they are not connected by reason of their remote and common cause, which is God.

Reply to Obj. 14: Among the intellectual virtues prudence is special in having a connection with the moral[71] virtues, by reason of its matter, for it concerns things to be done.

Reply to Obj. 15: In heaven, though hope and faith pass away, certain higher perfections–vision and comprehension–will replace them. And these are connected to charity.

Reply to Obj. 16: In angels and separated souls temperance and courage will not be directed toward those actions which they engender in the pre-

[64] non *P7,O2,V9*; *om. M.*
[65] P. 180.
[66] Pp. 176-7.
[67] P. 177.
[68] et *P7,O2,V9*] ad *M.*
[69] Pp. 176-7, 181.
[70] Augustine, *De Trin.* 6.4.6, CSEL 50: 233.1-234.11.
[71] moralibus *P7,O2,V9*; *om. M.*

sent life, moderating the passions of the sensitive part of the soul. Rather, they will be directed to other actions, as Augustine makes clear in *On the Trinity* 14.[72]

Reply to Obj. 17: The powers of the soul cannot be interchanged with its essence. For though no power of the soul can exist apart from its essence, the essence of the soul can exist without certain powers. For example, it can exist without the powers of sight or hearing, owing to destruction of the organs of which powers of this sort are the proper acts.

Reply to Obj. 18: A human is not outstanding simply due to possessing all the virtues, but due to having them in the highest degree.

Art. 3. *The third issue: In an individual[1] human are all the virtues equal?*[2]

It seems they are not:

1. 1 Cor [13:13] says: "So faith, hope, and love abide, these three; but the greatest of these is love." But greatness excludes equality. Therefore, in an individual human the virtues are not equal.

2. He replied[3] that charity has a greater act, but is not a greater habit. *To the contrary*: Augustine says in *On the Trinity* that "in things which are not great in size, being greater and better amount to the same thing."[4] But the habit of charity is better than the other virtuous habits, because it attains God more, according to *1 John* [4:16]: "he who abides in love abides in God." Therefore, the habit of charity is greater than the other virtues.

3. Perfection has precedence over what is perfected by it. But charity is the perfection of the other virtues, according to *Col.* [3:14]: "And above all these put on love, which binds everything together in perfect harmo-

[72] Augustine, *De Trin.* 14.9.12, CSEL 50a: 439.33-440.42. Cf. *CV* art. 4c, pp. 198-201 below.

[1] uno *P7,O2,V9*; *om. M.*

[2] Parallel passages: Aquinas, *In 2 Sent.*d.42. 2.5 ad 6m, 2: 1086-7; *In 3 Sent.* d.36. 4, 3: 1222-1224; *De malo* 2.9 ad 8m, ed. Marietti 2: 487; *ST* 1-2.66.2. Bonaventure, *In 3 Sent.* d.36. 1.5, ed. Quaracchi 3: 802-804.

[3] dicebat *P7,Am2*] dice *O2,V9*; dicendum *M.* "He replied (*dicebat*)," is a vestige of the actual classroom disputation and refers to the student respondent who offers the seven arguments *sed contra* and takes the side opposed to the objector.

[4] Augustine, *De Trin.* 6.8.9, CCSL 50: 238.8-9.

ny."[5] And *1 Tim.* [1:5] says: "the aim of our charge is love." Therefore, charity[6] is greater than the other virtues.

4. What is unconnected with imperfection is more perfect and greater, as what is less mixed with black is whiter. But the habit of charity is not mixed with imperfection. Faith and hope, however, are somewhat mixed with imperfection.[7] For faith concerns what is *not* manifest, and hope with what one has *not* attained. Therefore, charity, even when considered as a habit, is more perfect and greater than faith and hope.

5. In the *City of God* Augustine says: "Unless the virtues refer to God, they are vices."[8] From this one can conclude that the nature of virtue is perfected through being ordered to God. But charity orders a human more closely to God than do the other virtues, because it unites a human to God, according to *1 Cor* [7:17]: "he who is united to the Lord becomes one spirit with him." Therefore, charity is a greater virtue than the others.

6. The infused virtues have their origin in the grace which perfects them. But charity participates in grace more perfectly than the other virtues; for grace and charity are inseparable companions. Faith and hope, by contrast, can exist without grace. Therefore, charity is greater than the other virtues; and so the virtues are not all equal.

7. In *On Consideration* 1, Bernard says that "prudence is the mother[9] of courage,"[10] since without prudence courage falls down. But whatever is a principle and cause of something is greater and more powerful than that thing. Therefore, prudence is greater than courage; and so the virtues are not all equal.

[5] Paul uses a clothing metaphor to describe Christian virtue. Charity is like a belt or an outer garment which binds all the parts of the outfit together: "So put on, as the chosen of God, holy and beloved, heartfelt compassion, kindness, humility, modesty, patience. Bear with one another, if one of you has a complaint against another. As the Lord has forgiven you, so must you forgive one another. And over all these put on charity, which binds all together perfectly. And in your hearts let the peace of Christ rule, for which you have been called together in one body. And be thankful." *Col.* 3: 12-15.

[6] caritas *P7,O2,V9; om. M.*

[7] Fides autem et spes habunt aliquid imperfectionis admixtum *P7,V9; om. M,O2.*

[8] Augustine, *De civ. dei* 19. 25, CCSL 48: 696.7-10.

[9] mater] materia *M,P7,O2,V9.*

[10] Bernard of Clairvaux, *De consid.* 1.8.9, 3: 404.12.

8. The Philosopher says in *Nic. Eth.* 5 that justice "is the whole of virtue,"[11] while the other virtues are like parts. But the whole is greater than the part. Therefore, justice is greater than the other virtues, and so the virtues are not all equal.

9. In his *Literal Commentary on Genesis*, Augustine proves that if all things in the universe were equal, they would not be "all things."[12] But the virtues are possessed together, because they are connected, as has been shown.[13] Therefore, the virtues are not all equal.

10. The virtues are opposed to the vices. But the vices are not all equal. So neither are the virtues all equal.

11. We ought to praise virtuous actions. But some people are praised for one virtue, others[14] are praised for other virtues. This is why Cassian says in *Institutes* 5: "One is adorned with blooms of knowledge; another is firmly fortified with discretion; yet another is strengthened by the weight of patience; one is admired for the virtue of humility, another for the virtue of continence."[15] Therefore, not all virtues in an individual human are equal.

12. He said[16] that this inequality concerns acts, not habits. *To the contrary*: According to Aristotle in *Post. Anal.* 1, relatives must be intended together. But the proper definition of habit makes reference to act. For a habit is that "whereby someone acts when the time is right,"[17] as Augustine says in *On the Good of Marriage* 21. Therefore, if the action of one virtue is greater in a given human than the action of another virtue, it follows that the habits are also unequal.

13. Hugh of St. Victor says that acts augment habits.[18] Therefore, if virtuous acts are unequal, the virtuous habits will also be unequal.

[11] Aristotle, *Nic. Eth.* 5.1 (1130a9)

[12] Augustine, *De gen. ad lit.* 11.8.10, CSEL 28: 341.1-8.

[13] Pp. 174-8.

[14] quidam *P7,O2,V9*] quam *M.*

[15] John Cassian, *De. inst. coenob.* 5.4, 194.7-10.

[16] dicebat *P7,Am2*] dice *O2,V9*; dicendum *M.*

[17] Augustine, *De bono coniug.* 21.25, CSEL 41: 219.17-18. Augustine in this passage distinguishes two kinds of virtues, those working openly, and those which lie hidden, like the virtue of a martyr for withstanding trials yet to come (219:1-2).

[18] Hugh of St. Victor, *De sac.* 2.13.1, PL 176: 525c: "Thus then vices are the origin of sins from which are born the works of iniquity." 2.13.2, PL 176: 527a: "The soundness of vices is the integrity of virtues. The sound man operates; operating he is remunerated" tr. Deferrari.

14. A virtuous habit is related to its proper act in the moral realm, as a form is related to its proper motion or action in the natural realm. But in the natural realm, the more something possesses a form, the more it exhibits its operation or motion. For example, a heavier object tends downward more rapidly, and a hotter object heats things more. Therefore, in the moral realm the acts the virtues engender cannot be unequal, unless the habits of those virtues are unequal.

15. Perfections are proportional to the things which can be perfected. Now the virtues are perfections of the soul's powers, which are unequal, since reason exceeds the inferior powers it rules. Therefore, the virtues are also unequal.

16. In *Moralia* 22[19] Gregory says: "Blessed Job called increments in virtue steps, because he saw that the supreme munificence has given them to humans one by one, so that through them one might ascend, in order to[20] arrive at the rewards of heaven."[21] But where there are increments and steps, there is no equality. Therefore, the virtues are not equal.

17. All things so related that when one increases the other decreases are necessarily unequal. But it seems that when charity grows, faith[22] wanes; because the heavenly state, where charity is perfected, is the opposite of the state of the wayfarer, where faith finds a place. Now when one opposite increases, the other decreases. Therefore, charity and faith cannot be equal; and so the virtues are not all equal.

On the contrary:

1. Apocalypse [21:16], says that the sides of the city are equal. Now the gloss on this text says that these sides signify[23] the virtues.[24] Therefore, the virtues are equal.

2. In *On the Trinity*, Augustine says: "Those who are equal in courage are equal in prudence and temperance. For if you say they are equal in courage, but one person surpasses another in prudence, it follows that the courage of the second person is less prudent than the first. But for this rea-

[19] Moralium *P7,O2,V9*] et homil 15 in Ezech *add. M.*

[20] ut *P7,O2,V9*] et *M.*

[21] Gregory, *Moralia* 22.20.51, CCSL 143a: 1130.163-166. Cf. *Hom. in Ez.* 2.3.3, CCSL 142: 238.60-239.65.

[22] fides *P7,O2,V9*] aliud *M.*

[23] significantur *P7,O2,V9*] signantur *M.*

[24] *Glossa ordin.* on *Apoc.* 21: 16, ed. princeps, 1480, rpr.1992, 4: fol. 575.

son, they will not be equal in courage, since the courage of the first is more prudent than the second. And you will find the same thing is true about the other virtues, if you take the same approach to all of them."[25] But those who are equal in one virtue would not necessarily be equal in the other virtues, unless all the virtues in an individual human were equal to each other. Therefore, all the virtues in an individual human are equal.[26]

3. In his *Homilies on Ezechiel* Gregory says that faith, hope, charity, and action are equal.[27] Therefore, for the same reason all the other virtues are equal.

4. Ez. [46:22] reads: "the four compounds measured the same." The Glossa on this says: "by which we come to virtue." But things which are measured the same are equal. Therefore, all the virtues are equal.

5. John Damascene says: "The virtues are natural, and they exist in all things in equal measure, in the way accidents exist."[28] Therefore, the virtues are equal in their being.

6. A greater reward is owed to an action coming from a greater virtue. Therefore, if one virtue were greater than another in a given human, it would follow that both a greater and a lesser reward would be owed to the same person. But this is incorrect.

7. If the modality "simple being" entails a consequence in the modality "simple being," then the modality "more" entails a consequence in the modality "more." But simply possessing one virtue entails simply possessing all the virtues, because the virtues are connected, as has been said.[29] Therefore, possessing more of one virtue entails possessing more of all the virtues. Therefore, all the virtues are necessarily equal.

Response:

Equal and unequal refer to quantity, for the equal is[30] one in quantity, as the similar is one in quality, and the same one in substance, as *Met.* 5 makes clear.[31] Now quantity includes the notion of measure, which is found

[25] Augustine, *De Trin.* 6.4.6, CCSL 50: 233.3-234.10.

[26] Ergo omnes virtutes in uno homine sunt aequales *P7,O2,V9*; *om. M.*

[27] Gregory, *Hom. in Ez.* 2.10.17, CCSL 142: 392.445-450. At 40:47 Ezekiel is describing the square inner court in his dream-vision of the temple. Gregory interprets the square allegorically, to refer to four equal virtues.

[28] John Damascene, *De fid. orth.* 3.14.24, 226.210-211.

[29] Pp. 174-178.

[30] aequale *P7,V9*] dicitur *add. M*; facit *prae. O2.*

[31] Aristotle, *Met.* 5.15 (1021a8-12).

first of all in numbers, secondly in magnitudes, and in other ways in all other genera, as *Met.* 10 makes clear.[32] For in every genus, what is most simple and most perfect is the measure of everything else–whiteness for colors, and for motions the daily rotation of the heavens. So each thing is more perfect to the extent that it more closely approaches the first principle in its genus. From this it is clear that the perfection of each thing, in so far as one measures it[33] in relation to its first principle, is called its quantity.[34] This is what Augustine says in *On the Trinity*: "For those things which are not great in size, being better and being greater amount to the same thing."[35]

Since for every non-subsistent form being consists in being in a subject or matter, its quantity or perfection can be considered in two ways: in one way, by looking at the *nature of its proper species*; in a second way, by looking at the *existence* which it has in its matter or subject.

Looking at the nature of their proper species, the forms of different species are unequal, while within one species, it is possible that some of the forms are equal and others are not. For the principle specifying the species must necessarily reside in something indivisible. For differences in this kind of principle change the species. Therefore, if there were addition or subtraction to this principle, the species necessarily would be changed. This is why the Philosopher says in *Met.* 8 that the species of things are like numbers, where adding or subtracting unity changes the species.[36]

Now there are some forms which receive their *species* through something in their own essence, for example, all absolute forms, whether they are substantial or accidental. It is impossible that within the same species one such form turn out in this respect to be greater than another. For one white color, considered in itself, is not more a white color than another.

There are other forms, however, which receive their species from something extrinsic, toward which they are ordered. For example, motion receives its species from its terminus. Consequently, one motion is greater than another, based on how near or far it is from its terminus.[37] Likewise, there are some qualities which are dispositions ordered to some end. For

[32] Aristotle, *Met.* 10.1 (1053b4-8). Cf. 5.15 (1021a12-14).

[33] eius *P7,O2,V9*] est *add. M.*

[34] dicitur quantitas *Am2,O2,V9*] dicitur quod *P7*; similiter quantitas *M.*

[35] Augustine, *De Trin.* 6.8.9, CCSL 50: 238.8-9. Cf. n. 3.

[36] Aristotle, *Met.* 8.3 (1043b33-1044a2).

[37] Unde unus motus est maior alio secundum propinquitatem vel distantiam a termino *P7,O2,V9*; *om. M.*

example, health is a certain balance of the humors ordered to the nature of the animal which is called healthy. Therefore, a certain level in the balance of the humors in a lion is health, which in a human would be illness. Therefore, since health does not attain its species because of the level of balance alone, but is also based on the nature of the animal to which it is ordered, it can happen that one level of health can be greater than another in the same animal, as is said in *Ethics* 10.[38] This happens when there can be different levels of balancing the humors suitable to human nature. And the same relation holds for knowledge, which receives its unity from the unity of the matter known. Consequently, one student can know more geometry than another, when he has learned more conclusions ordered to understanding the matter of geometry: magnitude.

When we turn to the quantity of perfection forms of this sort have because they *exist* in matter or in a subject, the case is similar. Some forms within one species can be unequal, in so far as they can exist more or less in a subject. Other forms, however, cannot exist more or less in a subject. For every form specifying the species for the subject it is in cannot exist[39] more or less. The reason for this, as has been said, is that the specifying principle must be understood as indivisible. And from this it follows that[40] no substantial form is open to more and less.

Likewise, if some form takes its species from something which is indivisible in its own nature, it is not said to be more or less. This is why two, and every the other species of number specified by adding one, is not open to more and less. The same point holds for figures specified by number, such as triangle and quadrilateral; for determinate quantities, like three cubits or four cubits; and for numerical relations, like double and triple.

On the other hand, forms which do not specify a species for their subjects and do not take their species from something which is indivisible in its own nature, can exist more or less in something, for example, white, black, and other things of this sort.

From all this, therefore, it is clear that different forms are related to[41] equality and inequality in four ways:

Some forms in the same species are not open to inequality, either in their nature, as though one of these forms were greater than another of the

[38] Aristotle, *Nic. Eth.* 10.3 (1173a23-28).

[39] esse *P7*] inesse *M,O2,V9*.

[40] quod *P7,O2,V9*] quia *M*.

[41] se ad *Am2*] ad *P7*; se *O2*; si *V9*; potest aliquid se ad *M*.

same species, or in their existence, as though one could exist more in a subject. All substantial forms are like this.

Some forms are not open to inequality in their nature, but are open to inequality in their existence in a subject, for example, white and black.

Some forms are open to inequality in their nature, but not in their existence in a subject. For example, one triangle is said to be larger than another because the sides of the one are larger than those of the other, even though they fall under one specific description. But one side is not more triangular than another.

Some forms are open to inequality both in their natures and in their existence in a subject, for example, health, knowledge, and motion. For motion can be unequal, either because it covers more distance or because the moving subject moves more rapidly. Likewise, the scientific knowledge of one person is greater than another's, either because of having learned more conclusions or knowing the same conclusions better. Likewise, health can be unequal, either because the level of balance in one animal is nearer to what perfect equality would be than the level of balance in another, or because one animal holds the same level of balance more securely and better than another does.

In light of these considerations, concerning equality and inequality among the virtues,

I reply:

If we are speaking about the inequality of the virtues considered in their natures, *different species* of virtues can be unequal.

Since virtue is "a disposition of the perfect for the best act,"[42] as is said in the *Physics*[43] 7, that virtue is more perfect and greater which is ordered to a greater good. In this respect, the theological virtues, whose object is God, are more important than the others. And charity is the greatest of these, because it conjoins us more closely to God. And hope is greater than faith, for hope in a way moves our affections up to God, while faith brings God down to exist in us in a cognitive way.

Prudence, which[44] is a kind of governess for the rest, is the greatest of the other virtues. After prudence comes justice, by which a human is well ordered, not just internally but in relation to others. After justice comes

[42] Aristotle, *Physics* 7.3 (246b23-24).
[43] Phys *P7,O2,V9*] Eth *M.*
[44] quae *P7,O2,V9*] quia *M.*

courage, by which a human disregards mortal dangers for the sake of the good. And after courage comes temperance, by which a human disregards even very attractive bodily pleasures for the sake of the good.

Now the sort of inequality found in *one species* of scientific knowledge cannot be found in one species of virtue, because it is not part of the nature of scientific knowledge that a person possessing a given science should know all the conclusions of that science. But it is part of the nature of virtue that one possessing a certain virtue should do well in all the actions pertaining to that virtue.

When we consider the perfection or quantity of a virtue in the aspect of existing in a subject, then there can be inequality, even within one species of virtue. This happens when one person having this virtue is better at the actions which belong to it than another; or when one person has a better natural disposition; or when one has more experience; or when one is better at making rational judgments; or because one has been given more grace. These things can happen because virtue does not specify a species for its subject, nor does it have something indivisible in its definition, except according to the Stoics.[45] They said that no one possesses virtue without possessing it to the highest degree, and for this reason all those[46] who possess the same virtue have it[47] equally. But this does not seem to be part of the nature of any virtue, for differences in the way we participate in the virtues follow what has already been said, and these differences are not limited to the nature of some particular virtue, for example, chastity, or virtues like it.

Therefore, *in different people*, the virtues can be unequal, both with regard to the different species of virtue, and also concerning their existence in a subject, even within one species of virtue.

Now *in one and the same person*, virtues can be unequal in the quantity or perfection the virtues have in their own natures. But when we turn to the quantity or perfection a virtue has, in so far as it exists in a subject, then, absolutely speaking, it is necessary that all virtues be equal for the

[45] Aquinas knew about this doctrine of the Stoics from Albert, *In 3 Sent.* d .36. 1c; Jerome, *Ep.* 66.3; and Augustine, *Ep.* 167.4,12. On the knowledge Ambrose and Jerome had of Stoicism, see M. Colish, *The Stoic Tradition* 2: 48-91, though she wrongly attributes Stoic equality of the vices to Jerome in *Ep.* 66. On Augustine's understanding of the Stoic sage possessing all the virtues, 165-9, 213-220. On the Stoic doctrine of the equality of vices, see J.M. Rist, *Stoic Philosophy* c.5.

[46] omnes *P7,O2*] deus *Am2,V9*; sunt *add. M.*

[47] eam *P7,O2,V9*; *om. M.*

same reason that they are connected to each other. For equality is simply a kind of connection with regard to quantity.

Consequently, some thinkers[48] give an argument for equality of this sort[49] in which the four cardinal virtues are understood as the general modes of virtue. Augustine's argument in *On the Trinity* 6 is like this.

A second way of arguing for equality can be taken from the dependence the moral virtues have on prudence, and the dependence of all the virtues on charity. Where charity is equal, all the virtues are necessarily equal, with respect to the formal perfection of virtue. And the same argument can be made about prudence in relation to the moral virtues.

The virtues in one and the same person, however, when looked at in certain respects, *can* be unequal, just as they do not have to be connected to each other. This is due to the varying tendencies powers have for their respective acts, and comes from nature or some other cause. For this reason, some say that the virtues are unequal in their actions. But this must be limited to unequal tendencies to act of the sort we have described.[50]

[*Replies to objections*:]

Reply to Obj. 1. This argument concerns the inequality which[51] is found in the very nature of the virtues, not the inequality which follows their existence, which is the issue we are presently addressing. For, as has been said,[52] charity in its nature is greater than all other virtues. Yet when it grows, all the other virtues existing in one and the same human grow pro-

[48] Cf. Art. 1, Reply to Obj. 1; pp. 164-5.

[49] huiusmodi *P7,O2,V9*; *om. M.*

[50] huiusmodi *P7,O2,V9*; *om. M.* Considered in their *nature*, the seven virtues form a hierarchy: charity, hope, faith, prudence, justice, courage, temperance. Considered in their natures, none of these virtues vary in degree. But they can vary in their *existence* in different people. In one and the same person, their equality is a function of how the virtues are connected. Consequently, when understood as the general modes of virtue, the cardinal virtues are equal to each other, because no act can be completed unless it has its four cardinal aspects. The specific cardinal virtues must be connected to prudence, and all true virtue must be connected to charity. Consequently, all subordinate virtues depend equally on their superior virtues–the other cardinal virtues on prudence and all virtues on charity. Only when considering the tendencies, natural or otherwise induced, an individual may have, is there no necessary connection, and so no equality, among the virtues.

[51] quae *P7,O2,V9*] est et *add. M.*

[52] P. 192.

portionally. It is like the fingers of your hand; though unequal in nature, they grow in proportion to each other.

A similar reply should be given to *Objections 2 - 6*, and also to the *seventh objection*, which argues in the same way that prudence[53] is greater than the other virtues.

And a similar reply should be given to the *eighth objection*, which argues in the same way concerning justice, though the justice which is virtue entire is not the justice placed among the cardinal virtues.

A similar reply can be given to the *ninth objection*. Though all the virtues exist in this human, they are distinguished by the greater or lesser perfection of their species.

Again, a similar reply should be given to the *tenth objection*, that the vices are also unequal in the way outlined.

Reply to Obj. 11: An individual is praised more for one virtue than another because it leads more promptly to virtuous action.

Reply to Obj. 12: Where there is a greater habit, there must necessarily be more action following the inclination of that habit. Yet there can be something impeding or disposing a human to act, which is related accidentally to the habit. For example, the habit of knowledge is impeded from producing its act owing to drinking wine. Consequently, owing to these sorts of impediments and aids to acting, at times there can be something augmenting the act, even though the augment is not part of the relevant habit.

Reply to Obj. 13: More exercise of an acquired habit causes a greater habit. Yet a habit already acquired as a result of many acts can be impeded accidentally, so that it can no longer produce its proper action, as was said.[54]

Reply to Obj. 14: In the natural realm, there can be inequality of act where there are equal forms, because of some accidental impediment.

Reply to Obj. 15: The powers are essentially unequal, in as much as one power in its own nature is more perfect than another. And in this respect we have said that the virtues are unequal.[55]

Reply to Obj. 16: The virtues exist proportionally, as has been said.[56] But it does not follow from this that we possess them unequally.

[53] prudentiam] fortitudinem *M,P7,O2,V9.*

[54] Pp. 190-2.

[55] P. 190.

[56] Reply to Obj. 1, pp. 192-3.

Reply to Obj. 17: The heavenly state is opposed to faith because it is an unimpeded vision of God. But increasing charity does not guarantee the consequence that someone will obtain this vision. Therefore, it is not necessary that increasing charity diminishes faith.

[*Replies to arguments to the contrary*:]

The *reply to the arguments to the contrary 1 - 4* is clear from what has been said.

To argument to the contrary 5, I reply: Damascene understands that the virtues equally existing in all persons means that they are common to all persons.[57]

To argument to the contrary 6, I reply: Our reward corresponds essentially to the root of charity. Therefore, even if an individual's virtues are not equal, the same reward is due a given human, because of one level of charity.

Art. 4. *The fourth issue: Will the cardinal virtues remain with us in our heavenly homeland?*[58]

It seems not:

1. Gregory, in his *Moralia*, says: "the deeds of the active[59] life pass away with the body."[60] But the cardinal virtues perfect a human in the deeds of

[57] inesse, id est, communiter *P7,O2,V9*] esse *M*.

[58] Parallel passages: Aquinas, *In 3 Sent.* d.33. 1.4, 3: 1039-1041; *ST* 1-2.67.1. Alexander of Hales, *Glossa in 3 Sent.* d.33, n. 8, ed. Quaracchi 3: 392-3. Bonaventure, *In 3 Sent.* d.33. 1.6, ed. Quaracchi 3: 726-7.

[59] activae *P7,O2,V9*] accidentia *M*.

[60] Gregory, *Moralia* 6.37.61, CCSL 143: 331.204. In commenting on *Job* 5:26, Gregory refers to the story of Martha and Mary (*Luke* 10:38-42), interpreting it allegorically: "What is meant by Mary, who is sitting listening to the words of the Lord, if not the contemplative life? And what is signified by Martha, busy with external tasks, if not the active life? Now Jesus does not censure the concerns of Martha. But the concerns of Mary are praised, because, as great as the merits of the active life are, those of the contemplative life are better. Consequently, Scripture never says Mary's part will be 'destroyed,' because, though the deeds of the active life pass away with the body, the finer joys of the contemplative life will win out in the presence of our end–God" (331.198-205).

the active life. Therefore the cardinal virtues pass away with the body.[61] Therefore, they will not remain with us in heaven.

2. Once the end has been achieved the means leading to the end are no longer needed. For example, once you have made port, you no longer need a ship. But the cardinal virtues are different from the theological virtues in just this way. The theological virtues have the ultimate end as their object, while the cardinal virtues concern what leads to that end. Therefore, once one has attained the ultimate end in heaven, no cardinal virtue will any longer be needed.

3. Take away the end and you also take the means leading to the end. But the cardinal virtues are ordered to the good of the civil community, which will not exist in heaven. Therefore, neither will the cardinal virtues exist in heaven.

4. Things which will remain in heaven, not in their own proper species but only in their common genera, are not said to remain,[62] but to pass away. For example, faith is said to pass away, even though thought will remain, which is the genus of faith. But in heaven the cardinal virtues will not remain with us in their proper species, which distinguish them from each other. For in his *Literal Commentary on Genesis* Augustine says that "there the one and complete virtue is to love[63] what you see."[64] Therefore, in heaven the cardinal virtues will not remain but will pass away.

5. The virtues take their species from their objects. Now the objects of the cardinal virtues will no longer exist in heaven: For prudence concerns doubts we have about our moral deliberations. And justice concerns contractual relations and legal judgments. Courage concerns the danger of death. And temperance is about desires for eating, drinking, and sex. But none of these things will exist in heaven. Therefore there will be no cardinal virtues in heaven.[65]

[61] Sed virtutes cardinales perficiunt hominem ad opera activae. Ergo virtutes cardinales cum corpore transeunt *P7,O2,V9*; *om. M.*

[62] manere *P7*] in patria *add. M,O2,V9.*

[63] amare *P7,O2,V9*] amari *M.*

[64] Augustine, *De gen. ad lit.* 12.26.54, CSEL 28: 419.19. "There [in heaven] the virtues of the soul are not difficult and laborious. For there temperance does not have to work to restrain desire, nor courage work to withstand adversity, nor justice work to punish iniquity, nor prudence work to avoid malice. There the one and complete virtue is to love what you see, and the greatest happiness is to have what you love" (419.15-20).

[65] Ergo virtutes cardinales non erunt in patria *P7,O2,V9*; *om. M.*

6. He replied[66] that in heaven the cardinal virtues will have different acts. *But to the contrary*: Diversity about what falls within a definition produces difference in species. Now act falls within the definition of habit. For in his book on *The Good of Marriage*, Augustine says "habit is that whereby an act is performed when the time is right."[67] Therefore, wherever there are different acts, there must also be habits different in species.

7. Macrobius reports that Plotinus said the virtues of the purified mind are different from the political virtues.[68] But the virtues of the purified mind seem to be the virtues which will exist in heaven; while the virtues of the present life are the political virtues. Therefore, the virtues which exist here will not remain with us there,[69] but will pass away.

8. There is a greater distance in state between the blessed and wayfarers, than the difference in state in the present life between master and slave, or man and woman. But according to the Philosopher in *Politics* 1, there is one virtue for a master, another for a slave, and likewise, one virtue for a man, another for a woman.[70] Therefore, there is even more difference between the virtues of wayfarers and the virtues of the blessed in heaven.

9. We require virtuous habits in order to activate our ability[71] to do things. But in heaven, the light of glory will be enough to produce this sort of activation. Therefore, virtuous habits will no longer be necessary.

10. At *1 Cor* 13:8, the Apostle proves that charity is better than the other virtues, because it will not pass away. But faith and hope, which will pass away, are finer than the cardinal virtues; because they have a finer object–God. Therefore, the cardinal virtues will pass away.

[66] dicebat *Am2*] dicebant *P7*; dice *O2,V9*; dicendum *M*.

[67] Augustine, *De bono coniug*. 21.25, CSEL 41: 219.17-18.

[68] Macrobius, *In som. Sci*. 1.8.5, ed. Teubner 37.22-8. Macrobius reports that Plotinus (†270) "says there are four types of the four virtues. The first of these are called political virtues, the second purify*ing* virtues, the third the virtues of a puri*fied* mind, and fourth are the exemplar virtues." The political virtues, with their subordinate virtues, "make a man good in himself and thereby a leader of the republic." Purifying virtues make a human "open to the divine." Third are the virtues possessed by a mind which has "turned away from the bitterness of this world." Exemplar virtues are those found "in the divine mind itself." Cf. Plotinus, *Enneads* 1.2.1-7, 1: 126-147.

[69] ibi *P7,O2,V9*; *om. M*.

[70] Aristotle, *Pol*. 1.13 (1259b21-1260b7).

[71] passibilitatem *P7,O2,V9*] possibilitatem *M*.

11. The Philosopher[72] in *Nic. Eth.* 6 makes it clear that the intellectual virtues are finer than the moral virtues.[73] But the intellectual virtues will not remain with us, since knowledge "will pass away," as it says in *1 Cor.* [13:8]. Therefore, neither will the cardinal virtues remain with us in heaven.

12. At *James* 1:4 it says "patience produces a complete work." But only the reward for patience, not patience itself, will remain with us in heaven, as Augustine says in *The City of God* 14.[74] Therefore, even less will the other moral virtues remain with us in heaven.

13. Some of the cardinal virtues, temperance and courage, exist in the sensitive powers of the soul. For at *Nic. Eth.* 3 the Philosopher makes clear that they belong to the irrational parts of the soul.[75] But the sensitive parts of the soul are not found in angels, nor can they exist in a soul separated from the body. Therefore, there are no such virtues in heaven, neither in the angels, nor in separated souls.

14. In *The City of God* Augustine says we shall be free and shall see, and will love and will praise.[76] But being free is an act of wisdom, seeing is an act of mind, while loving is an act of charity, and praising an act of worship. Therefore, only these acts will be found in heaven, not the cardinal virtues.

15. In heaven, humans will be "like angels," as it says in *Mat.* [22:30]. But as far as sobriety is concerned, humans cannot be like angels, since angels do not eat and drink. Therefore, there will be no sobriety in heaven; and the same argument holds for other virtues of this sort.[77]

On the contrary:

1. is what is said in the book of *Wis.*: "Justice is perpetual and immortal."[78]

2. About divine wisdom, *Wis.* [8:7] says: "she teaches temperance and prudence, justice and courage; nothing in life is more profitable for men than these." But in heaven there will be the fullest possible participation in

[72] per philosophum *P7,O2,V9*; *om. M.*
[73] Aristotle, *Nic. Eth.* 6.7 (1141a16-1141b3).
[74] Augustine, *De civ. dei* 14.9, CCSL 48: 429.136-9.
[75] Aristotle, *Nic. Eth.* 3.10 (1117b23-4).
[76] Augustine, *De civ. dei* 22.30, CCSL 48: 866.145-7.
[77] That is, for the other "subjective parts" of temperance.
[78] *Wis.* 1:15 (Vulgate).

wisdom. Therefore, these virtues will exist fully in heaven.

3. The virtues are spiritual riches. But there will be[79] a greater abundance of spiritual riches in heaven than there is in the present life.[80] Therefore, virtues of the sort under consideration will abound even more fully in heaven.

Response:

The cardinal virtues will remain with us in our heavenly homeland, and there they will produce different actions from what they produce here, for as[81] Augustine says in *On the Trinity* 13: "What justice does now in giving aid to the wretched, and prudence in anticipating problems, and what courage does in withstanding troubles, and temperance in restraining evil pleasures, these actions will not exist there, where there is no evil at all.... But justice will consist in submitting to the rule of God ... and prudence in neither preferring nor even equating any other good with God, and courage will be to cling as closely as possible to God, while temperance will be to enjoy nothing hurtful at all."[82]

As proof of this one should understand that, as the Philosopher says in *On the Heavens* 1,[83] virtue involves the ultimate end of a power. Now it is clear that the powers of things differing in nature will have different ulti-

[79] erit *P7,O2,V9*] est *M.*

[80] vita *P7,O2,V9*] via *M.*

[81] ut enim *Am2,V9*] enim *P7*; ut *M,O2.*

[82] Augustine, *De civ. dei* 14.9.12, CCSL 50a: 439.29-30,36-42.

[83] Aristotle, *On the Heavens* 1.11 (281a10-12;14-15). Ultimate end (*ultimum*) describes the maximum achievement of a virtue or power. This term, taken from Philip and Albert, Aquinas uses first to contrast the cardinal virtues found in God and humans, then to compare the way humans employ the cardinal virtues in the present life with the way they will function in heaven. Since the character of habits is set by the kinds of acts they engender in relation to their objects, it might seem that different kinds of actions would always signify different virtues. The main theme running through the objections is that this principle would exclude the cardinal virtues from heaven, since their normal work would be superfluous there. Aquinas distinguishes the ultimate end of a virtue from the kinds of actions it normally produces, in order to do two things: (1) to show against the too worldly ancient pagans that the cardinal virtues have an ultimate end which goes beyond their normal realm of action; and (2) against the too otherworldly Christian objector to create logical space for the cardinal virtues to have two sets of actions not just one, while remaining the same virtues, whether exercised by the wayfarer or the blessed.

mates, since a higher nature has more power extending to more and greater things. Therefore, what is a virtue for one is not a virtue for another. For example, human virtue is determined in relation to those traits which are most important for a human life. So human temperance consists in not departing from reason in order to maximize pleasure, but moderating such pleasures under the direction of reason. Human courage consists in standing firm in the face of the greatest danger, the danger of death, for the sake of the good discerned by reason. The ultimate end of a divine power, however, is not understood in relation to such lower things, but in relation to something higher, the infinitude of God's own power. Therefore, divine courage consists in God's unchanging character. And divine temperance will be the divine mind turning toward itself. Divine prudence is the divine mind itself. While the justice of God is his everlasting law.

One should note, however, that there are two ways of understanding ultimates when they differ from each other. One way is when the different ultimates fall within one line of motion. The other way is when the different ultimates are completely separate, not related to each other at all.

So different ultimates falling within one line of motion are different, and produce specifically different motions; but they do not produce specifically different motive principles, because the same principle operates from the beginning to the end of a motion. We can draw an example of this sort of thing from architecture, where the ultimate result is the finished form of a building. But integrating the different parts of the building allows other ultimates to enter into the building process. Consequently, as the Philosopher says in *Nic. Eth.* 10, laying a foundation, which terminates in that foundation, is one kind of motion; erecting the columns is another; and finishing the structure a third. Nonetheless, skill in building construction is one and the same skill, and is the principle for these three types of motion.[84] And the same thing is true for other motions.

Alternatively, different ultimates, which are separate and do not fall within one line of motion, but are completely separate, produce specifically different motions, and specifically different moving principles. For example, the skill which is the principle of constructing buildings is different from skill at building ships.

Therefore, where there is specifically the same ultimate, there will also be the same species of virtue, and[85] that virtue will produce the same action

[84] Aristotle, *Nic. Eth.* 10.4 (1174a9-29).
[85] et *P7,O2,V9*; *om. M.*

or motion. For example, it is clear that temperance in me and in you achieves specifically the same ultimate result: moderating the pleasures of touch. Therefore, neither temperance nor its action are specifically different in me and in you.

But where the ultimate results in virtues that attain are not the same[86] in species and are not connected by being in one line of motion, then not only in the action the virtues produce, but in the virtues themselves, they must necessarily differ in species. For example, this is clearly the case when it comes to predicating the cardinal virtues of God and man.

Yet where the ultimate results differ in species, but fall under one line of motion, as when one proceeds from one to the other, then some[87] of the actions produced differ in species, while the virtue is the same. For example, courageous action produces[88] one ultimate result before battle, another during battle, and yet a third in victory after the battle. So moving forward to battle is an act specifically different from bravely standing one's ground in battle, and different still from rejoicing over a battle won. Yet courage is one and the same. Likewise, loving, wanting, and rejoicing are acts of one and the same power.[89]

From what has been said it is clear that, since the heavenly state is higher than the state of being on the way to that end, it necessarily follows that heavenly virtue[90] attains a more perfect ultimate result than does the virtue of the wayfarer. Therefore, if the ultimate result which the wayfarer's virtue attains is ordered to the ultimate result which heavenly virtue attains, it necessarily follows that there is specifically the same virtue, though

[86] idem *P7,O2,V9*] in eadem *M.*

[87] quidam *P7,O2,V9*] quidem *M.*

[88] determinatur *P7*] derivatur *M,O2,V9.*

[89] The first and second of these three situations are more familiar. Temperance has the same purpose for all people; while temperance and courage are essentially different, because they have different purposes. In these cases the "ultimate end" and the virtue itself are interchangeable. By distinguishing the ultimate end from the habit and the actions it produces in the third group, however, Aquinas ties together different kinds of actions under one virtue, in the case where their purposes feed into one another. Such can be called subordinated habits, since the actions of the cardinal virtues in the present life are (or should be) subordinated to the final end which these same virtues will attain in the next. This subordination allows the virtue to be one and the same, while exercised in different ways.

[90] necesse est quod virtus patriae *Am2,O2,V9*] necesse est quod unius patriae *P7; om. M.*

it produces different actions. On the other hand, if the one is not understood as[91] ordered to the other, then the virtues will not be the same, either in the acts they produce, or when viewed as virtuous habits.

It is clear that the acquired civil[92] virtues the philosophers described are ordered only to fulfilling humans in their civic lives, not as they are ordained to seek heavenly glory. Therefore, the philosophers held that such virtues will not remain with us after the present life, as Augustine said of Cicero.[93] But the cardinal virtues, as they are infused by grace and as we now speak about them, fulfill a human in the present life as[94] ordered to heavenly glory.

Therefore, it is necessary to reply: These cardinal virtues have the very same habit here and there, though their acts are different. For here they produce acts which are appropriate to those moving in the direction of their ultimate end; while there these virtues will produce acts appropriate to those already resting in that ultimate end.

[*Replies to objections*:]

Reply to Obj. 1: Virtues like the cardinal virtues perfect a human in the active life, which is like a road we travel to arrive home at our destination: heavenly contemplation. Therefore, in our heavenly homeland the cardinal virtues will remain with us, in acts consummated by achieving our end.

Reply to Obj. 2: The cardinal virtues concern the means leading to the end, but not as though their ultimate destination resided in such means. That would be as though the ultimate destination of a ship were merely sailing around. But the cardinal virtues concern the means in this way: Through the means leading to the end, the cardinal virtues are ordered to the ultimate end. For example, the temperance given through grace does not have moderating desires concerned with touch as its ultimate end. But it moderates such desires as a likeness of the temperance found in heaven.

Reply to Obj. 3: The civil good is *not* the ultimate end of the infused car-

[91] ut *P7,O2,V9*; *om. M.*

[92] civiles *P7,O2,V9*; *om. M.*

[93] Augustine, *De Trin.* 14.9.12, CSEL 50a: 438.1-439.20. Augustine introduces the re-definitions of the virtues given in n. 11 with Cicero's comment that the virtues seem useless in heaven, a point Cicero made in his lost *Hortensius*, the book which fired Augustine with a love of philosophy. Cf. *Conf.* 3.4.

[94] ut *P7,O2,V9*; *om. M.*

dinal virtues we are speaking about, but of the acquired cardinal virtues the philosophers presented, as has been said.[95]

Reply to Obj. 4: There is no reason why one and the same thing cannot be the end of different virtues and different skills. For example, preserving the civil good is the end and goal of both military skill and the positive law. Therefore, both these skills or virtues engage in actions which concern the civil good as their final good. But military skill looks to preserve[96] the civil good by fighting courageously to achieve this good, while the positive law looks to[97] the same end by ordaining the laws to preserve the civil good.

Likewise, finding joy in God in heaven is the end of all the cardinal virtues. And there each virtue will rejoice over that end, because it is the end of all its acts. Therefore, it is said that in heaven there will be "one virtue," in the sense that there will be a subject over which all the virtues rejoice. But there will be different acts and different virtues, owing to the different ways of rejoicing.

Reply to Obj. 5: Something is said to be the object of a virtue in two ways: In one way the virtue is ordered to its object as to an end. For example, the highest good is the object of charity, and eternal happiness is the object of hope. In a second way, the object of a virtue is the area the virtue concerns, so that it redirects us from this area to something else. This is the way sexual pleasure is the object of temperance. For the purpose of temperance is not to fix on such pleasures, but rather[98] by limiting them to redirect us to more rational goods. In a similar way, the purpose of courage is not to keep us in dangerous situations, but[99] by overcoming dangers[100] to follow what reason says is good. And the same thing is true for prudence, in relation to the quandries of conscience, and for justice, in relation to the necessities of the present life. Therefore, the more the progress of our spiritual life moves us away from such worldly concerns, the more perfect will be the actions the cardinal virtues produce. For the claims made in this objection apply to how the cardinal virtues work as points of departure on our spiritual journey, more than how they will work at our destination. But the latter respect is what truly gives the cardinal virtues their species.

[95] P. 201.
[96] conservatione *P7,O2,V9*; *om. M.*
[97] providet] gaudet *M,P7,O2,V9.*
[98] potius *P7,O2,V9*; *om. M.*
[99] sed *P7,O2,V9*; *om. M.*
[100] pericula *P7,O2,V9*] sed *add. M.*

Reply to Obj. 6: Not every way of distinguishing actions signifies a diversity of moral habits, as has been said.[101]

Reply to Obj. 7: The virtues of the purified mind, as Plotinus defined them, seem appropriate for the blessed in heaven. For there the role of prudence will be to gaze only on divine realities. There the function of temperance will be to forget worldly desires. There courage will ignore the passions. And there justice will be to maintain an eternal contract with God. But the political virtues Plotinus presents are ordained *only* to the civil good in the present life, as has been said.[102]

Reply to Obj. 8: The ultimate goals toward which the virtues of slave and master, woman and man, are directed, are not found on the field of their mutual relations, as if[103] the ultimate consisted in changing from one of these states to another. Therefore, the argument by analogy set out in the objection breaks down.

Reply to Obj. 9: The activation for performing virtuous deeds which is produced or perfected by the light of glory, is a feature of the very nature of virtuous habits.

Reply to Obj. 10: Faith is ordained to truth which is not manifest, and hope is ordained to an arduous goal not yet attained. These[104] negative notes give these virtues their species. Therefore, though these virtues are better than the cardinal virtues, due to having a higher object, they will pass away, because they take their species from what will not remain in heaven.

Reply to Obj. 11: The habit of science will not be destroyed but will produce different acts.

Reply to Obj. 12: Patience will not remain with us in heaven, as far as the action of enduring tribulations, which it produces in this life, is concerned. But it will remain with us, exercising an act appropriate to our final end, as was said of the other virtues.[105]

Reply to Obj. 13: Some thinkers have said that the emotion and desire which are the seat of temperance and courage, exist in the superior part of the soul, not in the sensitive part of the soul.[106] But this is contrary to the

[101] P. 200.
[102] P. 201.
[103] si *P7,V9*] sic *M*; scilicet *O2*.
[104] ad quod *P7,V9*] a *M*; *om. O2*.
[105] P. 201.
[106] Bonaventure, *In 3 Sent.* d.33. 1.3, 3: 717: "Although this way of speaking

Philosopher at *Nic. Eth.* 3, where it is said[107] that these are "the virtues of the irrational parts."[108]

On the other hand, some say the powers of the sensitive part of the soul remain in the soul separated from the body, either merely in potency,[109] or also[110] in act.[111] But this is impossible, for no sense power can act apart from the body. Otherwise, the sensitive souls of many[112] animals would be[113] incorruptible, which is false.

Now the actions of the soul are built on the powers of the soul.[114] It follows necessarily that powers of sensation exist in a soul joined with a body. Consequently, after death the powers of sensation will not remain in a separated soul in act, though they do remain virtually, in their root, as it were, since the powers of the soul flow from its essence.

The virtues of temperance and courage, then, do exist *in* the emotional [and desiring] part of the soul, as far as their derivation is concerned. But they originate and begin to develop *from* reason and will, since the principal act of moral virtue is choice, an act of rational appetite. But this choice terminates in an application of temperance and courage to the pas-

---

[that temperance and courage are in the inferior part of the soul] seems probable to moral philosophers, to the moral *theologian* it does not seem reasonable to say that some cardinal virtues find their place in the superior part of the soul, while others find their place in the inferior part of the soul. For all the cardinal virtues are equal in dignity when it comes to merit, since all cause merit. Therefore, since merit is rooted in free choice, the virtues, whether cardinal or theological, can exist only in those powers having freedom of choice. Therefore, since there is only freedom of choice in the rational part of the soul, where rational means partaking of reason, it follows necessarily that the other cardinal virtues find their place *in that part* of the soul."

[107] dicitur *P7,O2,V9*] dicit *M.*

[108] Aristotle, *Nic. Eth.* 3.10 (1117b23-4).

[109] ps.-Augustine, *De spiritu et anima* 15, PL 40: 791.

[110] etiam *P7,O2,V9; om. M.*

[111] ps.-Augustine, *De spiritu et anima* 30, PL 40: 800.

[112] multorum *P7,O2,V9*] brutorum *M.*

[113] esset *P7,O2,V9*] etiam *add. M.*

[114] This point is central to Aquinas' argument for the spirituality and immortality of the soul, because he reasons from act to power to the nature of the soul. Intellectual acts are purely spiritual and therefore require the intellectual power of the soul to be spiritual, separated from the physical body. But sensory actions involve the body, so they require that the power of sensation exist in a soul united to a body.

sions of the emotional and desiring elements of the soul.

Reply to Obj. 14: All four of the acts mentioned in the objection pertain to each and every act[115] as its end, since heavenly beatitude consists in these actions.

Reply to Obj. 15: Sobriety does not make us like the angels as an act the wayfarer performs, concerned with eating and drinking. But the sobriety which makes us like angels is an act done in heaven, concerned with our ultimate end. And the same can be said of the other virtues.

[115] actum *P7,O2,V9*] virtutum *add. M.*

Appendix 1
Patristic Texts on the Cardinal Virtues

A. AMBROSE

Exposition of the Gospel according to Luke 5. 49, 62-68[1] [date: 385-95].

49. *Blessed are the poor in spirit, for yours is the kingdom of God. Blessed are those that hunger now, for they shall be satisfied. Blessed are you that weep now, for you shall be glad. Blessed shall you be, when men hate you.* [*Luke* 6:20-22] Saint Luke listed only four of our Lord's beatitudes, while St. Matthew listed eight. But the four are in the eight, and the eight are in the four. For Luke has treated the four as like the *cardinal* virtues, while Matthew in the eight has unlocked a mystical number. For many of the psalms are entitled "for the octave"; and you accept the requirement "to give a portion to eight" [*Eccl.* 9:2], perhaps meaning benedictions, for just as eight is the perfection of our hope, so eight is the totality of the virtues. ...

62. Now let us say how St. Luke includes in his four beatitudes the eight beatitudes [of St. Matthew]. We know there are four cardinal virtues: temperance, justice, prudence, courage. Now whoever is poor in spirit is not greedy, whoever weeps is not proud, whoever is meek is also peaceful, whoever mourns is made humble, whoever is just does not deny what he knows, which is given for the common use of all, whoever shows mercy has his own wealth increased, whoever gives of his own does not seek what belongs to another nor do evil to his neighbor.

63. Therefore, the virtues are so connected and chained together, that whoever has *one* seems to have them all. And there accrues to the saints *one* virtue, but whose [virtue] is more fruitful gets the more fruitful reward. How much hospitality was there in Abraham, how much humility, how much sanctity, so that he saved the son of his brother from the enemy, and

[1] CCSL 14: 152, 156-7.

how great was his abstinence, so that he sought no booty! But since he stood out in faith, he deserved to be first in faith before all others. Therefore, for each there are a multitude of rewards because there is a multitude of incentives to virtue, but where the merit is more bountiful there will be greater rewards.

64. Therefore, *blessed are the poor in spirit*. You have *temperance*, which abstains from sin, tramples the present age, and does not seek seductions.

65. *Blessed are they who hunger and thirst.* For whoever thirsts has compassion for the thirsty, and being compassionate leads to largesse, and by bestowing largesse he becomes *just*, because *his justice remains forever* [*Ps.* 111:9]. Consequently, in Matthew we understand spiritual thirst and hunger, where the food and drink of justice is what is desired, because a virtue is like a kind of matter. In this way the just person sets himself equal to his inferiors, leaves evil aside, and seeks truth.

66. *Blessed are you who weep now, for you shall laugh.* You have *prudence*, whose task is to weep for what is under the setting sun but to seek what is eternal, to mourn for worldly powers which fight among themselves but to look for the God of peace, who *has chosen the foolish of the world to confound the wise* and who *destroys the things which are not in order to attain the things that are* [*1 Cor.* 1: 27-8].

67. *Blessed are you, when men hate you.* You have *courage*, the kind which does not merit hatred because of crime, but suffers persecution because of faith. For thus one attains the crown of suffering, if you neglect the favor of men and seek the favor of God. Finally, so you can know that the consummation of courage is suffering, he said *according to what their fathers did to the prophets*, because the prophets of Juda were persecuted even unto the death of the body. It also belongs to courage to conquer anger and control wrath, and this is how courage ensures control of mind over body and does not allow us to be perturbed by fear and sorrow, which overcome us like depraved soothsayers.

68. Therefore, temperance is in possession of purity of heart and mind, justice of mercy, prudence of peace, and courage of meekness (*mansuetudinem*).

B. Augustine

On the Customs of the Catholic Church 1.15[2] [date: 388-390].

[Augustine defines virtue in general as love of God. He then gives two definitions of the cardinal virtues, first in terms of love, then in terms of the love of God.]

If virtue leads us to the blessed life, I would say virtue is altogether nothing but the supreme love of God. For in talking about fourfold virtue, so far as I understand the matter, one is talking about various dispositions of love itself. So these four virtues–would that they were in your minds like their names are on your lips–I do not hesitate to define thus: Temperance is love giving itself wholly to what is loved. Courage is love readily enduring everything for what is loved. Justice is love serving the beloved alone, and ruling rightly for the sake of the beloved. Prudence is love wisely preferring what aids it over what impedes it. Now this love we have talked about is not love of just anything at all, but is love of God, that is, is love of the supreme good, the supreme wisdom, and the supreme harmony. Consequently, we can also define the virtues thus: Temperance is love keeping itself whole and uncorrupted for the sake of God. Courage is love easily enduring all things for the sake of God. Justice is love only serving God, and to this end ruling well those things subject to man. Prudence is love rightly distinguishing what helps from what hinders us reaching God.

C. Jerome

Letter 66, to Pammachius 66.3[3] [date: 397].

[Jerome uses the four cardinal virtues in a letter of consolation to Pammachius, a Roman Senator, over the death of his wife Paulina, daughter of Paula (one of Jerome's many aristocratic female disciples) and sister of Eustochium.]

1. After a wound has healed and a scar formed, treatment to remove the mark, while it seeks to return beauty to the body, must renew the original pain. So I, your tardy consoler, after two years of silence, fear that my present counsel may still be untimely, and tear open the wound in your

[2] PL 32:1322.

[3] CSEL 54: 647.5-650.12.

heart which time and meditation have cured. For who can have ears so dull or heart so hard as to hear the name of your Paulina without weeping? ...

2. The good ground we read about in the parable [*Matt.* 13:23] brought forth three harvests, one hundred-, sixty- and thirty-fold. I see here three gifts from Christ in three women united by blood and virtue. Eustochium reaps the flowers of virginity; Paula sweeps the threshing-floor of widowhood; Paulina keeps the chaste bed of matrimony. The mother, sustained by such companionship from her daughters, protects on earth all that Christ promised in heaven. And so that one household might send to the race a four-horse chariot of sanctity, and to match manly virtue with those of the women, Pammachius is added, truly a cherub like Ezekiel describes, brother-in-law to Eustochium, son-in-law of Paula, husband, or perhaps I should say, loving brother, to Paulina, for the language of marriage fails to describe the holy union of spirits.

3. Now let me say something about the philosophers. The Stoics say the four virtues are so closely connected to each other and mutually conjoined that whoever does not have one, lacks all: prudence, justice, courage, temperance. Each of you has all of them, yet each is eminent in one: prudence in you, justice in your mother-in-law, courage in the virgin, and temperance in your wife.

For who is wiser than you who have followed Christ, "the virtue of God and the wisdom of God" [*1 Cor.* 1:24], in rejecting the folly of the world? Or who is more just than your mother-in-law, who has divided her wealth among her children to teach them, following her own example, to spurn wealth, and to teach them what they really should love?

Or who has more courage than Eustochium, who, by choosing virginity, has torn down the gates of the nobility and the pride of the consular class, and has brought chastity to the first class in the first city of Rome?

And who has more temperance than Paulina, who, when she read the words of the apostle "matrimony is honorable, and chaste is the marriage bed" [*Heb.* 13:4], did not want to aspire to the felicity of her sister or the continence of her mother, but proceeded on the safe and lesser way, rather than becoming lost in the clouds. Once she married, her one thought day and night was that, once blessed with children, she would then live at the second level of chastity, and, "though woman, a leader in action," she would link her husband together with her in this new way of life, not leaving each other behind, but together looking forward to the fellowship of salvation.

D. JEROME

Exposition of Isaiah 56:1[4] [date: 410].

Just as the harp does not emit a harmonious sound, when even one of its strings is broken, so, if he lacks one string among the virtues, the spiritual womb of the prophet will not make sweet sounds, he will be like one trying to scream at the top of his lungs through a brick wall. And the opinion of the philosophers is that the virtues are all connected together; and the apostle James [*Jas.* 2:10] says that whoever lacks one virtue lacks them all.

E. AUGUSTINE

Letter 167 to Jerome[5] [date: 415].

1. ... I ask you, and in God's name beseech you, to explain to me something I think will help many ... how to understand these words in the epistle of James: "Whosoever shall keep the whole law, and yet offend in one point, is guilty of all" [*Jas.* 2:10]. ...

3. ... Unless another way of understanding it can be proven, the consequence seems to be that whoever said to the rich man "sit here" and to the pauper "sit there," giving greater honor to the one than the other, is also an idolater, a blasphemer, an adulterer, and a murderer, and, not to recall them all, which would take too long, is judged guilty of all crimes. Offending in one he is made guilty of all.

4. But whoever has one virtue has them all, and whoever lacks one, lacks all. If this be true, the sentence of the apostle is confirmed. But what I want is to have the sentence explained, not confirmed, since we hold that this sentence stands firmer by itself than by all the authority of the philosophers. But even if what has been said about the virtues and vices were true, it would not follow that all sins are equal. For the doctrine of the inseparability of the virtues, perhaps I am wrong, yet if I remember rightly what I hardly remember this doctrine was accepted by all the philosophers, who said these virtues are necessary for living rightly. The doctrine of the equality of sins, however, only the Stoics dared to maintain, against the unanimous consent of the human race. Arguing from the Scriptures, you

[4] CCSL 73: 264.17-24.
[5] CSEL 44: 586-609.

clearly refuted their vanity in the person of Jovinian, whom you called a Stoic in this opinion, but an Epicurean in following and defending pleasure. In that delightful and lucid disputation you made it clear that the idea that all sins are equal is inconsistent with our authorities and with that Truth who has spoken through them. I shall now do my best, with the help of God, to show how it is that, even if the doctrine of philosophers about the virtues is true, we do not have to admit that all sins are equal. Where I succeed, I hope you will approve; where my case is weak, you will improve it.

5. To be sure, those who maintain that whoever has one virtue has all, and that whoever lacks one lacks all, are persuaded in this way: Prudence cannot be cowardly or unjust or intemperate, for if it were any of these it would no longer be prudence. Conversely, if there is prudence only if (*si et*) it is brave and just and temperate [$\sim(C{\cdot}J{\cdot}T) \supset \sim P$], then wherever there is prudence it must have the other virtues along with it [$P \supset (C{\cdot}J{\cdot}T)$]. Likewise, courage cannot be imprudent or intemperate or unjust. And temperance must necessarily be prudent, brave, and just. And there is no justice if it is not prudent, brave, and temperate. Therefore, wherever any one of these virtues truly exists, the others also are found; and where the others are missing, one of these cannot truly be there, even if something somehow similar seems to be there. ...

10. Let us inquire more carefully into the matter. For the statement that "whoever has one virtue has all, and whoever lacks one lacks all" is not a scriptural statement. But this is the way things have appeared to men, to be sure to very clever men, learned men, cultured men, but still just men. ... Now fidelity (*puditia*) in marriage between men and women of faith is undoubtedly a virtue–for it is not nothing, nor is it a vice–yet it does not carry with it all the virtues. For if all virtues were there, there would be no vice; and if no vice, no sin at all. But who is altogether without sin? Therefore, who is without any vice, that is, without what is, as it were, the kindling or the root, of sin, when the apostle John, who rested his head on the breast of the Lord, says: "If we say that we have no sin, we deceive ourselves, and the truth is not in us" [*1 John* 1:8]? ...

11. Far be it from any believer to think that so many thousands of the servants of Christ, who sincerely confess that they are sinful, in order not to deceive themselves and the truth should not be in them, are altogether without virtue. For wisdom is a great virtue, and "he has said to man: Behold, piety is wisdom" [*Job* 28:28]. ...

12. The Stoics, therefore, seem to me to make a mistake, because they deny that a human progressing in wisdom has any wisdom at all, but then

say he has it when he is completely perfect in wisdom. Not that they deny he has progressed, but unless he suddenly emerges from the deep into the free air of wisdom, they say he in no way is wise. For just as for a drowning man there is no difference between being under many stadia of water or at the depth of a hand or even a finger, so they say those who are advancing toward wisdom make progress like those who surge up into the air from the bottom of the sea. But if their progress has not lifted them totally out of foolishness, like emerging from waves breaking over them, then they do not have virtue and are not wise. But when they have emerged, they immediately possess all of wisdom, and no foolishness, which is the source of every sin, remains.

13. This simile, where foolishness is like water and wisdom is like air, so that the mind emerging from suffocating foolishness breathes in wisdom all at once, does not seem to me well accommodated to the authority of our Scriptures. A better simile, so far as intelligible matters can be illustrated by similes borrowed from material things, is to compare vice or foolishness to darkness, and virtue or wisdom to light. So the way to wisdom is not like suddenly breaking from the deep to the air, beyond the highest waves, and breathing easily and all at once, but like proceeding gradually from darkness to light, progressively illumined. Until this happens completely, we say he is like a person climbing out of the depths of a cave toward the region of light, illumined more the closer he gets to the mouth of the cave. So the shining on him comes from the light he seeks, but the obscurity still there comes from the dark he is leaving. ...

14. But what am I doing? I forget to whom I speak, one learned, such as I make myself out to be when I propose to teach what I want to learn from you. But because I hit on the issue of the equality of sins in my topic, I set out my own view for you to examine. Now I bring that topic to a conclusion because, even if it is true that "whoever has one virtue has all the virtues," and "whoever lacks one virtue lacks all," it does not follow that all sins are equal. For where there is no virtue there is nothing right, but it does not follow that there cannot be more and less depravity, more and less distortion. If this be so, and I think this view more in agreement with Scripture, then intentions in the soul are like the parts in the body, not because they can be seen, but because they can be perceived in our affections. And one part is illuminated more, another less, and a third is without light and surrounded by darkness. And if so, as someone is touched by holy charity is in one act more, in another act less, and in a third act not at all good, so that person can be said to have one virtue, not to have another, and to have one more than another. For about that charity

which is piety, we are right to say "there is more charity in this person than in that," and "there is some charity in this one but none in that." And in relation one and the same human, we can say that he has more fidelity (*puditiam*) than patience, and more today than yesterday, and, if he is progressing in virtue, he still does not have continence but has not a little mercy.

15. To sum up briefly the general view I have about virtue so far as relates to right living: Virtue is the charity by which what ought to be loved is loved. This charity exists more in some, less in others, and in some not at all; but the greatest charity, which admits no increase, exists in no human living here on earth. So long as it admits of increase, what makes it less than it ought is due surely to vice. ...

16. If these things be so, how shall a person who has kept the whole law, yet offends in one point, be guilty of all? Perhaps because "the fulfilling of the law is that charity" [*Rom.* 13:10] whereby God and neighbor are loved, on which precepts of charity "hang the whole law and the prophets" [*Matt.* 22:40]. So whoever works against that charity, on which all hangs, is rightly said to be guilty of all. ...

17. Then why are sins not said to be equal? Perhaps because the graver the sin the more one acts against charity, the lesser the sin the less one acts against charity. And the very fact that sin admits of more and less is how one becomes guilty of all. But a graver sin or sinning more makes one more guilty; lesser sin or sinning less makes one less guilty. The greater the guilt the greater the sin, the less the guilt the less the sin. So even if one offends in only one instance, one is guilty of all, because acting against that charity, on which all hangs. ...

21. I have said many things, which may have been tedious for you, because, even if you approve them you do not expect to learn them, since you are accustomed to teach them. If there is anything in these points, about the matter–I don't care much about the style–if there is anything in them which offends your erudite mind, I ask you to tell me in reply, and do not hesitate to correct me.

F. JEROME

Letter 134 to Augustine[6] [date: 416]. Quoted in Augustine, *Letter 202a*[7] [date: 420].

[Jerome replies to Augustine's critique:]

1. Difficult times have come upon us, when it seems to me better to keep silent than to speak, so that our studies can continue, even while the hounds are howling along the Appian way. So I don't have time to respond to the two small treatises, very erudite and overflowing with the splendor of eloquence, you have dedicated to me; not that I think anything in them needs refutation, but, as the Apostle says: "Let each abound in his own sense; one in this way, another in that" [*Rom.* 14:5; *1 Cor.* 7:7]. I am sure that whatever a great mind can say about drinking in the waters of holy scripture, you have set down and discussed. But I ask your grace to allow me just to praise your abilities for awhile. For we have had discussions between ourselves for the sake of learning. But others, who are jealous of us, especially the heretics, will distort any differences of opinion they see in us, dragging things down to the gutter, where their own minds work. As for myself, I have decided to love you, and esteem you, and honor you, and wonder at you, and defend your works as though they were my own. ...

G. GREGORY THE GREAT

Moralia on Job 22:1[8] [date: 602].

[Gregory devotes Bks. 22 and 23 of his commentary to *Job* 31, where Job protests his innocence against the accusations of Eliphaz, Bildad, and Zophar. They had argued (*Job* 3-28) that Job must have sinned, because God would not have allowed Job to be punished had he not sinned. The verses Gregory quotes in sec. 3 below contain Job's main claims of innocence in c. 31. Immediately after the portion translated here, Gregory returns to his line-by-line commentary. But here he steps back from the text and uses Job as an example to explain the unity of the virtues. Following his usual allegorical method, Gregory moves quickly from Job, to the New Testament beatitudes, to the cardinal virtues, and back to Job. His descrip-

[6] PL 22: 1161-2.

[7] CSEL 57: 303.7-22.

[8] CCSL 143a: 1092.1-1093.62

tion of the cardinal virtues is a close paraphrase of Augustine's *Letter 167,* n.5, p. 212 above.]

1. I say what I have often said, and is no burden for me to repeat, because the great preacher has said it: "For me it is not fruitless to write the same things to you, but for you it is needful" [*Phil.* 3:1]. Blessed Job narrates his virtuous deeds because, caught between the reproaches of his accusers and the blows of his trials, he wonders whether his mind is losing the confidence of hope. To be sure, he has heard from the rebukes of his friends the many evils he has done. So his mind would not despair under the combined assault of words and events, he reforms it in the direction of hope by remembering his virtues. And in order not to suffer a great loss, his mind, at a tranquil moment, recollects the great deeds he has done. Therefore, since we have related the reason for his intention, it remains for us closely to examine the virtues he recounts.

2. The first thing to understand is that whoever is believed to prevail in some virtue truly prevails when it is not connected with vices coming from another part. For if it is connected to vices coming from elsewhere, it won't stand solid when we think it will. For each virtue is less to the extent that the other virtues are missing. Now it often happens that we see those who are modest but not humble; those who seem humble but not merciful; those who seem merciful but not just; those who seem just but have more confidence in themselves than in the Lord. But it is certain there is no true chastity in the heart of whomever lacks humility, because, owing to internal corruption from pride, by loving himself his fornication removes him from the love of God. Nor is that humility true which has not been joined to mercy, because what knows not how to bend to a brother's misery ought not be called humility. Nor is that mercy true which stands apart from the rectitude of justice, because what could be defiled through injustice doubtless does not know how to be merciful. Nor is that justice true which places its trust, not in the creator of all, but in itself perhaps, or in created things, because, in dragging hope away from the creator it perverts the order coming from the highest justice. Therefore, one virtue without the others is either nothing at all or imperfect.

For when I speak of what have appeared to some as the four primary virtues–prudence, temperance, courage, and justice–each single one of them is perfect to the extent it is joined in turn to the others. When disunited they cannot at all be perfect, because that prudence is not true which is not just and temperate and brave; nor is that temperance complete which is not brave, just and wise; nor is that courage whole, which is not prudent, temperate, and just; nor is that justice true which is not prudent, brave, and temperate.

3. So blessed Job, because he had, not one virtue without another, but all joined together, shows us this by enumerating the virtues one by one. Introducing the goodness of modesty, he says: "If my heart was seduced by a woman."[9] And to show that the grace of humility was not absent from modesty, he adds: "If I refused to subject myself to the judgment of the law over my man-servant."[10] And to show that mercy was joined to his humility, he adds: "If I denied the poor what they wanted."[11] And to show that his mercy comes from the root of justice, a bit earlier he said: "If I have walked in vanity, or hastened my steps toward deceit."[12] And to show how concerned he was about all the virtues, and how he considers all of them, he adds: "For I have always feared God, like waves breaking over me."[13] No one lifted up to prosperity and filled with an abundance of goods, who places hope in his own actions or in his circumstance, truly can be just. But when did this holy man put his hope in himself, since he clearly says: "Behold, help within me there is none"?[14] What remains but for you to learn the great inner wealth he possessed?

[9] *Job* 31:9-10: "If my heart was seduced by a woman, and if I waited at the door of my friend, then may my own wife be another man's mistress, and others have her to bed."

[10] *Job* 31:13-14: "If I refused to subject myself to the judgment of the law over my own man-servant or my serving-girl when they disputed with me, then what shall I do when God stands in judgment?"

[11] *Job* 31:16-17: "If I denied the poor what they wanted, and made the eyes of the widow wait in longing; if I have eaten my portion alone, and the orphan has had none of it."

[12] *Job* 31:5-6: "If I have walked in vanity, or hastened my steps in deceit, let him weigh me with the scales of justice, God will know my simplicity."

[13] *Job* 31:23: "For I have always feared God, like waves breaking over me, and I could not bear his weight."

[14] *Job* 6:13.

Appendix 2
Texts of the Masters on the Cardinal Virtues

A. Bernard of Clairvaux

On Consideration to Pope Eugenius III, Bk. 1. VII.8–VIII.11[1] [date: 1148-53].

[In 1145 Bernard Pignatelli, former monk of the Cistercian Abbey of Clairvaux in France and Abbot of St. Anastasio in Rome, was elevated to a pontificate marked by repeated conflicts with secular rulers. Bernard of Clairvaux then wrote him this long treatise, whose basic argument was that now, more than ever, his former student needed to rely on virtue, and chiefly on the intellectual practice Bernard calls, using a Stoic term, "consideration." No small advantage of consideration is in how it leads directly to the cardinal virtues, which are required for success in the practical world outside the cloister. In the following passage, Bernard uses the strong, Stoic sense of the unity of the cardinal virtues to show how they derive from "consideration." His argument is classical in relying on how the cardinal virtues mutually entail each other, and it shows how sensitive Bernard was to reductionism. For he raises the possibility of reducing all the cardinal virtues to temperance, then shies away from this unhappy consequence for no very strong reason. When Philip the Chancellor read this passage, two things struck him: the connection of the virtues, and certain phrases (here italicized) that he thought uncovered the very nature of the cardinal virtues and helped him develop scholastic, formulaic definitions for them. Philip summarized what he found in Bernard at pp. 97, 101-102 above.]

1.vii.8. You ask: "What is piety?" It is leaving time for consideration. Perhaps you tell me that in this I dissent from him who defined piety as "worship of God" [*Job* 28:28]. But this is not true. If you consider the matter well, I have expressed his sense in my own words, though only partly so. What pertains to the "worship of God" as much as what he exhorts us

[1] 1: 403.8-407.8.

to in the *Psalm*: "Leave time and see that I am God" [45:11]? And this is the most important part of consideration. In the end, what is as powerful as consideration, for through a kind of benign anticipation it produces the parts of action itself, by in a way acting out and ordering beforehand what ought to be done? Such consideration is necessary, otherwise actions which, if foreseen and premeditated could turn out propitious, might rather precipitate disaster. I doubt not that such things have happened to you with some frequency, if you remember certain actions in law, certain important negotiations and plans for great projects. First, consideration purifies that very font, that is, the mind, from which such endeavors flow. Next it governs the affections, then directs actions, corrects excesses, composes our morals, makes for a good and orderly life, and finally bestows knowledge of things both divine and human. This it is which puts limits to confusions, closes lacunae, pulls together what is dispersed, discloses secrets, investigates truths, weighs probabilities, exposes falsities and counterfeits. This it is which arranges things before and analyzes them after, so that nothing incorrect or needing correction resides in the mind. This it is which in prosperity anticipates adversity and in adversity does not fall victim. Of these virtues, one is courage, the other is prudence.

viii.9. Here you should observe there is the sweetest harmony and connection among the virtues, so that one depends upon the other. In the present case, you see that prudence is the mother of courage, and any confrontation not born of prudence should not be called courage, but foolhardiness. Again, it is consideration that finds the mean between pleasures and necessities, sitting as a kind of judge, she sets definite limits, assigning what is enough for one side, for the other that too much is foolish, and from both forming a third virtue called temperance. For consideration judges whoever stubbornly denies himself necessities is as intemperate as whoever indulges in superfluities. Therefore, temperance consists both in *cutting out superfluities* and in using necessities. Of this the Apostle seems to be not just a supporter but its author, for he teaches that care of the flesh is not perfected in desire. When he says that "the care of the flesh is not perfected" he checks superfluities; and when he adds "in desire" he does not exclude necessities [*Rom.* 13:14]. Therefore, it seems to me not completely absurd to define temperance as neither cutting off necessities nor exceeding them, following the philosopher's maxim: "Nothing to excess."

10. Now about justice, which is one of the four, is it not true that the mind must proceed through consideration before achieving the form of justice? For the mind must first reflect in order to develop out of itself the

norm of justice: not to do to another what it would not want done to itself, and not to deny to another what it would want for itself. In these two injunctions is clearly found the whole state of justice. But justice is not alone. Look now with me at the beautiful connection and conjunction between justice and temperance, and between both of these and the two virtues mentioned above, that is, prudence and courage.

Since half of justice is "not to do to another what you would not want done to you," while its perfect half, as the Lord says, is "do unto others as you would have them do unto you" [*Matt.* 7:12], neither half comes about unless the will, which wholly forms an action, is so ordered that it wills nothing superfluous and does not superstitiously refuse to will anything necessary. But this is precisely the function of temperance. Again, for justice to be just, temperance must impose the mean. "Be not too just" [*Eccles.* 7:17] says the sage, showing that justice which is not reined in by the mean given by temperance is minimally worthwhile. And why is it that wisdom itself does not spit out the bridle of temperance, as Paul says, following the wisdom given him by God: "Be not wiser than one ought, but be wise soberly" [*2 Pet.* 3:15]?[2]

Conversely, the Lord shows that justice is necessary for temperance, arguing against the temperance of those who abstain in order to seem to men to be fasting [*Matt.* 6:16]. Here was temperance about food but no justice in the mind, because they did not intend to please God, but men.[3]

Again, how can there be justice or temperance without courage? For it is true that the essence of courage, and no mediocre courage, consists in this: to confine one's choices and denials within the narrow way between too little and too much, so that the will is content with that mean which lies in the middle, bare, pure, alone, constant in itself and equitable to others, so that in every part it is equally trimmed? For it is agreed that in this alone consists the essence of virtue.[4]

11. Tell me, I ask, if you can, to which of these three virtues [justice, courage, temperance] do you think you should cede this middle ground which so borders on all that is seems to be the property of each? Is virtue this middle ground, and nothing else? If so, virtue would not be many, but all the virtues would be one. Is it not better to say that without this middle ground there would be no virtue? For it is in a way the one, internal power,

[2] $\sim T \supset \sim J$.

[3] $\sim J \supset \sim T$.

[4] $(\sim C \supset \sim J), (\sim C \supset \sim T)$.

the marrow of all the virtues, in which they are so united that they all seem to be one, especially because when they participate in it they do not send it from one to another but each possesses it whole and entire. For example, what is more a part of justice than the mean? If justice gave something beyond the mean, clearly it would not *render to each his own*, which is the very function of justice. Again, what else is temperance but to admit nothing immoderate? But I think you will confess that this mean is no less the essence of courage, since courage powerfully preserves the mean, keeping it pure from vices which assault it and attempt, as it were, to suffocate it. And courage *protects* it as the stable foundation of the good and the seat of virtue. Therefore, to hold to the mean is justice, it is temperance, it is courage. But look, perhaps they differ in this way, that the reality of justice exists in the affections, but its efficacy comes from courage and its possession and use is found in temperance.

It remains for us to prove that prudence is not excluded from this communion of virtues. Is not prudence what first finds and attends to the mean, long undervalued because neglected by the mind, as it were hidden away because of the envy of the vices and covered by the darkness of ancient habit? So I say to you: few attend to the mean because few are prudent.

And so justice seeks, prudence finds, courage protects, and temperance possesses the mean. This does not seem to me the place to dispute what I have offered you about the virtues, but I have said this much in order to exhort you to leave time for consideration, for its benefits consist in adverting to these and similar truths. To give no effort in life to such pious and useful employment of leisure, is this not to lose life itself?

B. Peter Lombard

Sentences, Bk. 3, d. 33 and 36[5] [date: 1155-58].

d. 33. c.1.1. Next we should discuss the four virtues which are called principal or cardinal virtues. They are justice, courage, prudence, temperance.

2. About them Augustine says: "Justice consists in helping the miserable, prudence in taking precautions to avoid traps, courage in enduring difficulties, temperance in restraining depraved pleasures."[6]

[5] 2: 187-8, 202-5.

[6] Augustine, *De trin.* 14.9.12, CCSL 50a: 439.

3. About them it says in the book of *Wisdom* [8:7]: "Sobriety and prudence she teaches, justice and truth." *Sobriety* signifies *temperance* while *truth* signifies *courage*. These virtues are called cardinal, as Jerome says,[7] "by which in this mortality one lives well" and afterwards attains eternal life.

c. 2. These virtues were and are to the fullest extent in Christ, "from whose fullness we have received them" [*John* 1:15]. In him they had the same use in heaven as on earth.

[c. 3 omitted]

d. 36. c. 1.1. It is usual to ask whether the virtues are so connected to each other that they cannot be possessed separately by anyone, that whoever has one has all. On this issue Jerome says: "All the virtues are so connected together that whoever lacks one lacks all,"[8] and whoever has one has all.

2. Now this seems probable. For since charity is the mother of all the virtues, wherever the mother is, that is, charity, there all her children, that is, the virtues, are rightly believed to be. Consequently, Augustine says: "Where there is charity, what can be lacking; and where there is no charity, what can be there?"[9] "Therefore, why do we not say that whoever has this virtue has all the virtues, since 'charity is the fullness of the law' [cf. *Rom.* 13:10]? The more charity there is in a man the more he is endowed with virtue, and the less charity, the less virtue is in him; and the less virtue, the more vice."[10]

c. 2.1. It is a genuine question whether someone possesses all the virtues equally (*pariter*), or some more and others less fervently.

2. For it seems to some that some are possessed more and others less by a given person. For example, patience stands out in Job, humility in David, and mercy in Moses. They also concede that someone has more merit through one virtue than through another, as he has one virtue more fully than another. But they say that one does not have more merit through any virtue other than charity, nor does one have another virtue more fully than one has charity. Therefore, they say there can be more of some and less of other virtues in someone, but none more than charity, which gener-

[7] Actually Augustine, *De trin.* 14.9.12, CCSL 50a: 438.

[8] Jerome, *In Isaiam* 56:1, CCSL 73: 264.17-24. See above, p. 211.

[9] Augustine, *In Ioannem* 15:12, 83.3, CCSL 36: 536.

[10] Augustine, *Ep. 167* to Jerome 3.11, CSEL 44: 599. See p. 212 above.

ates the others. And they call these the many faces the Apostle remembers when he says "from persons of many faces."

3. Others say what is truer, that all the virtues are together and on a par in whomever they exist, so that whoever is on a par with someone else about one virtue is equal to him in all the virtues. Consequently, Augustine says: "The virtues which exist in the human soul, although they are understood individually in this way and the other, can in no way be separated from one another, so that whoever are equal, for example, in courage, are also equal in prudence and justice and temperance. For if you said they are equal in courage, but one is better in prudence, it would follow that his courage would be less prudent. Consequently, they would not be equal in courage, because the courage of the other would be more prudent. And you will find the same thing is true of the other virtues, if you give them all this same consideration."[11]

4. From these points it becomes clear that all the virtues are not only connected to each other but also are on a par in the mind of man. Therefore, when someone is said to stand out in some virtue, say Abraham in faith or Job in patience, this must be understood about exterior uses of the virtue, or in comparison with other humans. For either he stands out especially in the preceding *habit* of humility or in the succeeding deed of faith or some other virtue, and this is why this virtue is said to prevail over other virtues, or he is said to excel other men in one virtue.

5. In this respect, that is, based on exterior acts, Augustine says in another text that in one person there can be more of one virtue and less of another, or one virtue can exist but not another. For he says: "In your lucid disputation it is clear that the idea that all sins are equal is inconsistent with our authorities and with truth itself, even if the doctrine about the virtues is true."[12] "Even if it is true that whoever has one virtue has all the virtues, and whoever lacks one virtue lacks all, it does not follow that all sins are equal. For where there is no virtue there is nothing right, but it does not follow that there cannot be more and less depravity, more and less distortion. If this be so, and I think this view more in agreement with Scripture, then intentions in the soul are like the parts in the body, not because they can be seen, but because they can be perceived in our affections. And one part is illuminated more, another less, and a third is without light. And if so, as someone is touched by holy charity is in one act more,

[11] Augustine, *De trin.* 6.4.6, CCSL 50: 233ff.

[12] Augustine, *Ep. 167* to Jerome, 2.4, CSEL 44: 592. See pp. 211-12 above.

in another act less, and in a third act not at all good, so that person can be said to have one virtue, not to have another, and to have one more than another. For about that charity which is piety, we are right to say there is more charity in this person than in that, and there is some charity in this one but none in that. And in relation one and the same human, we can say that he has more fidelity (*puditiam*) than patience, and more today than yesterday, and, if he is progressing in virtue, he still does not have continence but has not a little mercy. To sum up briefly the general view I have about virtue so far as relates to right living: Virtue is the charity by which what ought to be loved is loved. This charity exists more in some, less in others, and in some not at all; but the greatest charity, which admits no increase, exists in no human living here on earth."[13]

6. Here it seems implied that by this argument someone can be said to have one virtue more than another, because through charity more is done in the act of one virtue than in the act of another. Based on this difference in their acts it can be said that one has these virtues more or less, or that one does not have some virtue, even though one has them all together and equally in regard to habits of mind and their essences. In act, then, one has one virtue more and another less and another not at all, as the just man, making use of his wife, does not have continence in act even though he has the habit of it.

[c. 2.7 and c. 3 omitted]

C. THOMAS AQUINAS

Commentary on the Nicomachean Ethics, Bk. 2, lec. 8[14] [date: ca. 1270].

[Having formulated a definition of moral virtue in 2.6, Aristotle devotes 2.7 to a preliminary description of the moral virtues he later treats in detail. Aquinas makes the transition from a general definition of virtue to specific virtues by pausing at the mid-point between them–the cardinal virtues–and he raised a "consideration" not in Aristotle's text: what is the nature of the cardinal virtues?]

It should be noted that some thinkers have distinguished the virtues in two ways:

[13]Augustine, *Ep. 167* to Jerome, 4.14-15, CSEL 44: 601-2. See above, pp. 213-14.

[14] Ed. Leonine, 47: 102.33-103.97.

Certain thinkers view the distinctions among the virtues according to the general modes of the virtues, which are four. Now the root of virtue consists in that rightness of reason which one must follow in guiding one's actions and passions. But we direct actions and passions in different ways. For in their own nature actions, like buying and selling, are not resistant to reason. Therefore, for actions reason need only establish their rightness in some sort of equity. But the passions add a kind of inclination which can resist and battle reason. This can happen in two ways. In the first way passion draws reason away toward something else. This is clearly so for all the passions which pertain to following our appetites, such as desire, hope, anger, etc. For these passions reason has to establish rightness by repressing them and reining them in. In the second way passion pulls us back from what is in accord with reason. This is clear for all the passions which pertain to fleeing the appetites, such as fear, hatred, and such things. In passions of this sort reason has to establish rectitude by fortifying the mind for what is in accord with reason. Based on these considerations, the virtues are said to be four, and some call these four the principal virtues. For to prudence pertains the rightness of reason itself; to justice pertains the equity we put into our actions; to courage pertains firmness of mind; and to temperance pertains reining in or repressing the passions, as the very names of the virtues indicate.

Therefore, some have understood these virtues in a general way, supposing every cognition of truth pertains to prudence, every equity in actions pertains to justice, all fortifying the mind pertains to courage, and all restraining or repressing the passions pertains to temperance. Cicero and Seneca and certain others have spoken about these virtues in this way. Consequently, they have posited these virtues to be as it were general virtues and have said that all the virtues are species of these general virtues.

But this does not seem to be a good way of distinguishing the virtues. First, because these four virtues are such that without them no virtue can exist. Consequently, the species of virtues cannot be distinguished using them. Second, because the species of the virtues and vices are not determined by looking to reason, but by looking to their objects, as was said above.

Therefore, Aristotle's way of distinguishing the virtues in relation to their objects, or their matter, is better. In this way the four virtues in question are not called principal because they are general virtues, but because their species are understood in relation to certain principal concerns. For example, prudence is not about every cognition of truth, but specifically about the act of reason which is applying practical precepts. Justice is not about all equity in actions, but only about those actions toward others in which producing equity is the better thing to do. Likewise, courage is not about every firmness of mind, but only when fear of the danger of death is present. And temperance is not about all restraining, but only concerns the desires connected with the pleasures of touch. In addition, there are other virtues which concern secondary matters. Therefore, these additional virtues can be reduced to the four already mentioned, not as species to their genera, but as secondary to principal virtues.

The Development of the "Parts" of Courage: andreia, fortitudo

Cicero *De inv.* 87 BC	Andronicus *De pass* 50 BC	Diogenes *Vitae 7* 250 AD	Stobaeus 400	Macrobius *In som. Scip.* 400	Philip *De bono* 1225	Albert *De bono, Sent* 1248	Aquinas *ST,CV* 1270s	
General courage:								
	stouthearted Eupsychia	good tone eutonia	stouthearted eupsychia	firmness firmitas	confront difficulty	confront difficulty	firmness firmitas	
Special courage:								
					exterior passions	death	death	
Parts of courage:							**potential parts:**	**integral parts:**
(1a) magnificence								
magnificence magnificentia	magnificence magnificentia			magnificence magnificentia	magnificence magnificentia	magnificence magnificentia	magnificence magnificentia	execution executio
(1b) magnanimity								
	magnanimity magnanimitas	magnanimity megalopsychia	magnanimity megalopyschia	magnanimity magnanimitas			magnanimity magnanimitas	
(2) confidence								
confidence fidentia	manliness virilitas andragathia	unchangeable aparallaxia	confidence tharraleotes	confidence fiducia	confidence fidentia	confidence fidentia		confidence fidentia
(3) patience								
patience patientia		patience karteria	patience karteria	tolerance tolerantia	patience patientia	patience patientia	patience patientia	sustenance sustenentia

(4) perseverance

perseverance	perseverance		industriousness	constancy	perseverance	perseverance	perseverance	constancy
perseverantia	perseverantia		philoponia steadiness securitas	constantia	perseverantia	perseverantia	perseverantia	constantia
	linea?							

The Development of the “Parts” of Temperance: sôphrosynê, temperantia

Cicero *De inv.* 87 BC	**Andronicus** *De pass* 50 BC	**Diogenes** *Vitae 7* 250 AD	**Stobaeus** 400	**Macrobius** *In som. Scip.* 400	**Philip** *De bono* 1225	**Albert** *De bono, Sent* 1248	**Aquinas** *ST,CV* 1270s
General temperance:							
	[bona ordinatio	eutaxia	eutaxia]	moderatio	moderatio	moderatio	moderatio
							Integral parts:
				honestas verecundia		honestas	honestas verecundia
Special temperance					bodily passions	touch and taste	touch
Parts:							**Subjective parts:**
							[food]
				abstinentia		abstinentia	abstinentia
				sobrietas	sobrietas	sobrietas	sobrietas
							[sex]
				castitas	continentia	castitas	castitas
					virginitas	virginitas	virginitas
					aureola	viduitas	
				puditia		puditia	puditia
							Potential parts:
continentia	continentia		egkrateia			continentia	continentia
clementia						clementia	clementia
modestia			aidemosyne	modestia	modestia	modestia	modestia

bona ordinatio	eutaxia	eutaxia				bona ordinatio
ornatus	kosmiotes	kosmiotes				ornatus
austeritas					austeritas	austeritas
per se sufficientia			parcitas		parcitas	parcitas
simplicitas						simplicitas
humilitas						humilitas

The Development of the “Parts” of Justice: dikaiosunê, iustitia

Cicero	Andronicus	Diogenes	Stobaeus	Macrobius	Philip	Albert	Aquinas	
De inv.	*De pass*	*Vitae 7*		*In som. Scip.*	*De bono*	*De bono, Sent*	*ST,CV*	
87 BC	50 BC	250 AD	400	400	1225	1248	1270s	
General justice:								
						rectitudo	rectitudo render ius to other = community/ruler/God	
Special Justice								
[par		isotês	eukoinônêsia]			aequalitas	j. particularis aequalitas other = individual	others’
Parts							**Integral parts**: Do good to others Avoid evil to others	
						j. distributiva j. restitutiva	**Subjective parts**: j. distributiva: ruler to individual j. commutativa: individual. to individual	
religio pietas gratia observatia	eusebia eucharistia eugnômosunê	eugnômosunê	eusebia eusunallaxia	religio pietas concordia humanitas			**Potential parts**: religio pietas gratia observantia	

bona

commutatio

benignitas amicitia amicitia

vindicatio vindicativa vindicatio

veritas chrêstotês veritas

affectus

innocentia

pactum

par isotês eukoinônêsia equitas

iudicatum legispositiva

liberalitas liberalitas

sanctitas

Glossary of Latin Terms

ad aliquid: relative, relative to some particular matter, in one area of life
appetitus: appetite, inclination
ars: craftsmanship, art, skill
attenduntur secundum: understood in relation to

cognitio: thinking, thought, knowledge
cognitio rationalis: rational direction
concupiscibilis: desire, desiring
constantia: constancy
consuetudo: pattern of behavior
conveniens, convenienter: good, right, well, appropriate

electio: choice
evacuo: lay aside

firmitas: resoluteness
fortitudo: courage

habitus: habit
homo: a human, the human, man, person

infusio, infusa: infusion, outpouring, infused
intemperans: intemperate
irascibilis: emotional, emotion, emotive, irascible
ius: right, due, law
iustitia: justice

moderatio: moderation, limit, measure
modificatio: modification

opus: function, deed

passio: passion
passio concupiscibilis: desiring passion, desiderative passion
passio irascibilis: emotive passion

perfecta: complete, perfect; *imperfecta*: incomplete, imperfect
potentia: power
praedictae: the ones mentioned, those under consideration
prudentia: prudence

quantum: in so far as, to the extent that, as
rectitudo: correctness, right, propriety, rightness
refrenatio: restraint, reining in

simpliciter: absolute, essential, intrinsic; general, concerning one's whole life
sobrietas: sobriety
sustinentia: endurance

temperantia: temperance; *intemperantia*: lack of temperance, intemperance

vindico: protect
virtus: virtue
vitium: vice

Terms for the Powers of the Soul

- *cognitio*: cognition
  - *apprehensio*: apprehension
  - *sensitivus*: sense
  - *intellectualis*: intellectual
- *appetitus*: appetite, desire
  - *appetitivus*: appetitive
- *passio*: passion
  - *appetitus intellectualis*: intellectual appetite
    - *voluntas*: will
  - *appetitus sensitivus*: sense appetite
    - *appetitus irascibilis*: emotion(al)
    - *appetitus concupiscibilis*: desiring, desire, desiderative, appetite

Bibliography

A. PRIMARY SOURCES FOR PHILIP, ALBERT, AND AQUINAS

Albert the Great. *Opera omnia*. ed. Borgnet. Paris: Vives, 1894-1902.
——. *Opera omnia*. Cologne: Aschendorff, 1951-.
——. *De bono*. ed. H. Kühle, C. Feckes, B. Geyer, W. Küble. Ed. Cologne 28, 1951.
——. *Ethica*, ed. Borgnet 7.
——. *In 3 Sententiarum*. ed. Borgnet 28, 1890.
——. *Super ethica commentum et quaestiones*. W. Kübel. Cologne 14.1, 1968.

Philip the Chancellor. *Summa de bono*. ed. N. Wicki. Bernae: Francke, 1985.

Thomas Aquinas. *Opera omnia*. ed. Leonine. Rome: Typographia Polyglotta, 1882-.
——. 34 vols. Paris: Vives, 1871-1880.
——. *Quaestiones quodlibetales*. ed. R. Spiazzi. 8th ed. Turin-Rome: Marietti, 1949.
——. *Scriptum super sententiis magistri Petri Lombardi,* vol. 3. ed. M.F. Moos. Paris: 1933.
——. *Sententia libri Ethicorum Aristotelis*. ed. Leonine. Rome, 1969. vol. 47, 47.2. Tr: *Commentary on the Nicomachean Ethics*. tr. C.I.Litzinger. 2 vols. Chicago: 1964. rpr. Notre Dame, IN: Dumb Ox Press, 1993.
——. *Summa theologiae*. 5 vols. Ottawa: 1941.
——. *Summa theologiae*. ed. T. Gilby. 60 vols. London-New York: 1964-1969.
——. *De virtutibus in communi,* in *Quaestiones disputatae,* vol. 2. ed. P. Bazzi et al. 9th ed. Rome-Turin: Marietti, 1953. Tr: *St. Thomas Aquinas on The Virtues (in General)* tr. J.P. Reid. Providence, RI: Providence College Press, 1951. *Disputed Questions on Virtue*. tr. R.M. McInerny. South Bend, IN: St. Augustine's Press, 1999.
——. *De virtutibus cardinalibus,* in *Quaestiones disputatae,* vol. 2. ed. P. Bazzi et al. 9 ed. Rome-Turin: Marietti, 1953. *Disputed Questions on Virtue*. tr. R.M. McInerny. South Bend, IN: St. Augustine's Press, 1999.

B. Other Ancient and Medieval Authors

Anonymous. "The Anonymous Scholia on Books II,III, and IV", *The Greek Commentaries on the Nicomachean Ethics of Aristotle: In the Latin Translation of Robert Grosseteste, Bishop of Lincoln (†1253)* vol. 1, *Corpus Latinum Commentariorum in Aristotelem Graecorum* vol. 6.1. ed. H.P.F. Mercken. Leiden: Brill, 1973.

Alexander of Hales. *Glossa in quatuor libros sententiarum Petri Lombardi*. vol. 3. Florence: Quaracchi, 1954.

Ambrose. *De excessu fratris Satyri* ed. O. Faller. CSEL 73. 1955. Tr. M. McGuire et al, *Funeral Orations by Gregory Nazianzen and St. Ambrose*. The Fathers of the Church, vol. 22. New York: 1953.

——. *De fide 5 ad Gratianum Augustum*. PL 16.

——. *De Ioseph*. Ed. C. Schenkl. CSEL 32.2. Prague, Vienna, Leipzig: 1897.

——. *De officiis*. PL 16.

——. *De paradiso*. ed. C. Schenkl. CSEL 32.1. Prague, Vienna, Leipzig: 1898.

——. *De spiritu sancto*. PL 16.

——. *Exemeron*. ed. C. Schenkl. CSEL 32.1. Prague, Vienna, Leipzig: 1898.

——. *Expositio evangelii secundum Lucam*. ed. M. Adriaen. CCSL 14. Turnhout: Brepols, 1957. Tr: *Traité sur l'Evangile S. Luc*. G. Tissot. Paris: Editions du Cerf, 1956, 1971.

Apuleius. *De Platone et eius dogmate*. Ed. Beaujeau. Paris: Les Belles Lettres, 1973.

Aristotle. *Ethica Nichomachea*. ed. I. Bywater. Oxford: Clarendon, 1894, rpr. 1962. Tr: W.D. Ross. in *The Works of Aristotle*, vol. 9. Oxford: 1925. rev. J.O. Urmson. in *The Complete Works of Aristotle*, vol. 2. Princeton: 1984. Lat. Tr. R.A. Gauthier, ed. *Aristoteles Latinus* 26.1-3.1-5. Leiden: Brill, 1972-74.

Augustine. *Contra Julianum*. PL 44: 641-874. Tr: *St. Augustine: Against Julian*. tr. M.A. Schumacher. in *The Fathers of the Church*, vol.35. New York: 1957.

——. *De civitate dei xi-xxii*. ed. B. Dombart, A. Kalb. CCSL 48. Turnhout: Brepols, 1955.

——. *De genesi ad literam*. ed. J. Zycha. CSEL 28. Vienna: 1894. Tr: *St. Augustine: The Literal Meaning of Genesis*. tr. J.H. Taylor. in *Ancient Christian Writers*, vol. 41-2. New York: Newman Press, 1982.

——. *De libero arbitrio*. ed. W.M. Green. CCSL 29. Turnhout: Brepols, 1970.

——.*De moribus ecclesiae*. PL 32: 1309-1378. Tr: *The Catholic and Manichaean Ways of Life*. tr. D. and I. Gallagher. in *The Fathers of the Church*, vol. 56. Washington: Catholic University Press, 1966.

——. *De Trinitate*. ed. W.J. Mountain. CCSL 50, 50a. Turnhout: Brepols, 1968. Tr: *St. Augustine: The Trinity*. tr. S. McKenna. in *The Fathers of the Church*. vol. 45. Washington: Catholic University Press, 1963.

——. *Epistulae*. ed. A. Goldbacher. CSEL 44. Vienna: 1904. Tr: *Letters of Saint Augustine*. tr. J.G. Cunningham. Edinburgh: 1875.

——. *Retractationes*. ed. A. Mutzenbecher. CCSL 57. Turnhout: Brepols, 1984.

Bede. *In Lucae evangelii expositio*. ed. D. Hurst. CCSL 120. Turnhout: Brepols, 1960.

Bernard. *De consideratione ad Eugenium papam*. in *Opera omnia*, vol. 3. ed. J. Leclercq, H.M. Rochais. Rome: Editiones Cistercienses, 1963. Tr: *Five Books on Consideration*. J.D. Anderson, E.T. Kennan. Kalamazoo, MI: Cistercian Publications, 1976.

Biblia Latina cum Glossa Ordinaria. ed. princeps. Strassburg: Adolph Rusch, 1480-1. repr. Turnhout: Brepols, 1992.

Bonaventure. *Commentaria in quatuor libros sententiarum magistri Petri Lombardi*, vol. 3. in *Opera omnia*, vol. 3. Florence: Quaracchi, 1887.

Cicero. *De officiis*. ed., tr. Walter Miller. Cambridge, MA: Harvard, 1975.

Cyprian. *De habitu virginum*. in *Opera omnia*. ed. G. Hartel. CSEL 3. Vienna: 1868. tr. Sr. A.E. Keenan, *St. Cyprian: Treatises*. in *The Fathers of the Church*, vol. 36. New York: 1958.

Gregory the Great. *Homiliae in Hiezechihelem prophetam*. ed. M. Adriaen. CCSL 142. Turnhout: Brepols, 1971.

——. *Moralia in Job*. ed. M. Adriaen. CCSL 143, 143a. Turnhout: Brepols, 1979-80. Tr: *Morals on the Book of Job*. Tr. J. Bliss. in *A Library of Fathers of the Holy Catholic Church*,ed. E.B. Pusey, John Keble, C. Marriott. Oxford: 1845.

Hugh of St. Victor. *De sacramentis christianae fidei*. PL 176: 183-618. Tr: *Hugh of St. Victor on the Sacraments of the Christian Faith*. tr. R.J. Deferrari. Cambridge, MA: Mediaeval Academy, 1951.

Isaac of Stella. *Epistola de anima*. PL 194.

Jerome. *Commentariorum in Hiezechielem Libri XIV*. ed. F. Glorie. CCSL 75. Turnhout: Brepols, 1964.

——. *Epistulae*. ed. I. Hilberg. CSEL 54. Vienna: 1904-10. PL 22: 325-1191. Tr: *St. Jerome: Letters and Select Works*. in *Nicene and Post-Nicene Fathers*, vol. 6. W.H. Fremantle. New York: 1893.

John Damascene. *De fide orthodoxa*, tr. Burgundio. ed. E. Buytaert. St. Bonaventure, NY: Franciscan Institute Press, 1955. Tr. from Gk: *John of Damascus: Writings*. in *The Fathers of the Church*, vol. 57. New York, 1955.

Macrobius. *In Somnium Scipionis*. Ed. Eyssenhardt. Leipzig: Teubner, 1893. Tr. W. Stahl, *Commentary on the Dream of Scipio*. New York: Columbia, 1952.

Peter Lombard. *Sententiae in iv libris distinctae*, 2 vols. 3rd ed. Rome: Grottaferatta, 1981.

Plato. *Platonis Opera*. ed. J. Burnet. Oxford: Clarendon, 1901.

Ulrich of Strasburgh. *Summa de bono*. Ed. J. Daguillon, *La Summa de bono, lib. 1*. Paris: Vrin, 1930. Ed. F.J. Lescoe, *God as First Principle in Ulrich of Strasbourg*. New York: Alba, 1979. *De summo bono*, ed. K. Flasch and L. Sturlese (Corpus Philosophorum Teutonicorum Medii Aevi) 1 (1989), 2.1-4 (1987), 4.1-2 (1987).

Xenophon. *Memorabilia*. Ed., tr. E.C. Marchant. New York: Putnam, 1968.

C. Modern Authors

Abba, Giuseppe. *Lex et virtus: Studi sull'evoluzione della dottrina morale di san Tommaso d'Aquino*. Rome: Libreria Ateneo Salesiano, 1983.

Aertsen, J. *Medieval philosophy and the transcendentals: the case of Thomas Aquinas*. Leiden: Brill, 1996.

——. *Nature and Creature: Thomas Aquinas's Way of Thought*. Leiden: Brill, 1988.

Algra, Keimpe, et al., eds. *The Cambridge history of Hellenistic philosophy*. Cambridge: Cambridge University Press, 1999.

Annas, J. *Platonic Ethics, Old and New*. Ithaca: Cornell, 1999.

Anscombe, G.E.M. "Modern Moral Philosophy," in *Collected Philosophical Papers*, vol. III: *Ethics, Religion, and Politics*. Minneapolis: University of Minnesota Press, 1982, 26-42.

Barnes, J., ed. *The Cambridge companion to Aristotle*. Cambridge: Cambridge University Press, 1995.

Benson, H.H., ed. *Essays on the Philosophy of Socrates*. Oxford: Oxford University Press, 1992.

Bloomfield, Morton. *The Seven Deadly Sins*. 2nd ed. East Lansing, MI: Michigan State Press, 1967.

——. *Incipits of Latin Works on the Virtues and Vices, 1100-1500AD*. Cambridge, MA: Harvard, 1979.

Bourke, V. *Ethics: A Textbook in Moral Philosophy*. New York: Macmillan, 1966.

——. *Will in Western Thought: An Historico-Critical Survey*. New York: Sheed and Ward, 1964.

Boyle, Leonard E. *The Setting of the Summa theologiae of St. Thomas*. Toronto: Pontifical Institute of Mediaeval Studies, 1982.

Bradley, Denis J.M. *Aquinas on the Twofold Human Good*. Washington: Catholic University of America, 1997.

Broadie, Sarah. *Ethics with Aristotle*. Oxford: Oxford University Press, 1991.

Brown, Oscar. *Natural Rectitude and Divine Law in Aquinas*. Toronto: Pontifical Institute of Mediaeval Studies, 1981.

Bullet, G. *Vertus morales infuses et vertus morales acquises selon saint Thomas d'Aquin*. Fribourg: Éditions universitaires, 1958.

Carr, David. "The Cardinal Virtues and Plato's Moral Psychology," *Philosophical Quarterly* 38 (1988) 186-200.

Casey, John. *Pagan Virtue*. Oxford: Clarendon, 1990.

Castiello, J. "The psychology of Habit in St. Thomas," *The Modern Schoolman* 14 (1936) 9-12.

Cessario, Romanus, OP. *The Moral Virtues and Theological Ethics*. Notre Dame, IN: University of Notre Dame Press, 1991.

Chenu, M.D. *Introduction à l'étude de S. Thomas d'Aquin*. Paris: 1950. Tr.*Toward Understanding St. Thomas*. tr. A.M. Landry op, D. Hughes op. Chicago: Regnery, 1964.

——. *Saint Thomas d'Aquin et la théologie*. Paris: Éditions du Seuil, 1959.

——. *La théologie au treizieme siecle*. Paris: Vrin, 1969.

——. *La théologie comme science au treizeme siecle*. 3rd ed. Paris: Vrin, 1957.

Colish, Marcia L. *The Stoic Tradition from Antiquity to the Early Middle Ages*. Leiden: Brill, 1985.

——. *Peter Lombard*. Leiden: Brill, 1994.

Cooper, John M. *Reason and the Human Good in Aristotle*. Cambridge, MA: Harvard, 1975.

Corbin, M. *Le chemin de la théologie chez saint Thomas d'Aquin*. Paris: Beauchesne, 1974.

Courcelle, P. "Ambroise 'professeur de philosophie' (Paulin de Milan, *Vita Ambrosii*, VII,9)," *Recherches sur S. Ambroise*. Paris: Études augustiniennes, 1973.

——. *Recherches sur les Confessions de S. Augustin*. Paris: Boccard, 1968.

Dalcourt, Gerard. "The Primary Cardinal Virtue: Wisdom or Prudence?" *International Philosophical Quarterly* 3 (1963) 55-79.

Delhaye, P. *Le Decalogue et sa place dans la morale chretienne*. Brussels: La Pensée catholique, 1963.

Deely, John. *Four Ages of Understanding: The First Postmodern Survey of Philosophy from Ancient Times to the Turn of the Twenty-first Century*, Toronto: University of Toronto Press, 2001.

Dent, N.J.H. *The Moral Psychology of the Virtues*. Cambridge: CUP, 1984.

Dewan, L. "*Obiectum* Notes on the Invention of a Word," *Archives d'histoire doctrinale et littéraire du moyen age* 48 (1981) 37-96.

Dörnemann, H. *Freundschaft als Paradigma der Erlösung: eine Reflexion auf die Verbindung von Gnadenlehre, Tugendlehre und Christologie in der Summa theologiae de Thomas von Aquin*. Würzburg: Echter, 1997.

Dumont, S. "The Necessary Connection of Moral Virtue to Prudence According to John Duns Scotus–Revisited," *Recherches de Théologie ancienne et médiévale* 55 (1988) 184-206.

Elders, L. "La méthode suivie par saint Thomas d'Aquin dans la composition de la *Somme de théologie,*" *Nova et Vetera* 66 (1991) 178-192.

Emery, Kent, Jr. "Reading the World Rightly and Squarely: Bonaventure's Doctrine of the Cardinal Virtues," *Traditio* 39 (1983) 183-218.

Eschmann, I.T. "St. Thomas's Approach to Moral Philosophy," *Proceedings of the American Catholic Philosophical Association* 31 (1957) 25-33.

——. *The Ethics of Saint Thomas Aquinas: Two Courses.* Ed. E.A. Synan. Toronto: Pontifical Institute of Mediaeval Studies, 1997.

Finance, J. de. *Être et agir dans la morale de S. Thomas.* Rome: Grégorienne, 1965.

Finnis, John. *Natural Law and Natural Rights.* Oxford: Clarendon, 1980.

Flannery, Kevin L. *Acts Amid Precepts: The Aristotelian Logical Structure of Thomas Aquinas's Moral Theory.* Washington: Catholic University of America Press, 2001.

Foot, Philippa. "Virtues and Vices," in *Virtues and Vices and Other Essays in Moral Philosophy.* Berkeley: University of California Press, 1978.

Gauthier, R.-A. *Magnanimité.* Paris: Vrin, 1951.

Geach, Peter T. *The Virtues.* Cambridge: Cambridge University Press, 1977.

Gilson, E. *Le thomisme : introduction a la philosophie de Saint Thomas d'Aquin.* 6th ed. Paris: Vrin, 1965. Tr. *Thomism: The Philosophy of Thomas Aquinas.* A. A. Maurer. Toronto: Pontifical Institute of Mediaeval Studies, 2002.

——. *Le thomisme : introduction a la philosophie de Saint Thomas d'Aquin.* 5th ed. Paris: Vrin, 1944. Tr. *The Christian Philsophy of St. Thomas Aquinas.* L.K. Shook. New York: Random House, 1956.

Gracia, J., T. Noone, eds. *A Companion to Philosophy in the Middle Ages.* Oxford: Blackwell, 2003.

Grisez, G. *The Way of the Lord Jesus,* vol. I. *Christian Moral Principles.* Chicago: Franciscan Herald Press, 1983.

——, with J. Boyle. *The Way of the Lord Jesus,* vol. 2. *Living a Christian life.* Quincy, Ill.: Franciscan Press, 1993.

Hall, P. *Narrative and Natural Law.* Notre Dame, IN: University of Notre Dame Press, 1994.

Hamelin, A.M. *L'ecole franciscaine des debuts a l'occamisme.* Louvain: Nauwelaerts, 1961.

Hankinson, R.J. *The Skeptics.* London: Routledge, 1995.

Hauerwas, Stanley. *Character and the Christian Life: A Study in Theological Ethics*. San Antonio: Trinity University Press, 1975.

Hedwig, K. "Über die Theorie der Praxis bei Thomas von Aquin," *Philosophisches Jahrbuch* (1992) 202-222.

Houser, R.E. "*Chronos* and *Logos*: Rhetoric and the Rise of Philosophy," *ACPQ* 68 (1994) 247-258.

——. "The Cardinal Virtues: Aquinas and the Fathers," in *Les philosophies morales et politiques au Moyen Âge*. Ed. B. C. Bazan et al. Ottawa: LEGAS, 1995. 2: 699-708.

——. "The *De virtutibus cardinalibus* and Aquinas' doctrine of happiness," in *Atti del IX Congresso tomistico internazionale*. Vatican City: Libreria Editrice Vaticana, 1991. 3: 250-9.

Hughes, W.D., tr. Thomas Aquinas, *Summa theologiae, vol. 23: Virtue* (1a2ae 55-67), vol. 23. NY: McGraw-Hill, 1968.

Hutchinson, D.S. *The Virtues of Aristotle*. London: Routledge, 1986.

Inglis, John. "Aquinas's Replication of the Acquired Moral Virtues: Rethinking the Standard Interpretation of Moral Virtue in Aquinas," *Journal of Religious Ethics*. 27 (1999) 3-27.

——. *On Aquinas*. Belmont, CA: Wadsworth/Thomson, 2002.

Irwin, Terence. *Aristotle's First Principles*. Oxford: Clarendon, 1988.

——. *Platonic Ethics*. Oxford: Oxford University Press, 1995.

Jordan, Mark D. "Aquinas's Construction of a Moral Account of the Passions," *Freiburger Zeitschrift Fuer Philosophie und Theologie* 33 (1986), 72-97.

——. *The Alleged Aristotelianism of Thomas Aquinas*. in *The Etienne Gilson Series* 15. Toronto: Pontifical Institute of Mediaeval Studies, 1992.

——. tr. *On Faith: Summa Theologiae 2-2, qq. 1-16 of St. Thomas Aquinas. Readings in the Summa theologiae*, vol. 1. Notre Dame: 1990.

Keenan, J.F. *Goodness and Rightness in Thomas Aquinas's Summa Theologiae*. Washington: Georgetown University Press, 1992.

Kelly, J.N.D. *Jerome, His Life, Writings, and Controversies*. London: Duckworth, 1975.

Kent, Bonnie. *Virtues of the Will: The Transformation of Ethics in the Late Thirteenth Century*. Washington: Catholic University of America, 1995.

Kerferd, G.B. *The Sophistic Movement*. Cambridge: Cambridge University Press, 1981.

Kissinger, W.S. *The Sermon on the Mount. A History of Interpretation and Bibliography*. Metuchen, NJ: Scarcrow Press, 1975.

Klubertanz, George. *Habits and Virtues*. New York: Appleton-Century- Crofts, 1965.

Kluxen, W. *Philosophische Ethik bei Thomas von Aquin*. Hamburg: Meiner, 1980.

Kraut, Richard. *Aristotle on the Human Good*. Princeton: Princeton University Press, 1989.

——, ed. *The Cambridge Companion to Plato*. Cambridge: Cambridge University Press, 1992.

Kretzmann, N., A. Kenny, J. Pinborg, eds. *The Cambridge history of later medieval philosophy: from the rediscovery of Aristotle to the disintegration of scholasticism, 1100-1600*. Cambridge: Cambridge University Press, 1982.

Langan, John P. "Augustine on the Unity and the Inter-connection of the Virtues," *Harvard Theological Review* 72 (1979) 81-95.

Lee, W.P. "The Permanence of the Ten Commandments: St. Thomas and his Modern Commentators," *Theological Studies* 42 (1981) 422-443.

Lenox-Conyngham, A. "Ambrose and philosophy," *Christian faith and Greek philosophy in late antiquity*. Leiden: Brill, 1993. 112-128.

Libera, Alain de. *Albert le Grand et la philosophie*. Paris: Vrin, 1990.

Long, A.A. and D.N. Sedley. *The Hellenistic Philosophers*. 2 vols. Cambridge: University Press, 1987.

Lottin, Odon, OSB. *Psychologie et morale aux XIIe and XIIIe siecles*. Paris: Gembloux, 1942-1960. 6 vols.

Lutz-Bachman, Matthias. "The Discovery of a Normative Theory of Justice in Medieval Philosophy: On the Reception and Further Development of Aristotle's Theory of Justice by St. Thomas Aquinas," *Medieval Philosophy and Theology* 9 (2000) 1-14.

MacIntyre, A. *After Virtue*. Notre Dame: University of Notre Dame Press, 1981.

——. *Dependent Rational Animals: why human beings need the virtues*. Chicago: Open Court, 1999.

——. *Three Rival Versions of Moral Enquiry*. Notre Dame: University of Notre Dame Press, 1988.

——. *Whose Justice: Which Rationality?* University of Notre Dame: Notre Dame Press, 1988.

Madec, Goulven. *Saint Ambroise et la philosophie*. Paris: Études Augustiniennes, 1974.

Mähl, Sibylle. *Quadriga Virtutum: die Kardinaltugenden in der Geistesgeschichte der Karolingerzeit.* Beihefte zum Archiv für Kulturgeschichte 9. Cologne, Vienna: Böhlau, 1967.

Maurer, A.A. *Medieval Philosophy*. 2 ed. Toronto: Pontifical Institute of Mediaeval Studies, 1982.

McInerny, Ralph. *Ethica Thomistica: The Moral Philosophy of Thomas Aquinas*. Washington: Catholic University Press, 1982, 1997.

——. "Naturalism and Thomistic Ethics," *The Thomist* 40 (1976) 222-244.

Metz, W. *Die Architektonik der Summa theologiae des Thomas von Aquin*. Hamburg: Meiner, 1998.

Milbank, John and C. Pickstock. *Truth in Aquinas*. London: Routledge, 2000.

Mitsis, P. *Epicurus' Ethical Theory*. Ithaca: Cornell, 1988.

Mongillo, D. OP. "La struttura del 'De justitia', *Summa theologiae* II-II qq. 57-122" *Angelicum* 48 (1971) 355-377.

Moorhead, John. *Ambrose: Church and Society in the Late Roman World*. London: Longman, 1999.

Mulcahey, M. Michelle. *"First the Bow is bent in Study...." Dominican Education before 1350*, Toronto: Pontifical Institute of Mediaeval Studies, 1998.

Müller, Jörn. *Natürliche Moral und philosophische Ethik bei Albertus Magnus*. Munich: Aschendorff, 2001.

Nelson, D.M. *The Priority of Prudence: Virtue and Natural Law in Thomas Aquinas and the Implications for Modern Ethics*. University Park, PA: Pennsylvania State University Press, 1992.

Newhauser, Richard. *The Treatise on Vices and Virtues in Latin and the Vernacular*. Typologie des sources du moyen âge occidental 68. Turnhout: Brepols, 1993.

Nickl, P. "Habitus. Bemerkungen zu einem vergessenen Begriff," *Jahrbuch des Forschungsinstituts für Philosophie*. Hanover (1992-3) 174-192.

Nussbaum, Martha. *Aristotle's De motu animalium*. Princeton: Princeton University Press, 1978.

Oderburg, D. "On the Cardinality of the Cardinal Virtues," *International Journal of Philosophical Studies*. 7 (1999) 305-322.

Patfoort, A. *La Somme de saint Thomas et la logique du dessein de Dieu*. Paris: Cerf, 1997.

——. *Saint Thomas d'Aquin. Les clefs d'une theologie*. Paris: FAC, 1983.

Pence, Gregory E. "Recent Work on Virtues," *American Philosophical Quarterly*. 21 (1984) 281-297.

Pesch, Otto H. "Philosophie und Theolgie der Freiheit bei Thomas von Aquin in Quaest. disp. *de malo* qu. 6," *Münchiner Theologische Zeitschrift* 13 (1962) 1-25.

——. "The Theology of Virtue and the Theological Virtues," *Concilium* 191: *Changing Values and Virtues*, ed. D. Mieth and J. Pohier. Edinburgh: Clark, 1987.

Pieper, Josef. *The Four Cardinal Virtues*. Notre Dame, IN: University of Notre Dame Press, 1966.

Pinckaers, Servais (Th.) OP. *Les actes humaines*, 2 vols. Paris: 1962,1966.

——. "Habitude-Habitus" *Dictionnaire de Spiritualite* 7(1969) 2-11.

——. *Les sources de la morale chretienne. Sa methode, son contenu, son histoire.* Fribourg: Editions Universitaires, 1985,1990. Tr: *The Sources of Christian Ethics.* Tr. Sr. Mary Thomas Noble. Washington: Catholic University of America, 1995.

Pope, Stephen S., ed. *Aquinas on Ethics.* Washington: Georgetown University Press, 2002.

Porter, Jean. *The Recovery of Virtue: The Relevance of Aquinas for Christian Ethics.* Louisville: Westminster/Knox, 1990.

——. *Moral Action and Christian Ethics.* Cambridge: Cambridge University Press, 1995.

——. *Natural and Divine Law.* Grand Rapids, MI: Eerdmans, 1999.

Potts, T. *Conscience in Medieval Philosophy.* Cambridge: Cambridge University Press, 1980.

Principe, W. *Philip the Chancellor's theology of the hypostatic union.* Toronto: Pontifical Institute of Mediaeval Studies, 1975.

Ramsey, B., C. Harrison, eds. *Ambrose.* New York: Routledge, 1997.

Ratzinger, Josef. *Principles of Christian Morality.* San Francisco: Ignatius, 1986.

Reeve, C.D.C. *Practices of Reason.* Oxford: Clarendon, 1992.

Rhonheimer, M. *Natur als Grundlage der Moral: Die personale Struktur des Naturgesetzes bei Thomas von Aquin: Eine Auseinandersetzung mit autonomer und teleologischer Ethik.* Innsbruck: Tyrolia-Verlag, 1986. Tr. *Natural Law and Practical Reason*, Gerald Malsbary. New York: Fordham University Press, 2000.

——. *Praktische Vernunft und Vernünftigheit der Praxis.* Berlin: Akademie Verlag, 1994.

Riesenhuber, K. *Die Transzendenz der Freiheit zum Guten. Der Wille in der Anthropoligie und Metaphysik des Thomas von Aquin.* Munich: Berchmans-Kolleg, 1971.

Rist, J.M. *Augustine: ancient thought baptized.* Cambridge: Cambridge University Press, 1994.

——. *Epicurus: an Introduction.* Cambridge: Cambridge University Press, 1972.

——. *Stoic Philosophy.* Cambridge: Cambridge University Press, 1969.

Romilly, J. de. *The great Sophists in Periclean Athens.* Oxford: Clarendon, 1992.

Roton, Placide de. *Les Habitus. Leur caractere spirituel.* Paris: Labergerie, 1934.

Savon, H. *Ambroise de Milan.* Paris: Desclee, 1997.

Schneider, J. "Die Bestimmung des Tugendbegriffes in den Schriften Alberts *De natura boni* und *Summa de bono.*" In *Albertus Magnus–Doctor Universalis 1280-1980.* Mainz : Matthias-Grünewald, 1980. Pp. 295-322.

Schneyer, Johannes Baptist. *Die Sittenkritik in den Predigten Phillip des Kanzlers*, in *Beiträge zur Geschichte der Philosophie des Mittelalters*, 39/4. Münster: 1963.

Schockenhoff, E. *Bonum Hominis: Die anthropologischen und theologischen Grundlagen der Tugendethik des Thomas von Aquin*. Mainz: Matthias-Grünewald, 1987.

Sertillanges, A.D. *La philosophie morale de saint Thomas d'Aquin*. Paris: Aubier, 1942.

Sherman, N. *The Fabric of Character: Aristotle's Theory of Virtue*. Oxford: Clarendon, 1989.

——, ed. *Aristotle's Ethics: Critical Essays*. New York: Rowan and Littlefield, 1999.

Simon, Yves R. *The Definition of Moral Virtue*. ed. Vukan Kuic. NY: Fordham, 1986.

Slote, Michael. "Utilitarian Virtue," *Midwest Studies in Philosophy* 13 (1988) 384-397.

Steutel, Jan and Ben Spiecker. "Rational passions and Intellectual Virtues: A Conceptual Analysis," *Studies in Philosophy and Education* 16 (1997) 59-71.

Stegman, T.D. "St. Thomas Aquinas and the Problem of *Akrasia*," *The Modern Schoolman* 66 (1989) 117-128.

Strauss, Leo. *Xenophon's Socrates*. Ithaca: Cornell University Press, 1972.

Tarabochia-Canavero, A. *Alberto Magno: Il bene*. Mailand: 1987.

Torrell, J.-P. *Initiation a Saint Thomas d'Aquin : sa personne et son oeuvre*. Fribourg : Editions Universitaires, 1993. Tr. Robert Royal. *Saint Thomas Aquinas: v. 1. The person and his work* . Washington: Catholic University of America Press, 1996.

Tugwell, Simon. *Albert and Thomas: Selected Writings*. New York: Paulist, 1988.

VanderWaerdt, P., ed. *The Socratic Movement*. Ithaca: Cornell, 1994.

Verbeke, Gerard. *The Presence of Stoicism in Medieval Thought*. Washington: Catholic University of America, 1983.

Vlastos, G. *Socrates: Ironist and Moral Philosopher*. Cambridge: Cambridge University Press, 1991.

Wadell, P. *The Primacy of Love: An Introduction to the Ethics of Thomas Aquinas*. New York: 1992.

Wallace, James D. *Virtues and Vices*. Ithaca: Cornell, 1978.

Weisheipl, James A. ed. *Albertus Magnus and the Sciences*. Toronto: Pontifical Institute of Mediaeval Studies, 1980.

——. "Albertus Magnus," *Dictionary of the Middle Ages*. New York: Scribner, 1982, 1: 126-130.

——. *Friar Thomas d'Aquino*. Garden City, NY, 1974. 2nd ed. Washington: Catholic University of America, 1983.

Wenzel, J. *Augustine and the Limits of Virtue*. Cambridge: Cambridge University Press, 1992.

Westberg, Daniel. *Right Practical Reason: Aristotle, Action, and Prudence in Aquinas*. Oxford: Clarendon, 1994.

Wieland, G. *Ethica-scientia practica: Die Anfänge der philosophischen Ethik im 13. Jarhundert*. Münster: Aschendorff, 1981.

Wittmann, M. *Die Ethik des hl. Thomas von Aquin in ihrem systematischen Aufbau dargestellt und in ihren geschichtlichen, besonders in den antiken Quellen erforscht*. Munich, Frankfurt: Minerva, 1962.

Zimmerman, A. *Albert der grosse: seine Zeit, sein Werk, seine Wirkung*. Berlin: de Gruyter, 1981.

Index